Our Shared Witness
A Voice For Justice and Reconciliation

Munib A. Younan
Bishop of the Evangelical Lutheran Church
in Jordan and the Holy Land
President of the Lutheran World Federation

Fred Strickert, Editor

Lutheran University Press
Minneapolis, Minnesota

Our Shared Witness
A Voice for Justice and Reconciliation
By Munib A. Younan
Fred Strickert, Editor

Copyright 2012 Munib A. Younan. All rights reserved. Published by Lutheran University Press, an imprint of 1517 Media.
Cover design: Karen Walhof

Library of Congress Cataloging-in-Publication Data

Younan, Munib, 1950-

Our shared witness : a voice for justice and reconciliation / by Munib A. Younan ; Fred Strickert, editor.

p. cm.

Includes bibliographical references and index.

ISBN 978-1-932688-69-6 -- eISBN 978-1-942304-71-5

1. Lutheran Church–Israel. 2. Arab-Israeli conflict. I. Strickert, Frederick M. II. Title.

BX8063.I75Y68 2012

261'.10956—dc23

2011050484

Table of Contents

Biographical Sketch 5

Foreword 9

Part One: The Life and Work of Lutherans in the Holy Land 11

The Evangelical Lutheran Church in Jordan and the Holy Land: Adapting to a Changing Environment While Drawing Strength from Deep Christian Roots 13

Lutheran Interest in the Middle East: A Short Historical Survey 22

Fifty Years of Living Witness and Creative *Diakonia* 41

A Word for the Graduates 46

Part Two: Messages of Reconciliation for a World of Division 51

Justice, Reconciliation, and Hope: United for God's Mission 53

Reforming Luther: Toward a Prophetic Interfaith Dialogue Among Christians, Jews, and Muslims 57

Give Us Today Our Daily Bread 71

What's Lutheran About Health Care? Insights from Martin Luther 87

Ecumenism Is Reconciliation in the Middle East and in the World 92

Jerusalem Today and Tomorrow: Four Visions 112

What Does the Lord Require of Us? A Vision of Peace through Justice ... 124

The Church's Commitment to Nonviolence. 137

Bring Religion Back to the Front Lines of Peace 141

The Role of Religion in the Middle East 144

Why Lutherans Should Recognize Interfaith Harmony Week 150

Suggestions for Christian–Muslim Dialogue 153

Part Three: Sermons about Love for Neighbor and Reconciliation ... 167

Fear Not! (Luke 2:10) 169

Living Stones (1 Peter 2:5) 175

Reformed for Costly Discipleship and Creative *Diakonia* (Matthew 5:1-12) ... 182

With Eyes and Ears on Jesus (Matthew 17:1-9) 188

Jesus' Strategy Session for the Early Church (John 14:1-14) 192

I Am the Resurrection and the Life (John 11:25) 197

One in the Apostles' Teaching (Acts 2:42) 202

Living As the Children of Light (Ephesians 5:8) 208

Welcoming the Stranger (Matthew 25:31-46) 212

In Christ—Hope for the World (Ephesians 1:15-23) 218

Planting a Tree for the Future (Genesis 8:11) 224

List of Publications 227

Endnotes 229

Biographical Sketch

Munib Andria Younan was born in the old city of Jerusalem after his parents sought refuge in the Monastery of John the Baptist in the Muristan section during the war of 1948, what Israelis refer to as the War of Independence and Palestinians call *al-Nakba*, the Catastrophe. His parents lost everything and were never allowed to return to their homes. Still today he holds a United Nations Relief and Works Agency (UNWRA) refugee card, identifying with the millions of Palestinian refugees, mostly ignored and mischaracterized by the world for over six decades.

Younan likes to talk about how this misfortune was able to turn out for good. "My house was just a stone's throw from the Church of the Holy Sepulchre, just three minutes walk from the *Haram al-Sharif*, just five minutes from the Western Wall. Just around the corner was the Lutheran Church of the Redeemer where I was attracted as a youth to its evangelical theology." His location meant that he grew up playing in the streets with Muslim children and in a context of religious pluralism—the background that makes him a leading participant in ecumenical discussions and in interfaith dialogue. Muslim shopkeepers in the Old City *Suq* fondly call him their Muslim Bishop.

Still people often ask him, "When did your family become Christian?" His answer is quite clear. They were Christian long before missionaries set foot in places like Europe and North America, let alone Africa and China. His family goes back to the days of the Book of Acts, and he deeply treasures his deep roots in the land. He speaks fondly of the many hikes that he took while living in the boarding section of the Lutheran Boys Home in Beit Jala—hikes to get to know the land, its plants and animals, its geography, and its people.

After completing his primary and secondary education in the Lutheran schools in Palestine, Bishop Younan traveled to Finland where he studied diaconal ministry at Luther Opisto College in Järvenpää from 1969 to 1972, and theology at the University of Helsinki from 1972 to 1976. His thesis for a master's degree in theology was on "Election in Deutero Isaiah." Later, in 1988, he did graduate study at the Lutheran School of Theology at Chicago, Illinois (U.S.A.), where he was awarded an honorary doctor of divinity degree in 2011. He earlier was awarded an honorary doctorate by Wartburg College, Waverly, Iowa (U.S.A.), in 2001.

In 1976, Younan was ordained at the Lutheran Church of the Redeemer in Jerusalem. He then served pastorates in Jerusalem, Beit Jala, and Ramallah, as well as being called to leadership positions in youth ministry and religious education in the Lutheran schools. From 1990 to 1998 he also served as president of the synod for the Evangelical Lutheran Church in Jordan (ELCJ). On January 5, 1998, he was consecrated as bishop of the ELCJ. It was renamed Evangelical Lutheran Church in Jordan and the Holy Land (ELCJHL) in 2005. He also chairs numerous boards and committees within the ELCJHL.

In the field of interreligious encounter, Younan has been active since his work as co-founder of the Al-Liqa' Center for Religious Studies in 1982. Since 1991, with the Jonah Group, Younan has launched several long-running, informal dialogues providing space for joint reflection by local Christians and Jews. Younan is also a founding member of the Council for Religious Institutions in the Holy Land (CRIHL), an organization of interfaith trialogue with membership including the Heads of Churches in the Holy Land, the Chief Rabbinate of Israel, the Ministry of *Waqf* and Religious Affairs, and the Islamic *Shari'a* Courts of the Palestinian Authority.

Younan continues to make a substantial contribution to the life of the churches and ecumenism in the Middle East. Younan has been an active member of the Middle East Council of Churches, serving in various capacities since 1985, and he presently serves as president for the Evangelical Family of Churches. From 2004 to 2010, Younan served as president of the Fellowship of the Middle East Evangelical Churches (FMEEC), leading them to a unanimous vote in support of women's ordination in January 2010. A founding member of the World Council of Churches' Ecumenical Accompaniment Programme for Palestine and Israel (EAPPI), Younan has chaired its Local Reference Group since 2002. Bishop Younan is an active member of the Heads of Churches of Jerusalem, participating in the release of statements concerning Christians in the Middle East and concerning the Israeli-Palestinian conflict.

He is the recipient of a number of awards including

- 2011 St. Henrik Cross from the Evangelical Lutheran Church in Finland.

- 2008 Mikael Agricola Medallion, Finland
- 2007 Templar Peace Prize
- 2005 Bethlehem Star Award from Palestinian President Mahmoud Abbas
- 2004 Holyland Christian Ecumenical Foundation (HCEF) Prize, Washington, D.C.
- 2004 Bethanien (Bethany) Prize from the Methodist Church, Oslo, Norway
- 2001 Human Rights Award from the United Nations Association, Washington, D.C.
- 2001 The Finnish Peace Prize from the Finnish Christian Peace Movement

Younan has been involved with The Lutheran World Federation for three decades, including membership in its youth committee (1981-1984); adviser to the council (1990-1997); council member, vice-chair of the board of trustees of the Institute for Ecumenical Research in Strasbourg, and vice-chair of the LWF Program Committee for Mission and Development from 1997 to 2003. From 2003 to July 2010 Younan served as LWF vice-president for the Asia region and council member and member of the LWF executive committee and board of trustees.

Bishop Munib A. Younan was elected to the presidency of The Lutheran World Federation by the LWF Eleventh Assembly in Stuttgart, Germany, on 24 July 2010. As president, he also chairs the LWF council, executive committee, and board of trustees.

A high-profile lecturer and speaker, Younan is sought after for his perspective on just peace as a Palestinian Christian. Younan is also active in interreligious encounter, ecumenism, and reconciliation in his own region and internationally. His work has been recognized with a number of awards and prizes. He is author of *Witnessing for Peace: In Jerusalem and the World*, and he had translated the Augsburg Confession into Arabic, has delivered numerous lectures, and published a variety of articles relating to the life of Palestinian Lutherans in the Middle East.

Bishop Younan is married to Suad Yacoub; the couple has a son, two daughters, and a granddaughter.

Foreword

A bridge-builder. An ambassador of reconciliation. A prophetic voice, speaking truth to power. An advocate for justice, peace, and nonviolence. A witness to the liberating Gospel of Jesus Christ. A servant for the suffering.

These are some of the characterizations I had heard about Bishop Munib Younan long before I came to the Lutheran World Federation (LWF). And in my current capacity as general secretary, this is the way I have come to know him in his service as LWF president: As a pastor and a church leader he cares deeply both about his own church in the Holy Land and about the church universal. He cares both about the well-being of his own Palestinian people and about people around the world. He cares about violations of human rights wherever they occur and about what it takes to make for peace. As we say in the LWF, he lives "with passion for the church and for the world!"

As you will read in the present collection of sermons, speeches, and writings, Bishop Younan's theology is contextual—deeply rooted in his daily reality as a Palestinian Christian—while at the same time being universal—offering insights and principles that apply to other situations in vastly different parts of the world.

Let me in particular lift up two of his basic commitments. The first is to *principled nonviolence.* This is not a nonviolence that meekly submits to violence and oppression, nor is it a nonviolence that ignores violations of basic human rights or accepts them. Rather, it is an active nonviolence, which hears the cries of the oppressed, speaks the truth, engages those holding opposing positions—seeing in them a common humanity—and seeks mutual respect, calling to heed the "better angels" of our human nature.

The second commitment is to *peaceful human life in interfaith community.* Living and witnessing in Jerusalem and the Holy Land, Bishop Younan is aware of the special responsibility that religious communities carry in that particular context. He insists that religions have both the potential and the obligation to be agents of transformation, to overcome alienation, oppression, and violence. Religions are not meant to be stumbling blocks, but rather cornerstones of societies living in justice and peace. Even in his local context, where Christians are a small minority, currently under the immense pressure of the difficult conditions under which Palestinians live, he continues to offer the witness of mediation and dialogue.

Given the tragic history of failed Israeli–Palestinian peace efforts, it would be easy to become pessimistic, discouraged, and even bitter. You will see from this book that this is not the case with Bishop Younan. He suffers with his people and is rightly outraged at the violations of human dignity and human rights imposed upon them. But he continues to speak truth to power and is full of hope, the hope that comes from a deep faith. Again, as we say in the LWF, this is the testimony of a man "liberated by God's grace, working for a just, peaceful, and reconciled world."

Rev. Martin Junge, General Secretary
The Lutheran World Federation

The Life and Work of Lutherans in the Holy Land

The Evangelical Lutheran Church in Jordan and the Holy Land

Adapting to a Changing Environment While Drawing Strength from Deep Christian Roots

Published in *The Lutheran Forum* • Winter 2011

Often, one of the first questions asked when I give presentations is, "When did you convert to Christianity?" People are likely to assume that one whose mother tongue is Arabic is Muslim or that one who hails from Jerusalem is Jewish. But in Israel–Palestine, the cradle of the three great monotheistic faiths, Arabic-speaking Christians have existed since the church was born at the first Pentecost (Acts 2:11).

The Evangelical Lutheran Church in Jordan and the Holy Land (ELCJHL) has deep roots going back to those early days described in the Acts of the Apostles. Perhaps that is why the ELCJHL may be the longest acronym for any Lutheran group. Although we officially became a church only in 1959, we have a long and rich history. Our church members were deliberate in 2005 when calling their body **The Evangelical Lutheran Church in Jordan and the Holy Land**. Each component emphasizes a critical aspect of this church's story.

As **Church** we relish our continuity with the early church of the Acts of the Apostles. Like those early Christians, we are a small but vibrant community, led by the Spirit and bold in our witness. We are the descendants of those first Christians who struggled as a minority, yet who "devoted themselves to the apostles' teaching and fellowship, to the breaking of bread and the prayers" (Acts 2:42).

The historical development of the church in Jerusalem is quite complex, with immigrants drawn to Jerusalem from many countries and intermarrying to present a diverse heritage. Yet the witness has remained uninterrupted for two millennia. There were Arab bishops already at the Council of Nicea shaping orthodox theology and, since the seventh century, Arabic language and culture became predominant in the Holy Land.

The struggles during later centuries have been characterized more by diversity than unity. Throughout the centuries, the Jerusalem Church grew to include Greek Orthodox, Latin Catholic, Syriac, Armenian, Coptic, and Ethiopian. By 1852, the political arrangement known as the *Status Quo* appeared to fix responsibilities and territorial allotments for the Ottoman Empire and years to come.

At almost the same time—in the mid-nineteenth century the fruits of the Protestant Reformation began to reach the Holy Land. While the Ottoman Empire was beginning to crumble, new interest in the region came from Europe with biblical archaeologists wanting to make historical connections and pilgrims seeking spiritual edification. One cannot discount political and economic motives—this period of course coincided with the colonialist era. The British consulate was established in Jerusalem in 1838, followed by France, Russia, Prussia, and the United States. Along with the consulates came missionaries—thus the description of our church as **Evangelical Lutheran.**

This missionary effort from the start was ecumenical in nature. Not wishing to compete with each other, Lutherans concentrated their efforts from Jerusalem to the south, Anglicans from Jerusalem to the north, and Presbyterians in Lebanon. A joint bishopric was established in Jerusalem in 1841. The Anglican Michael Solomon was the first, followed by the Lutheran Samuel Gobat from 1846 to 1879. Then the bishopric split as a result of differing objectives. For the Anglicans of this era, missionary efforts flowed out of the London-based Society for the Conversion of the Jews, established in 1808. The Anglican Christ Church was built next to the British Consulate near Jaffa Gate. For the Lutherans the focus was not so much on conversion, but on *diakonia*, and the efforts were directed at the larger Arab population. (Gobat had previously learned to speak Arabic in Ethiopia.)

In 1851, the Kaiserswerth diaconate established an orphanage for girls in west Jerusalem that eventually became Talitha Kumi School. By the turn of the century it had over 500 students and also a deaconess program. In 1860 the Swabian missionary Johann Schneller established the "Syrian" orphanage when he brought ten orphans to Jerusalem from the area that is now Lebanon. Schools and orphanages became the backbone of diaconal efforts.

It was in these educational institutions that young Arab men and women began to learn the distinctive Evangelical Lutheran theology. Most were already Christian, but this Lutheran preaching of grace appealed to them. In 1883, graduates of these schools formed the first Lutheran congregation, followed by others in Bethlehem, Beit Sahour, Jerusalem, and Hebron. Our church was thus ecumenical and diaconal, but also confessional by nature. The hallmark of the Reformation, the Bible in the language of the people, became a reality in 1864 with the publication of the first Arabic Bible.[1] Printing presses, newspapers, and literary societies soon brought about a well-educated and well-read Arab Palestinian Christian society.

The Evangelical Lutheran church was given a prominent visible presence in gifts from these early missionaries. The Lutheran Church of the Redeemer with its 45.5 meter tower just a stone's throw from the Church of the Holy Sepulchre was dedicated by Kaiser Wilhelm on Reformation Day, 1898. Twelve years later the Augusta Victoria compound was established on the Mount of Olives. Christmas Lutheran Church in Bethlehem is also a reminder of that missionary era, where parishioners sing, pray, and hear the Gospel in Arabic while early stained-glass windows portray a blonde-haired, blue-eyed Jesus whose words are recorded in German inscriptions. So this is indeed an **Evangelical Lutheran Church.**

The descriptive **in Jordan** marks a major change that took place in 1948, the year Israelis refer to as their year of Independence and Arabs as *al-Nakba*, the catastrophe. The church was now located entirely within the Kingdom of Jordan. Older congregations in Bethlehem, Beit Sahour, and Beit Jala were now in the West Bank of Jordan. The city of Jerusalem was now divided, with Redeemer congregation located in East Jerusalem. We were severed from earlier Lutheran presence in the territory that became Israel. Church properties such as the Schneller School, Talitha Kumi School, and others in West Jerusalem were confiscated by the state of Israel. Lutheran communities in other locations such as Jaffa and Haifa were no more. Our recovery could not have taken place without the full assistance of The Lutheran World Federation (LWF).

The ELCJ was a refugee church. It is estimated that one-third of the Christian population from before the war became refugees, leaving homes in Ramle, Jaffa, Lydda, and West Jerusalem for the West Bank. This, of course, offered an influx of new members for existing congregations, but also called for economic and emotional assistance. With large numbers of Christian refugees fleeing to Ramallah, the church also took up the challenge of starting The Lutheran Church of Hope in 1954. Later, following the 1967 war, the ELCJ, with the help of the church in Finland and Sweden, began a mission outreach in Amman, Jordan, and established Good Shepherd Lutheran Congregation with over 200 members.

The 1948 war also left Jerusalem divided in resources with many Christian hospitals located on the "Israeli" side of Jerusalem. Of the eighteen hospitals in Jerusalem, all eighteen were on the West Jerusalem side of the border and none in East Jerusalem. The United Nation Refugee Relief and Works Agency and the International Red Cross, along with the Kingdom of Jordan, asked Lutherans to convert the Lutheran Pilgrims House on the Mount of Olives into Augusta Victoria Hospital (AVH), which soon became the premier hospital providing care both in Jerusalem and through mobile clinics in the West Bank. AVH has proved itself resilient and adaptable. Severely damaged by 1967 war bombing and cut off by later closures of the West Bank and the construction of the Separation Wall, the hospital has rebuilt and refocused its efforts in specialized care, especially cancer treatment and pediatric dialysis. This continues the long history of Lutheran *diakonia* in this land.

This period following 1948 marked the transition from mission field to independent church—a phenomenon paralleled in Africa and the church of the South. However, it is important to note that the Palestinian church was not just following a popular trend. It was a necessary development out of the political situation with the German church recovering from its losses in World War II and Palestine divided by war and partition. Evangelical Lutherans in Palestine stepped up to the challenge and in 1959 established the **Evangelical Lutheran Church in Jordan** (ELCJ).

Shortly after the 1970 Lutheran World Federation (LWF) Assembly in Evian, France, the ELCJ applied for LWF membership. That particular assembly, with the theme "Sent into the World," had created a greater focus on the church in the South and on human rights. Our acceptance of membership in the LWF in 1974 was conditional on the presence of independent Arab leadership and on the publication of the Augsburg Confession in the Arabic language. I was entrusted with the translation of the latter.[2] In 1979 Bishop Daoud Haddad was elected the first Palestinian bishop. He was succeeded in 1986 by Bishop Naim Nasser, who served until 1998 when I was chosen as bishop of the ELCJ.

This period was marked by a new understanding of church-to-church relationships, with older churches of the North and the younger churches of the South seeing one another as equal partners in an accompaniment model. In 1977, we established The Coordination Committee for Cooperation between the ELCJHL and Overseas Partners (COCOP) whose members included the Berliner Missionwerk (BMW), the Church of Sweden (CoS), the United-Evangelical Lutheran Church of Germany (VELKD), the Finnish Evangelical Lutheran Mission (FELM), the Lutheran Church in American (LCA), the Evangelical Church in Germany (EKD), the Northelbian Evangelical Lutheran Church (NEK), the Church of Norway (CoN), the Evangelical Lutheran Church in Canada (ELCIC), and The Lutheran World Federation (LWF) as an affiliated member.

In 2005, the church changed its name to the **Evangelical Lutheran Church in Jordan and the Holy Land.** The longer name better reflects the changing political realities (only the Amman congregation is now in Jordan) and also the indigenous character of the church.[3] Perhaps the dominant characteristic of Palestinian Lutherans is their minority status: politically an Arab minority in a land heavily populated by Israeli Jews; religiously a minority outnumbered by Muslims and Jews; denominationally a minority where Orthodox and Catholic Christians are prominent. This minority status has led Palestinian Lutherans to a particular contextual theology that reads the Bible from a bottom-up point of view, as Good News for the downtrodden and the politically oppressed, which witnesses in hope for peace with justice. Our theology of grace and the theology of the cross sets us in a unique position to be intermediaries in the current conflict, to be brokers for peace, advocates of human rights, apostles of love, and ministers of reconciliation.

The most pressing issue facing the Palestinian church today is Christian emigration with Christians now numbering less than 1.7 percent of the population, a vast decrease from ten percent prior to the events of 1948. Surveys about this phenomenon have shown the three reasons mostly commonly given for emigration are:

1. The continued situation of political occupation[4]
2. A lack of jobs
3. The growth of extremism among both Palestinians and Israelis

And we as the church are stressing a number of essential programs in order to face the problems of emigration:

1. Community-based education
2. Assistance in finding jobs
3. The building of affordable and secure housing[5]
4. The strengthening of Christian institutions serving every human being regardless of ethnicity, religion, or nationality

In response to the problem of emigration, we have recently identified thirty promising young people for an intensive educational program in the Bible and in Lutheran doctrine helping to prepare them for congregational leadership and work as Sunday school teachers and youth directors. The ELCJHL seeks to continue to meet the spiritual as well as material needs of its people and its communities in this Holy Land context as it has done so throughout its history.

In this **Holy Land** context, ecumenism is a high priority for the ELCJHL. I have often said, "Given the choice to live and witness together or to die alone, we choose life." Ecumenism, however, is not merely something of a theological debate, but a way of life. Ecumenism is seeking reconciliation and understanding with sisters and brothers in other streams of Christianity, which inspire hope and love in the hearts of others.

The history of earlier times includes many episodes of division, hostility, and competition among various Christian groups. However, the first *intifada* served as a catalyst for the heads of Jerusalem's thirteen churches to speak with one voice against the violence of occupations. Subsequently this group has issued various statements on issues of mutual interest. A current focus for the group concerns the status of Jerusalem as a city shared by three faiths—Jews, Christians, and Muslims—and by two peoples, Israelis and Palestinians, as a capital for their autonomous but interdependent states. The heads of churches work with Jewish and Muslim leaders in pursuit of an agreement that would preserve the religious, civil, and human rights of all inhabitants of and pilgrims to the great city.

Another group is the Fellowship of the Middle East Evangelical Churches (FMEEC), formed in 1974 to help Lutheran, Reformed, and Anglican churches work together to strengthen mission and to equip leaders and laity of both sexes for ministry. At its January general assembly, FMEEC members voted unanimously to urge member churches to ordain women as pastors. The ELCJHL joined with other regional churches in 2006 to sign the Amman Reformed–Lutheran Agreement, which in turn makes us part of the Leuenberg Agreement of Reformed and Lutheran churches.

On a more local level, the Lutheran congregation in Ramallah took the lead in joining with other Christians of that city to establish a common date for celebrating Easter.

Out of this shared Holy Land context the ELCJHL also gives high priority to interfaith work. This is only natural since we have always been a diaconal church; service is directed to all in need.

Today Muslims make up forty-five percent of the student body in our Lutheran schools where the focus is on teaching peace, coexistence, and democratic principles. These students learn side by side to live and laugh with one another. To this end, ELCJHL educators strive to provide quality, holistic education that inspires children to develop to their fullest. Through music, art, sports, drama, and other programs, they seek to help children build their hearts, their homes, and their nation, instilling in them the values of a modern, civil society that is based on human rights for all. Through peace education classes, they learn how to live and dialogue with other religions.

The schools also nurture Palestinian identity by teaching students traditional Palestinian arts and crafts, music and dance. Such cultural pursuits deepen a Palestinian identity which helps youth appreciate their cultural heritage and deepen their roots in the land. Culture transcends politics and borders, building bridges between peoples.

Similarly, our Augusta Victoria Hospital, with a staff of both Muslims and Christians, provides specialized health care predominantly to Muslims.

In addition to daily interaction between Christians and Muslims, the ELCJHL is involved in deliberate programs of dialogue and cooperation among religious leaders. The most important is the Council of Religious Institutions in the Holy Land. The council was formed in 2005 to bring together leaders of Jerusalem's Jewish, Muslim, and Christian communities to jointly promote coexistence, combat discrimination, and seek solutions to societal problems. Considering the political climate in which the council exists, what the council has achieved so far is no less than remarkable. One of the main projects is a hotline for calls about derogatory remarks made by clergy, imams, and rabbis about other faiths. Faith leaders receive reports about the remarks in order to hold their respective preachers accountable for contributing to interreligious misunderstanding. In a similar vein, academic consultants are currently studying hundreds of textbooks from Israeli and Palestinian schools in an effort to uncover and eliminate statements that promote interreligious discrimination. Accurate representation of other religious traditions is a core value of the council, as is securing access for all to Jerusalem, the spiritual home of all three religions.

Other interfaith efforts include the Jonah Group, which brings together Palestinian Christian and Israeli Jewish faith leaders and educators to make us more aware of each other's practices and beliefs.

Muslim–Christian interaction has taken various shapes, perhaps most prominently in the dialogue that has followed the 2007 "A Common Word

Between Us and You," an open letter from 138 Muslim scholars to Christian leaders that acknowledged love of God and love of neighbor as the essence of both religions.[6]

This Holy Land context also means that the ELCJHL is a global church through and through. Over the past decades its current and future pastors have studied in Germany, Finland, the USA, Tanzania, and Lebanon. Currently eighteen potential ELCJHL leaders—male and female alike—are engaged in a three-year online leadership training program with the American educational agency, Infinite Excellence. In addition to distance learning curriculum, the program includes on-site workshops and individual mentoring. Such activities, along with congregational exchanges, help Palestinian Lutherans understand themselves as part of the global church.

The church in Palestine hosts a constant flow of visitors, including tourists, pilgrims, and church delegations, and it also benefits short- and intermediate-term volunteers who come from churches spanning the globe in an accompaniment model of support. At the same time, ELCJHL leaders have become known locally and throughout the world through their speaking engagements and their writing.[7]

The ELCJHL is also a member of the Middle East Council of Churches (MECC), is active in and a candidate for membership in the World Council of Churches, is a signatory to numerous mutual recognition agreements; and enjoys relationships with many churches—Lutheran and others—around the world.

From its inception, The Lutheran World Federation (LWF) and the ELCJHL have worked hand in hand in health care and vocational training. The ELCJHL has actively involved itself in this federation of Lutheran churches. I myself have been privileged to serve as vice-president for the Asia region from 2003 to 2010 and now humbly, but eagerly, begin my responsibilities with my election as president at the July LWF Assembly in Stuttgart.

With the first apostles having been commissioned to be Christ's witnesses from Jerusalem to the ends of the earth, the ELCJHL can be nothing other than a global church. We are **church** with deep roots going back to the first Christians in the Acts of the Apostles. We are **Evangelical Lutheran**, confessing the unique Lutheran understanding of God's grace, showing faith active in love in our diaconal ministry, focusing heavily on education. We are **in Jordan** because of political circumstances of the mid-twentieth century, not despairing, but living in hope and developing strong Palestinian leadership to emerge as a vibrant, independent church. We are **in the Holy Land**, a place sacred to three religions, and therefore our faith calls us to dialogue and cooperation in a unique ecumenical and interfaith witness. We speak for nonviolent approaches to peace with justice and see ourselves as an integral part of the global church, receiving accompaniment from afar and sending out our undying witness to the whole world. Our strength is in our vital witness and creative *diakonia*.

Lutheran Interest in the Middle East

A Short Historical Survey

September 2011

Martin Luther had interest neither in Jerusalem nor the Middle East. He was too preoccupied with the divisions of Western Europe and in gaining political support for his fledgling Protestant movement. In a sense he benefited from the political threat of the expanding Ottoman Empire. The Holy Roman Emperor Charles V wanted to unite the West against the Ottomans, and he thus called for the Diet of Augsburg in 1530 which gave the Lutherans the opportunity to explain their doctrinal and ecclesiastical stance.

Luther's argument was with Rome and the papacy, and his debates were frequently sprinkled with comments concerning agreements with the Eastern church to justify his own theological positions. He was not hesitant to note that he and the Orthodox Church were in agreement over against the position of the Roman church on the issues of clerical celibacy, papal supremacy, purgatory, indulgences, and communion by bread alone.[8]

Dialogue with Orthodox Leaders

Luther's focus on the Reformation in Europe did not leave him time to pursue discussions with Orthodox leaders, which would have required him to travel east. However, in 1559, a good decade after Luther's death, Patriarch Joasaph II (1555-1565) sent a Serbian deacon, Demetrios Mysos, to Germany to engage in dialogue with the Lutherans. Philip Melanchthon, Martin Luther's colleague at the University of Wittenberg, a New Testament and Greek scholar, and the author of the Augsburg Confession, provided hospitality for this delegate at Wittenberg from May 20 through the end of September that year. Together they examined similarities of the Orthodox and Lutheran objections to medieval abuses seen at that time in the Roman church. Melanchthon also translated the Augsburg Confession for him to take back to Patriarch Joasaph II. However, this Greek edition is more than a strict translation.[9] Bernard Korte believes that a spirit of ecumenism was really at the heart of the accommodations and expansions in the *Augustana Graeca*:

> Accordingly the Greek rendering of the Augsburg Confession is not merely a translation but a revision in the interest of building a bridge between the East and the West. Terms of the Greek liturgy were employed not only to make matters clear to the Greek mind but very often to remove theological obstacles which hindered union.[10]

Many have wondered about the objectives of this visit from a delegate of the ecumenical patriarch. Was it merely theological interest about the Reformation and its followers? Were there also political objectives? It is perhaps a coincidence of history that the Reformation was occurring at a critical point in history for the Orthodox church. In 1453, the city of Constantinople had been sacked. The Ottoman Empire was now on the rise, providing new challenges for Orthodox Christians. For the Lutherans, contact with the East was important in their efforts to show themselves in agreement with the doctrines and practices of the church. The talks between Melanchthon and Mysos held the potential for further discussions. However, Melanchthon's letter and his copy of the Augsburg Confession in Greek did not reach the patriarch. The best explanation is that Deacon Mysos died in route to Constantinople.[11] Melanchthon himself was to die one year later (1560). Constantinople remained for a time unaware of the interest of the Lutherans.

The second Lutheran–Orthodox contact occurred, however, when a German Lutheran pastor, Stephan Gerlach, traveled to Constantinople in 1573. He had been chosen to accompany as chaplain the first ambassador to Constantinople, Baron David Ungnad von Sonnegk, a pious Lutheran who had studied law at the University of Tübingen. Tübingen had become an important theological center for Lutheranism within its second generation, including scholars such as Jakob Andreae (1528-90) and Martin Crusius (1526-1607), who had become familiar with Melanchthon's translation of the Augsburg Confession into Greek. One of Gerlach's first priorities was to meet with leaders of the Orthodox church in Constantinople, including Patriarch Jeremias II (1572-1595), presenting him with correspondence from Andreae and Crusius and a copy of the Augsburg Confession in Greek.

This developed into a serious exchange of three letters each over the next six years, producing over 400 printed pages. These letters have been characterized as "a friendly but candid exchange of extensive doctrinal correspondence."[12] Andreae wrote in 1575:

> If perhaps, we differ in some customs because of the great geographical distances that separate us, nevertheless, we hope that we have in no way innovated on the principal articles of salvation. As far as we know, we have both embraced and preserved the faith which has been handed down [to us] by the holy apostles and prophets, the God-bearing fathers and patriarchs, and the seven [ecumenical] synods that were built upon the God-given scriptures.[13]

Prominent topics discussed included the authority of scripture and tradition; the *filioque*; the nature of the church; grace, free will, and synergism; justification, faith, and good works; eucharistic practices; the priesthood and the ministry; prayers for the departed; the invocation of saints; feasts and fasting; and monasticism. In the end they reached an impasse. A third and final response from the patriarch concluded the dialogue in 1581, stating that he did not see any hope of reconciliation:

> Therefore we request that from henceforth you do not cause us more grief, nor write to us on the same subject if you should wish to treat these luminaries and theologians of the Church in a different manner. You honor and exalt them in words, but you reject them in deeds. For you try to prove our weapons which are their holy and divine discourses as unsuitable. And it is with these documents that we would have to write and contradict you. Thus, as for you, please release us from these cares. Therefore, going about your own ways, write no longer concerning dogmas; but if you do, write only for friendship sake. Farewell.[14]

Still, the Lutherans made one further attempt at dialogue:

> And even if you ask us to no longer trouble you with such writings (although we have conversed with you with much love and much kindness and with due respect) yet we are hopeful that the matters which have been written to you by us up to now will in time be reexamined and reconsidered more accurately and much better. . . . Therefore, standing together with Your Holiness, Patriarch and Most Reverent Sir, we offer to the God of all, our true friendship which we have shown to you and which we will continuously afterwards keep.[15]

Thus the year 1581 brought an end to this potentially fruitful exchange.

Now, 400 years later, we are thankful the situation has changed. We Lutherans have completed thirty years of fruitful dialogue with the Orthodox on "What is the mission of the church?" We look forward to continuing this dialogue.

Reluctance Toward Pilgrimage

Unlike earlier Christians in both the East and West, Lutherans had little interest in pilgrimages to the Holy Land. Part of this attitude came from Luther's own experience when he made pilgrimage to Rome as an Augustinian monk in 1510 at the age of twenty-seven. His decision to join the order had been influenced by a restlessness in his soul, how to satisfy a wrathful God. His superior had encouraged this act of piety. Instead of providing comfort for his soul and inspiring him, his experience was only negative as he observed the clergy in Rome living in luxury while occupied with selling indulgences to the common, uneducated Christians.

Back in Germany, Luther also was observing the transformation of local churches into pilgrimage sites through the collection of relics. The Reformation itself began when Luther nailed ninety-five theses for debate on the door of the Wittenberg Church, in the city where he was a professor at the university, at the church that his own regional ruler and protector, Frederick III, had turned into a pilgrimage center through the acquisition of 5,000 relics including a vial of Mary's milk and straw from Jesus' crib in Bethlehem.[16] By posting these theses, he was challenging the abuse of this practice of indulgences through pilgrimage on October 31, 1517, the eve of the most important pilgrimage day, All Saints Day.

However, Luther's aversion to pilgrimage arose not only from the abuses, but also from his theological understanding of faith. Luther was following in the tradition of Eusebius, who stated that "Everywhere the Holy Communion is celebrated, there is Jerusalem." His three basic principles of *sola fide, sola gratia,* and *sola Scriptura* gave an emphasis to the individual reading of the Bible as sufficient for faith. So there was no encouragement for Lutherans to travel to the Holy Land.

In a similar way, Luther was very critical about the crusades of earlier centuries and also about calls for a new crusade to fight the growing Ottoman Empire. In 1518 he asserted that "to fight against the Turk is to fight against God who is punishing our sins through them." Rather, Christians should focus on repentance. However, when Suleiman moved upon Vienna in 1529, Luther finessed his argument a little more carefully. In his pamphlets *On War Against the Turks* (1529) and *Military Sermon Against the*

Turks (1530), Luther clarified his position on the Christian response to Islam, rejecting such a crusade as a blasphemous confusion of the spiritual and the secular. "If I were a soldier and saw in the battlefield a priest's banner or cross, even if it were the very crucifix, I would run away as though the very devil were chasing me!" he wrote. The military was the realm of government, not the church. The church, however, should resort to spiritual weapons to oppose teachings it saw as false.

For 300 years there would be no impetus for Lutherans to travel to the Middle East.

Western Intervention in the Holy Land

In 1841, a joint Anglican–Lutheran bishopric was established in Jerusalem, bringing about a complete change in attitudes toward the Middle East. This occurred at a time when the Ottoman Empire was beginning to collapse and when Western governments were seeking a new role in this part of the world. In 1798 Napolean sent his army against Egypt and then the coast of Palestine. Beneficiaries of Napolean's campaign were Muhammad Ali, the Albanian Ottoman army general who stepped in as ruler of Egypt, and his son Ali Pasha, who gained French-backed control of Jerusalem from 1831 to 1840. This resulted in a number of reforms benefitting non-Muslims which later carried over to the Tanzimat reforms when the Ottomans regained control with the backing of British and Prussian (German) military.

In 1840, the population of Jerusalem was about 10,750—4,400 Muslims, 3,350 Christians, and 3,000 Jews.[17] Jerusalem could have been considered a poor town. All the Jews lived in poverty and were dependent upon contributions from abroad. The entire population was still suffering the affects of a severe 1834 earthquake which had destroyed many buildings, domestic as well as religious. Christians in particular were in transition, with many giving up farming and leaving villages for urban life.[18] So there were needs that the new consulates could fill.

The reward for regaining Jerusalem for the Ottomans was the right to establish permanent consuls in Jerusalem. Previously, France had gained consulate status as protectorate of the Catholic minorities, and Russia as protectorate of the Orthodox. The British consulate was established in Jerusalem in 1839 and the Prussian consulate in 1842. Other nations followed over the next decade. This led to a period to which some have referred as the "peaceful crusade." The West had come to stay. With Jerusalem as the holy city, missionaries came along with the consulates. So by an act of the British parliament the Anglican–Prussian bishopric was established in 1841. In reality, the Prussians were to play a secondary role. Since the Protestants of German lands did not have apostolic succession, all bishops were to be consecrated by the Archbishop of Canterbury under the authority of the Church of England. With this understanding, the British and Prussian governments would alternate in appointing bishops.

The First Protestant Bishop

There was another motive in the establishment of the joint bishopric. The early nineteenth century was an era of the development of Protestant missionary societies in Britain and the other Protestant countries of Europe. Among these was the London Society for Promoting Christianity amongst the Jews, founded in 1809. Lord Ashley, the Earl of Shaftesbury, who served as president of the Society for the Church's Ministry among Jewish People (CMJ), had approached Britain's foreign minister, Lord Palmerston, to seek the role of the British Consul as protector of the Jews of Jerusalem, just as the French had that role for the Catholics and Russia for the Orthodox. It was not coincidental that the British consul from 1846 to 1863, James Finn, was a lifelong member of the Society for the Conversion of the Jews and that his father-in-law was a missionary for CMJ in London.

The first Protestant bishop of Jerusalem was especially chosen for this task. He was Michael Solomon Alexander, who was born a Jew in Posen, Prussia, and who had served as a rabbi before coming to London where he converted to Christianity and became an Anglican priest serving as a missionary of the London Jews Society. He was consecrated as bishop in London in December 1841 and arrived in Jerusalem in January 1842. In the meantime, the British government that included the interventionist Foreign Secretary Lord Palmerston was voted out. The new foreign minister's office instructed diplomats in Istanbul and Jerusalem so that they opposed any efforts to convert either Jews or Muslims.

When Bishop Alexander arrived in Jerusalem, however, the CMJ was already in place. Its senior missionary, Danish clergyman Hans Nicolajsen, had arrived already in 1825 and by 1839 had baptized his first Jewish convert.[19] On February 10, 1840, he laid the foundation for the first Protestant church in Jerusalem, Christ Church, located next to the British consulate inside Jaffa Gate. However, as an unauthorized individual it was illegal for him to build a church, and he was not allowed to continue.[20] The establishment of the bishopric changed that. One of Alexander's first acts as bishop was to lay the first stone upon the foundation for this church that would eventually be completed in 1849—the first Protestant church in the Middle East. However, Bishop Alexander was in reality a bishop without a church. The handful of Jewish converts were not recognized by the Church of England. The rest of his congregation was made up of CMJ missionaries. After only four years in Jerusalem, he died in 1845.

Bishop Samuel Gobat

The second bishop, Samuel Gobat, would serve in Jerusalem for thirty-four years (1845-1879). According to the agreement of the joint Anglican–Lutheran bishopric, he was appointed by Prussian King Friedrich Wilhelm IV. A seminary graduate of Basel, Switzerland, and ordained in Germany, he then went to England in 1825 where he received Anglican ordination and membership in the Church Missionary Society (CMS) of London. He then spent twenty years in missionary work in Egypt and Abyssinia before coming to Jerusalem as bishop. This experience led the work in Jerusalem in a new direction. Fluent in Arabic, he placed a greater focus on the Arabs of Jerusalem, inviting new missionaries from the CMS while still offering support to CMJ endeavors. However, both remained problematic. Conversion of Muslims was against Ottoman policy, and the few who did convert were ostracized by families so that they became totally dependent upon the church. So converts among Jews and Muslims were few.

Gobat turned to diaconal work as the heart of his efforts, and this was carried out through dozens of German and Swiss missionaries—lay and clergy alike, especially pietists connected with Basel, Switzerland—where Gobat had gone to school and where Christian Friedrich Spittler had founded the Basel Mission Society. Among their early missionaries were laymen Conrad Schick and Ferdinand Palmer who focused on teaching clock-making, olive wood carving, and building trades.[21]

Schick soon became one of the most famous nineteenth-century architects in the city of Jerusalem. His skills as an architect and as a builder became known,[22] just as residents of Jerusalem were for the first time moving outside the Old City. His major project was the entire neighborhood of Mea Shearim with 100 apartments completed in 1874 for new Jewish immigrants. Nearby on Prophets Street he built the German Hospital, his own residence at Beit Tabor,[23] and St. Paul's Anglican Church, as well as other buildings throughout the city, some to be mentioned later.[24]

One cannot mention Schick without also noting his contributions to new archaeological study including Gordon's Golgotha, Hezekiah's Tunnel, the Temple Mount;[25] his mapping of Jerusalem; and his role in founding the Palestine Exploration Fund with publications sponsored by the British consulate in 1865.[26]

In 1854, Spittler sent another graduate of the Basel program, Johann Ludwig Schneller, who began teaching at the Gobat school. He was the first foreigner to live outside the walls, where he was quick to learn Arabic. When he learned of the massive numbers of deaths of Maronite Christians at the hands of the Druze in Lebanon, he journeyed north to investigate, returning with nine orphan boys. With his wife, Magdalene, he turned their home into an orphanage, called in German *Das Syrische Waisenhaus,* officially opened in 1860. He followed up with several more trips to Lebanon, so that within a year, they were caring for forty orphans.[27] He bought another twenty-five acres of land from the village of Lifta and, with Conrad Schick designing and building the compound, soon developed a rather innovative form of *diakonia,* providing for wholistic needs of individuals.[28] By 1868, he had added a dormitory for girls and a year later began a program for the blind. In addition to regular school work, students were provided with vocational training, including a shoe-making shop, a print shop, a laundry, a bakery, and a clinic.[29] The Schneller compound eventually exceeded the Old City of Jerusalem in size. At the time of his death in 1896 his sons took over his work.

Several years prior to the arrival of Schneller, Bishop Gobat had met Theodore Fliedner, who had recently established a program for deaconesses in the small village of Kaiserswerth on the Rhine River.[30] In 1851, four deaconesses from Kaiserswerth arrived to start a school for girls called Talitha Kumi and a hospital. Education was a rarity for young girls in the Middle East, but the school became quite successful, preparing many for careers as nurses. As the school grew, a new building was constructed by Schick in 1867, west of the city at a place called Gottfried's Height, with the capacity to accommodate 140 girls.[31]

Schools and orphanages became the backbone of diaconal efforts. It was in these educational institutions that young Arab men and women began to learn the distinctive Evangelical Lutheran theology. By 1864, with the Bible having been translated into Arabic in Lebanon, Gobat was able to encourage individual Bible reading for students.[32] Printing presses, newspapers, and literary societies soon brought about a well-educated and well-read Arab Palestinian Christian society.

Gobat's focus on education was diaconal by nature. Yet he faced a dilemma because he had no intention of creating friction with the already established churches. While some of the students were orphans, most of them came from the Orthodox or Catholic churches, along with a few Muslims, and from these students came the core of the Lutheran church in Jerusalem.

He tried his best to convince others that he was not deliberately proselytizing. Likely such criticisms grew out of frustrations from an 1850 *firman* from the Ottoman government that legalized conversions from other churches to Protestantism, a decision designed to steer these missionaries away from Muslims as possible converts.[33] However, during the early years of his tenure several hundred Arab Christians requested to be confirmed as Lutherans. For a while, Gobat encouraged students to remain within their churches, thinking that he could make them better Orthodox and better Catholics through their education and knowledge of the Bible. However, in some cases young Christians were excommunicated by zealous priests when they attended his schools. In 1910, after fifty years of the Schneller School, it was decided to examine the records of the hundreds of students who had gone through that program. There were only ten baptisms among all those students. Similarly, from the non-Protestant students at that institution, only about one-fifth of them were confirmed Lutherans.[34] Yet by the time of his death in 1879, the members of Gobat's churches numbered 1,000 members.[35]

While there was no shortage of missionaries, Bishop Gobat made it a priority to train local leaders, a decision that would bear much fruit in the long run. From the graduates of the schools, he appointed teachers, evangelists, and Bible readers. In 1871, he ordained the first Palestinian pastor. New church buildings were being constructed: Christ's Church in Nazareth (1871), St. Paul's Church outside the current New Gate in Jerusalem (1874), St. Philip's Church in Nablus (1882), and St. Andrew's in Ramallah (1888).[36] These congregations would form the nucleus of the Anglican church.

The End of the Joint Bishopric

When Bishop Gobat died in 1879, the British appointed as his successor Joseph Barclay, who had previously headed up the LJS mission in Jerusalem from 1856 to 1870, and who had been publicly critical of Gobat's work, saying that disproportional support had been given to the German work. As bishop, Barclay served primarily as pastor of the British-Jewish congregation and offered no new initiatives.[37] After only less than two years, Barclay died. At the request of the Germans, the joint bishopric agreement was terminated in 1886.

The *Jerusalemsverein* (Berlin Society for Mission)

In addition to important contributions from the Basel mission, Lutherans from Berlin were showing interest in Jerusalem. Already from 1844 to 1846, Friedrich Adolf Strauss, a Berlin pastor and professor, traveled through the Middle East, carefully noting the places related to the Bible. Upon his return he published these as *Sinai und Golgatha*, which became very famous in Germany through eleven printings. One of his illustrations, labeled as *Johanniterhospitaleta Portal*, was the northern portal of the ruins that would become the Lutheran Church of the Redeemer a half century later.[38] These reports sparked interest in the Holy Land.

In 1852, the Lutheran Pastor Strauss and others who had visited Jerusalem and had observed early mission work, established the Jerusalem Society of Berlin (*Jerusalemsverein*) to contribute financially to this work. One of Bishop Gobat's schools had been started in Bethlehem in 1854 and interest quickly grew to start a German Lutheran congregation. Gobat turned to the *Jerusalemsverein* to purchase land in the Muslim Quarter on the western edge of Bethlehem, away from the Church of the Nativity. Because of its connection with the *Jerusalemsverein,* the newly built school[39] was known as the German School—where girls were admitted from the beginning and where students were taught German language, math, and science, in addition to religion. By 1893, they were able to build the Evangelical Christmas Church. Other German-speaking congregations were established in Beit Jala (1886), Beit Sahour, and Hebron.

The *Jerusalemsverein* also sent pastors for a German language congregation in Jerusalem including, from 1866 to 1869, Carl Hoffmann, whose father was Pastor Wilhelm Hoffmann, the president of the *Jerusalemverein* in Berlin and a court chaplain for the Prussian King Wilhelm I.

This was an era when Prussia was growing in power leading up to the unification of Germany under the Emperor Wilhelm I, who ruled no less than twenty-one million subjects and saw himself as the new Charlemagne. Already envisioning this expansion of power, Wilhelm had secured in 1869 from the Ottoman Sultan Abdul Aziz I the ruins of St. Mary Latin Church and the Hospital of St. John on Muristan Road, just a stone's throw away from the Church of the Holy Sepulchre. The Order of the Knights of St. John had built the complex in the twelfth century to provide care for as many as 2000 persons at a time during the era of the crusades.[40] The first evangelical chapel there was named the Chapel of St. John, in 1871, restored from the ruins of the hospital refectory, and plans were made for the construction of a large church to represent German interests.

The German Colony

While these developments were taking place, there was a third strand developing in Jerusalem, a group that had arrived, not for mission, but to maintain their own existence in an end-of-the-world scheme. This movement had its beginnings among pietists in the Wuerttemberg region of southwest Germany. One of its leaders, Christoph Hoffmann, had studied theology at Tübingen and had served for several years with the Chrischona Mission in Basel. However, separating from the church, he and Georg David Hardegg formed the Temple Society (or Templers—not to be confused with the Templars) in 1861 with the goal of preparing for the rebuilding of the temple in Jerusalem and hastening the second coming of Christ. Condemned by the Lutheran Church in Wuerttemberg, they set out to build colonies in the Holy Land where their unique form of spirituality, combined with a carefully designed program to improve the quality of life in Palestine through building projects, agriculture, and economic development, would usher in the kingdom of Jesus. In 1868, they established a large, successful German colony in Haifa, which has subsequently been credited in shaping the character of the city.[41]

After a falling out between the two leaders of the sect, a schism resulted with Hoffmann leading his faction to settle first at Sarona near Jaffa, where they were the first to market Jaffa oranges,[42] and then by 1873 in the Rephaim Valley southwest of Old City Jerusalem, an area of carefully planned streets with houses resembling the two-story structures of Germany.[43] The Hardegg faction turned to the Church of Sweden and then the London Missionary Society for support, but were rejected. The Jerusalem colony, however, was in a somewhat different situation because Christoph Hoffmann's brother was Wilhelm Hoffmann, the former president of the Berlin-based *Jerusalemverein*, and his nephew, Carl Hoffmann, had served as Lutheran pastor in Jerusalem from 1866 to 1869.[44] With Germany now unified, there also seemed more openness from the Berlin-led church. Although the Templers had arrived for a different purpose, the *Jerusalemverein*, seeing itself to be the mother institution for German mission activity, sought to bring all the Germans under its wing. Many German colony residents sent their children to the German Lutheran School.[45] However, they built a separate church building in the colony.[46] Some estimates were that one-third of the colony movement eventually became connected to the Lutheran church. By 1886, a group from Haifa appealed for acceptance by the Prussian Lutherans. Five years later, the Berlin-based *Jerusalemverein* sent funding to help them build their church, dedicated by the Jerusalem Lutheran pastor, Carl Schlicht, and then provided financial support for their own pastor.[47] The German colony of Haifa soon grew to about 750 residents.

These developments lead to the presence of different factions among German Protestants in the Holy Land. The older faction of Schneller and the

Kaiserswerth deaconesses under Gobat came for *diakonia* to the Arab residents of the land, which resulted in the beginning of Arab congregations. The new immigrants had come to colonize the land and seemed to have little interest in the local population. The *Jerusalemverein*, which funded much good work among Arabs, was now funding congregations for German residents because it considered itself to be a mother institution for all German work in Palestine.

The Evangelical Lutheran Church of the Redeemer

The acquisition of this significant property as well as the expansion of German political power were factors in the withdrawal from the joint Jerusalem bishopric. The Anglican church would continue to thrive, and by October 18, 1898, they would be represented by the large St. George's Cathedral on Nablus Road. For the Germans there was now a new focus, beyond the diaconal programs already established, with a German church in Jerusalem created for the sake of German residents. On Reformation Day (October 31, 1898), the Evangelical Lutheran Church of the Redeemer (*Erlöserkirche*) was dedicated with enormous fanfare. Designed by the well-known German architect, Friedrich Adler, the magnificent church structure with its dominant tower[48] was funded by the *Jerusalem Stiftung* created from the remaining finances of the now defunct joint bishopric. It is said that the Romanesque Revival style was in some sense a return to the crusader era and became typical of German imperialism.[49] A note on Adler's drawing read: "His Majesty the Emperor has drawn the sketch for the bell tower with his own hand."[50]

Kaiser Wilhelm II and his wife the Kaiserin Augusta Victoria—accompanied by an entourage of thirty courtiers, sixty-five servants, and numerous security personnel, with 600 Turkish soldiers and 800 mule drivers for luggage making up a procession of over 2,000 persons and 1,300 horses and mules[51]— made their way to Jerusalem for this event with the greatest pomp and circumstance. Wilhelm saw himself as more than just the guardian of Protestantism; rather, he considered himself the Christian emperor of all Germans. On that same afternoon of October 31, Kaiser Wilhelm took possession and presented to German Benedictines property for the Church of Dormition outside Zion Gate. Similarly, he obtained property across from Damascus Gate for the Catholics to construct St. Paul's Hospice, which eventually became Schmidt's Girls School. Wilhelm also presented himself as protector of German Jews, meeting with Theodor Herzl.[52] Perhaps the crowning achievement of the kaiser's 1898 visit was the acquisition of 150 acres on the Mount of Olives for the construction of the Augusta Victoria Pilgrims Hospice and Ascension Church. The construction of the compound was even more of an imperial endeavor, with much of the building materials imported from Germany. Four large bells, the largest weighing six tons, were shipped from Hamburg for the fifty-meter high church tower. They were so large that the road from Jaffa to Jerusalem had to be widened before they could be transported. When the building was completed in 1910, it was considered the most modern in Jerusalem, the first building with electricity. No longer was the church in Jerusalem a sign of Lutheran presence; it was a symbol of German Lutheranism.

While the diaconal ministries in Jerusalem among the Arab population and Arab-speaking congregations were beginning to blossom, the German congregation continued to serve German expatriates.

First Half of the Twentieth Century: Setbacks of the War Years

All churches struggled through the years of World War I, with Christian institutions closed and personnel restricted following the arrival of General Allenby in Jerusalem on December 11, 1917. The Anglicans suffered because of a scarcity of funding due to the war efforts in Britain. However, with the British Mandate established from 1922 to 1948, the church in Jerusalem was bolstered by an influx of personnel.

The opposite was the case for the Lutherans. The German community, as citizens of an enemy nation of the British, were put under severe restrictions. The Schneller School was closed until 1921 in order to house displaced British citizens. Only a few Germans, such as Theodore Schneller and Deaconess Barkhausen of the Kaiserswerth Hospital, were allowed to stay. Most of the others, including the deaconesses at Talitha Kumi School, were imprisoned at Halwan, Egypt, for the duration of the war; the British took over the school until 1926. General Allenby took over the Augusta Victoria compound in 1917 as the British military headquarters and then as the administrative center of the British Mandate until 1928. During the 1930s there was something of a return to normality.

In the meantime, Arab leadership rose to the occasion with Fu'ad Kurban taking official responsibility for Redeemer Lutheran Church. Said Abbud served as pastor in Bethlehem, and Iskander Haddad in Beit Jala, elevated from their earlier status as assistant pastors. The Palestinian Protestant Congregation of Jerusalem was officially established on June 30, 1929. The name reflects the rising interest over the previous decade of Palestinian identity and a growing interest between Lutherans and Anglicans in eventually forming their own united

Protestant church. The congregation was placed under the direction first of the German Lutheran *propst* and second of the German director of the Schneller School, with Arab leadership assisting. The smaller Redeemer chapel was still designated as the place for the congregation's worship, with a second worship site near the orphanage. Purchase of Arabic language hymn books from Lebanon helped to establish an independent character for the congregation. With the retirement of Rev. Kurban in 1931, the Arab congregation joined in offering financial support for his successors, including Schedid Baz Haddad and Daoud Haddad, who had studied theology in Germany.[53]

However, with the onset of World War II, all German personnel were arrested and many were deported. The German Lutheran Propst Johannes Doering was interned in a prison camp from 1940 to 1945. The German colony and descendents of the Templer movement were cited for their strong pro-Nazi stance and deported. Once again, Lutheran institutions were closed. The deaconesses at Talitha Kumi were sent to Wilhelma near Lod, with the school itself torn down following the war to build a shopping center. The Schneller School was turned into the central British army camp during the war, then turned over to the Israeli army for an officers barracks until 2008; the orphanage was never rebuilt. British military barracks were erected on the Augusta Victoria compound, and the hospice was turned into a 1,400-bed military hospital. From 1940 on, the Lutheran Church of the Redeemer was closed for services.

The leadership of Palestinian Christians was tested by fire. Because many Arab Lutherans had learned to speak German, they were immediately considered suspect. From 1939 on, the British imprisoned Tawfiq Ca'naan, the son of the founding Arab pastor of the Beit Jala congregation, Bishara Ca'naan, because he had a German wife.[54] Daoud Haddad had just returned from four years of theological study at Neuendettelsau, Germany, and was interrogated thoroughly by British forces. However, he was ordained just days prior to the deportation of Propst Doering and served the families of the Schneller congregation through the war years without pay.[55] For the most part, all the Arab pastors and evangelists found themselves with additional responsibilities for much of the decade without receiving financial remuneration due to the extremely difficult circumstances.

The Post-War Era: ELCJ/ELCJHL

The difficult years of World War II were followed in the Holy Land by further conflict: the United Nations partition of Palestine, the Israeli-Arab war of 1948-49, and the flight of refugees, including a high number of Christian families. Already in 1946 Rev. Dr. Edward Moll arrived from the American Lutheran Church to negotiate for confiscated properties. Both the Schneller Orphanage and the Talitha Kumi School and hospital properties were lost to the church. The newly-formed Lutheran World Federation in Geneva was able to take over responsibility for the Augusta Victoria compound on the Mount of Olives and, in conjunction with the Red Cross and the United Nations Relief and Works Agency, was able to convert the institution into a hospital for Palestinians. Moll was able to reopen the Lutheran Church of the Redeemer, which had been closed since 1940, and to arrange for Rev. Daoud Haddad to serve as Redeemer's pastor. Haddad describes overflowing prayer services in St. John's Chapel every night of the conflict. On Sundays they were allowed to use the large sanctuary, including one Sunday worship when Israel shells hit the building, damaging stained glass windows; worshippers had to lie on the floor while gunshots penetrated the building.[56] By 1954, Haddad and others began to pastor in Ramallah where refugee families from Jaffa, Ramle, and Lod had fled. This led to the building of the first Arab Lutheran Church in Ramallah in 1964.

It was not until 1957 that German Lutheran personnel were again arriving in Jerusalem. Through the assistance of the LWF, ownership of the Lutheran Church of the Redeemer was retained by the *Jerusalem Stiftung*, with the understanding that it could never be sold. For seventeen years, Palestinian leadership not only had kept the church alive, but also had helped it thrive during extremely difficult circumstances. It was only natural for an independent Palestinian church to become an official entity. Because of the time involved to receive official recognition from Jordan, the year 1959 is considered the beginning of the ELCJ/ ELCJHL. On May 7, 1959, King Hussein recognized the Evangelical Lutheran Church in Jordan[57] as an autonomous religious community. The ownership of property, however, remained in the hands of the *Stiftung*. The Arab church was shaped significantly by Rev. Haddad who spent the post-war decades gathering and translating worship materials that eventually led to the publication in 1985 of a 600-page Lutheran liturgical book in Arabic.[58]

With the LWF having carried out significant work in Jerusalem in the post-war years, a natural development was that the ELCJHL became a member of the LWF in 1974, on the condition that it be lead by a Palestinian bishop and that the Augsburg Confession be translated into Arabic. In 1979, the first Palestinian Lutheran bishop was consecrated, Bishop Daoud Haddad, followed by Bishop Naim Nasser, and then myself, Munib Younan.[59] The *Propst*, however, was considered to represent the Evangelical Church in Germany (EKD). Congregations of the ELCJHL include the Arab congregations in Jerusalem, Bethlehem, Beit Jala, Beit Sahour, Ramallah, and Amman in Jordan, with about 3,000 members. Four schools have an enrollment of 2,000 students, and the church operates other educational ministries, women's and youth programs.

As a member church of the Lutheran World Federation and in my role as LWF president, the ELCJHL maintains a "companionship" relationship with Lutheran churches around the world who follow an accompaniment model of mission. The organizational name is the Coordination Committee of Overseas Partners for the ELCJHL (COCOP).[60] The Lutheran character of the ELCJHL was strengthened with my translation of the Augsburg Confession into Arabic,[61] in a sense carrying on the intention of Philip Melanchthon in translating this historic Lutheran document into Greek. Today dialogue and cooperation is common between the ELCJHL and the Greek Orthodox Church; I serve along with the Greek Orthodox patriarch as one of the Jerusalem heads of churches; the ELCJHL is an active member of the Middle East Council of Churches where I serve as president for the Evangelical Family of Churches while Patriarch Theophilus serves as president of the Orthodox family in the MECC. The ELCJHL in 2011 was accepted on an interim basis for associate member status in the World Council of Churches.

Conclusions

1. The arrival of Anglican and German mission personnel primarily in the middle of the nineteenth century has shaped the Protestant experience in a different way than the experience of the Orthodox church. The Orthodox still carry the burden of humiliation both by the European crusaders which sharpened the dispute between East and West churches and by the fall of Constantinople in 1453 to the Muslims resulting in the Ottoman Empire controlling the Middle East for four and a half centuries. The arrival of Protestantism came along with the establishment of British and German consuls in Jerusalem at the invitation of the Ottomans as a way of bolstering the disintegration of that once powerful empire. To some degree the Ottomans even encouraged competition and friction between Protestants and Orthodox with a *firman* in 1850 that permitted the conversions of Orthodox to Anglican and Lutheran. At the same time, the *Status Quo* agreement of 1852 recognized the priority of the Greek Orthodox patriarch in Jerusalem. Slowly by the late twentieth century relations began to improve. With this heavy historical baggage, one must ask if the Orthodox will ever be able to forgive. Or will they continue to be suspicious of Catholic and Evangelical churches?

I believe that we need, in an ecumenical sense, to accompany one another for the sake of the witness of the Arab church.

2. The diaspora in Jerusalem is different than any other, with some arriving for religious motives and others for political motives. Some came with a sense of individual pietism, others with a desire to establish evangelical work, and still others with a sense of ecclesiastical expansion. There is no doubt that some who came with the diaspora, like the German Templers, wanted to be in Jerusalem for the time of the parousia. Their group did not integrate themselves with the local grassroots but continued to stand apart from them, loyal to the regime that was governing their country without any critical questioning.

3. After World War II, at the same time as the rise of pan-Arabism, local churches that were the outgrowth of missionaries found themselves for a time on their own, benefitting from the nurture and edification of their own Arab leadership. Many missionaries saw the importance of this transformation and worked to strengthen the local churches in order to ensure the continuity of the work they had begun. Likewise, local government such as the Kingdom of Jordan offered encouragement. Beginning in 1957, Jordan was trying to formulate legislation supporting the indigenization of the Orthodox church to promote more local leadership. For the Anglicans, the Lutherans, and the Catholics these efforts succeeded in bringing to fruition this process of Arabization, especially with the consecration of Arab Palestinian bishops. How did the diaspora churches with their expatriate leaders and members respond? Usually they were challenged by this Arabization, which continues to be a source of tension. Some of the expatriates tended to align themselves with one political side or the other, but in fact their support of the government in power served to prolong their positions in Jerusalem. At the same time, the local church can move forward in a positive manner because of the freshness of the Gospel; the diaconal ministries of education and social work are a lasting benefit to the life of the local church.

4. Today's accompaniment model of inter-church relationships is one that has developed as an outgrowth of the missionary efforts of the Anglican and Lutheran churches in the nineteenth century. This certainly is not unique to Jerusalem, but is a global phenomenon as colonial empires have come to an end and as indigenous churches have emerged around the globe. How can North and South, East and West, cooperate with each other?

The LWF document *Mission in Context* speaks of this changing relationship among churches:

Given the increasing complexity of today's contexts in mission, partnership in mission is more crucial than ever before. New models of partnership that promote equal participation and sharing of responsibility are being tried. Churches in the North and in the South are now talking about *accompaniment* in mission. As the word accompaniment comes from companion, which means "sharing bread together," companion churches in mission share all their resources with one another. As in the Emmaus story, companions share the journey together with all the concerns, pains, hopes, and joys that each one brings. The resurrected Christ, who joins the journey, makes the companionship empowering and transforming for the church and the world.

In some churches, for historical and structural reasons, mission is still carried out through independent, church related agencies. This practice needs further and deeper theological reflection in light of the ecclesiological understanding of the church as missional. In order to avoid blurring the roles and responsibilities of the church itself in God's mission, some mission agencies have taken the initiative to challenge the church to reflect on the nature of the church as missional. Integrating mission into church structures, locally and globally, as well as bringing together witnessing through word and deed, into one structure, would be part of the discussion.[62]

Within the German diaspora, there were already three different groups in the Holy Land in the nineteenth century. The earliest missionaries were Swabian pietists from Basel who came not intentionally to start churches, but to provide *diakonia* through schools, hospitals, and social work. In particular, we hold up the work of Johannes Schneller and the Syrian Orphanage, the Kaiserswerth deaconesses and Talitha Kumi School, and the leadership of Bishop Gobat in promoting education. The second model is the establishment of German schools and churches for German expatriates. The third model is that of the Templer movement, who came to Jerusalem to hasten the second coming of Christ. Of these, the Templer movement is now gone, having been expelled for political reasons a generation ago. Interestingly, the early Jerusalem institutions of the first model, *diakonia*, are long gone, but their fruits live on in the children, grandchildren, and great-grandchildren of the early beneficiaries of these diaconal programs. The ELCJHL looks with appreciation on the work of its forbearers and on its seeds which blossomed during difficult circumstances in the twentieth and twenty-first centuries to be a partner church with Lutheran churches around the world who walk in an accompaniment model.

In particular, this accompaniment model is manifested in two ways:

a. Agreements with nine different churches led in 1977 to the idea of COCOP as a way for churches who shared part of this history in common to share together in mission.

b. The 2007 agreement between the ELCJHL and the EKD, which recognized the long history of mission shared together in this place that would continue in future years through accompaniment with the German ministries, the *Propst* representing the EKD and the bishop representing the ELCJHL as the local expression of the global Lutheran communion worldwide.

So the two models strengthen each other, with all respecting the local church and its history.

With this rich heritage, we can neither erase history nor change it. This history is only a mirror of the past, and we cannot relive the past. Nor can our history imprison us from future plans. It is essential that history becomes a tool by which we learn from the past, to frame the present, to inspire and shape the future.

In this world in which we live together with Christians and Jews, the church must be seen as working with one mission for the sake of the other. For this reason, when we celebrated 170 years of work in the Holy Land, our theme was "Living Witness and Creative *Diakonia*" to strengthen the local church as witnessing church. We ask you to carry us in your prayers.

Fifty Years of Living Witness and Creative *Diakonia*

Lutheran Church of the Redeemer, Jerusalem
Anniversary Worship Service • May 17, 2009

The grace of our Lord Jesus Christ, the love of God the Father, and the communion of the Holy Spirit be with you evermore.

> Remember your leaders, those who spoke the word of God to you; consider the outcome of their way of life, and imitate their faith. Jesus Christ is the same yesterday and today and forever (Hebrews 13:7-8).

Dear sisters and brothers in Christ,

One morning Napoleon Bonaparte stood on the balcony of the Louvre palace holding his son, the crown prince, in his arms. He declared to the people, "The future is mine." After many years, the well-known French poet Victor Hugo answered this emperor in a poem: "No! The future is God's."

Years passed, and Bonaparte was deposed from his office. He spent the rest of his life as a prisoner on St. Helene Isle, reviewing his past and present, his deeds and wars, his victories and losses, saying, "What I have established by the sword and the canon has collapsed. But what you, Jesus, the Nazarene, established by love and sacrifice, will endure forever."

This was the introduction of the sermon by the first president of the synod of the Evangelical Lutheran Church in Jordan and the Holy Land, the late Pastor Shadeed Baz Haddad, at the first session of the synod in 1959. Today we stand with those who preceded us and with those who are still working with us, to celebrate what the early missionaries established 170 years ago by love and sacrifice.

We stand with those who united the church by establishing the synod and with those who established the Arab bishopric in 1979. We stand with them in humility, yet are proud to know that the Holy Spirit is working in our church. We stand with *Propst* Weiggelt, who was the spiritual leader of this church at that time. At the first session of the synod he said, "For more than 130 years, Arab and German pastors and other lay members in the church and the Evangelical Lutheran schools, worked together inspired by the word of God and his Spirit from the spiritual side, and the moral and financial support given by *Jerusalemsverein* in Berlin."

This support was widened by the theology of accompaniment and by establishing the Coordinating Committee of Overseas Partners known as COCOP. We have developed church-to-church relationships with these partners. Our partner churches in Finland, Sweden, Germany, Norway, U.S.A., Canada, and the LWF have signed official accompaniment agreements. We thank all our partners, local and abroad, who have helped us to become a strong Arab Palestinian Evangelical Lutheran church that preaches the word of God and serves God's people. I agree with the poet Hugo when he says, "The future is God's." For we say the future is for every living church that serves with love and sacrifice. The future is for every church where the message of Christ never gets old, but continually revives the church, for "Jesus Christ is the same yesterday, today, and forever."

It is said that a famous evangelist asked a ministry candidate when he decided to study theology. The student answered, "It was when I heard a sermon in the school church." The evangelist asked him, "Who was the preacher?" The student said, "I do not remember his name. All that I know is that the preacher showed me the face of Jesus Christ."

For this reason, if you asked me today for a list of the names of those in the cloud of witnesses who labored to establish this church I would tell you, "I do not remember all their names. I only remember that they have shown us the face of Jesus Christ. They did not leave us anything except a living example and a renewed inspiration." We are able to be a church and to serve today because of their living witness and creative *diakonia*. For ever since the evangelical movement began in the Middle East in the nineteenth century, it has borne good fruit.

We also do not remember all the names of those who served the evangelical family, whether in the Holy Land or the whole Middle East. But what we do know is that God sent them to us as an example and an inspiration. Their message was very clear. They revived the word of God in the hearts of the local people. They established schools and universities. They translated the Bible into Arabic. They strengthened the awareness of being responsible for the land on which we live. They initiated the ecumenical movement. They built and established churches. They created social and medical ministries.

And since the establishment of our synod on May 17, 1959, the ELCJHL has continuously flourished. Our work has increased. Our structure is better organized. We have established churches in Ramallah and Amman. We respond to the needs of society by establishing services that implant Christians in their land and help them responsibly to continue to be a living witness. I am not in a position to count our work or boast, but I would say that this work attests to the fact that our Lord has sent his Holy Spirit to be among us. In spite of our mistakes and shortcomings, our risen Lord has made us a living church with a living witness and creative *diakonia*.

Thirty years ago, the Arab Evangelical Lutheran bishopric was established. Our synod unanimously voted for this blessed, historic decision. All our partner churches fully supported this. The first Arab Palestinian bishop was the late Bishop David Haddad and the second was the late Bishop Naim Nasser, both of whom handed on to me what they received. At my 1998 consecration, I declared the words of St. Paul: "For I am not ashamed of the gospel. It is the power of God for salvation for everyone" (Romans 1:16). I publicly declared that my mission is the mission of my church; that is, to proclaim the good news, to celebrate the sacraments, to educate the generations from the womb to the tomb, to work for the unity of the church, and to work for reconciliation among the people. I continue to stand with our church, its congregations, its schools and its educational, cultural, diaconal, and social institutions in asking God, "Lord, continue to make of us good examples by being living witnesses, renewing inspiration and offering vital *diakonia*, so that we continue to assure everyone that Jesus Christ is the same yesterday, today, and forever."

Dear sisters and brothers in Christ, the church of the resurrection teaches us that the strength of the Christian church is not in its numbers or its political power or its history or its buildings or property or its bank accounts. The strength of the church is always in its vital proclamation of the Gospel of salvation and its constructive, positive impact on society. The ELCJHL—like all churches in the Holy Land and the whole Middle East—is small in number. Its strength is that it made way for the Holy Spirit to work in us, to guide us, and to lead us, allowing us to become the local expression of worldwide Evangelical Lutheranism.

The love of God works in our church, and so we serve human beings regardless of religion, gender, doctrine, political, or religious affiliation. The love of Christ is reflected in us as we serve human beings for the sake of humanity. Our living witness and creative *diakonia* have shaped this church to be an instrument for peace based on justice, a ministry of reconciliation, a defender of human rights including women's rights, initiators of dialogue among religions, educators of the coming generations, and apostles of love. For this reason, I say our church has taken its pulpit to the streets, being a living witness in the streets of our land, thus responding to God's call for a vital *diakonia*.

Arab Christianity has existed since the first Pentecost. Our church, as part of the evangelical family, is an integral part of this ongoing Arab witness. If you read the history of our church, you observe that it has remained steadfast in the midst of political and economic turbulence. To that I respond simply that "God has put us here for a holy commission." The secret of our existence is our diversity, which serves as a living example and the source of inspiration. God calls all churches and Christians to be one, to work together, to witness together, to heal together and to work for justice together. So the ELCJHL continues to extend its hand to all our brothers and sisters in the churches of Jerusalem and tells them: God calls us to serve with you, to witness with you, and to pray and carry the message of love with you, in order that the banner of Christ will be over our land. To our sisters and brothers who live with us and serve the expatriate Christians in Jerusalem, we tell you that our church is at your service, to proclaim the message of Christ. And we tell our evangelical brothers and sisters in the Middle East, and the other church families in the MECC, that God has called us to be a witness of love together, for the world is waiting to hear from us a single voice speaking a common word of love, justice, and service.

We also want to tell the representatives of our partner churches in the world that the ELCJHL wants to carry with you the message of love and join you in our Christian vocations. We will work with you locally and globally for social justice, for gender balance, and for addressing such problems as climate change. We collaborate to oppose all forms of extremism, xenophobia, anti-Semitism, Islamophobia, or Christianophobia. Our church readily works with you, for we believe that this is an integral part of its living witness and creative *diakonia*. But allow me, a resident of Jerusalem, to remind you not to forget the Arab Christians in Jerusalem, whose numbers are declining. For what is Jerusalem without those who first carried Christ's message to the world 2,000 years ago?

The church of Christ does not live in shrines but in its people. For this reason, our church hears Christ when he says, "He has anointed me to bring good news to the poor; he has sent me to proclaim release to the captives and recovery of sight to the blind; to let the oppressed go free" (Luke 4:18).

Christ's message was one of peace and justice. Our church has existed amidst political and economic difficulties, leading many of our members to be displaced and some to emigrate. Our church suffers with all who suffer. We see religious fanaticism and political extremism growing, for the common denominator between the Israeli and the Palestinian peoples is fear. Our church is afraid that there are those who want to shift the political conflict into religious war. We are afraid that this fear, insecurity, and continuous denial of the other results in more hatred, more bloodshed, more violence. But our church wants to be a church with a prophetic vocation. It wants to heal the broken hearted, to call for release for the prisoners and restoration of sight for the blind. It wants to continue, with God's grace, to work for justice and reconciliation, peace, forgiveness, and coexistence with shared responsibility. For this reason, we say to all politicians at this celebration: Our nations are tired. It is time to implement justice in which both peoples can live in their own states with security, freedom, peace, and reconciliation. It is time that both people comprehend that their security and freedom are symbiotic. It is time to hear the position, articulated by the patriarchs and heads of local churches in Jerusalem, that calls for a Jerusalem that is shared between three religions and two nations, Palestine and Israel. Our church will work with all people of good conscience for Christian, Muslim, and Jewish peoples, and together seek the common values that allow for justice, peace, forgiveness, and the acceptance of the other. Our church desires that future generations may live in freedom and security, and that this Holy Land will be a lighthouse for all. Now is the *kairos* moment for justice and peace in Jerusalem.

Hugo said, "The future is God's." This saying comes right from God through the Holy Spirit working in us. It calls us to apostolic vocation, as Jesus succinctly described it, to love God and love the neighbor as yourself. If we heed our Savior's call, then our work will continue to be a living example and continuous inspiration, a living witness and creative *diakonia*.

A Word for the Graduates

Dar al-Kalima College

29 July 2011

"And the word became flesh and lived among us" (John 1:1).

Dear graduates,

The analysts are left asking, and the pundits left questioning, following the terrorist attack that took place last week in Oslo, Norway, taking the lives of more than ninety people: Why was such a horrendous act committed in such a safe, secure country we know Norway to be? What led this man to do such a thing? Is it truly because this man wants Norway to be a land only for Norwegians? Or are there other motives behind it?

One can say that this right-wing, fanatic, Norwegian man is himself a victim—a victim of education toward hatred and fear and instigation to violence. For hatred and fear, when introduced into the heart of any person, can instigate in that person a vicious cycle that, if left unchecked, can convince people of personal, cultural, or ethnic superiority, fomenting in them tendencies that may result in violent terrorist attacks that are acceptable neither to humanity nor to God.

This is a dangerous and threatening cycle, and we in the Arab Christian church vehemently denounce the attacks in Norway and the cycle of violence that leads to such attacks. We call those right-wing groups that instigate fear of the other and xenophobia to turn from such education of hatred and instigation to violence, which are capable of warping people to the point that they hate not only those around them, but themselves as well.

I want to also mention a second series of events which took place just six months ago. This past January, I was touched in my heart and my eyes filled with tears when I watched the news reports about the Egyptian revolution. What moved me deeply was the scene when Muslim Egyptians in Tahrir Square protected Christian Egyptians during their Sunday service. And then in a similar way, when the Christian Egyptians protected Muslim Egyptians during their Friday prayers.

What touched me the most was that this generous gesture occurred only one month after the treacherous New Year's Day bombing of the Coptic Church of St. Mark and Pope Peter in Alexandria. So to all those near and far, it was made known that the "Revolution of Freedom" in Tahrir Square was to be a revolution aimed at preserving Christian–Muslim unity in Egypt. For those who wanted to muddle with religion for their own narrow factional interests, these demonstrations of mutual respect proved that the unity of the people is embodied when there is a sincere call for freedom for all. Such unity does not discriminate between rich and poor, between one social group and another, between one religion and another. Rather such a call for freedom always promotes national cohesion while standing against partisans, radicals, and exploiters of religion for narrow personal interests.

And it is because of this that I speak to you today about two things:

First, I wish to speak of right religion. Right religion is religion that combats any phenomena of instigation against the other and any incorrect generalizations that misrepresent those with whom we are thought to differ. The essence of religion is not hatred and fear of the other. Rather, the essence of religion is love of God and love of neighbor.

And therefore, in true and right religion no one is discriminated against based on his or her ethnicity, religion, or gender. No one has cause for pride that places him or her above any other. No one is looked at with fear and suspicion because they are different. Rather, pluralism is respected in right religion as God has created us as unique and different individuals. And right religion is completely separate from that which is used to justify hatred, killing, and oppression of the other.

Second, right religion also combats any instigation to violence that is taught—whether taught at home, from the pulpit, in mass media, or in public places. Such instigation plays upon the emotions of people to lead them to a place of hatred. For this reason, whenever we hear such instigation to violence and hatred against the other, it is our responsibility to stand up and speak out against it with one united voice. We cannot stand idle while others work to instigate hatred, attempt to undermine and undercut, work to defame, or create prejudice against any other. Such indignation is like the fire that burns the green grass before the dry. And those who instigate hatred must realize that children will learn to hate their parents before they learn to hate the other their parents call enemy.

The core values of all religion are love of God and love of neighbor. With this fundamental grounding in faith, true religion calls for respect and tolerance, understanding and dialogue between peoples, no matter their thinking, opinions, and movements.

But why does a bishop speak with such language at a graduation, let alone at the graduation ceremony for Dar al-Kalima Evangelical Lutheran College? For, indeed, Dar al-Kalima Evangelical Lutheran College is an institution that equips its students with the strongest instrument that a human being can carry throughout his or her life. And that instrument is the Word. We believe that the Word has become flesh and dwells among us.

We in the ELCJHL have placed a high emphasis on education—as has been the case in this land for over a century and a half. From kindergarten through the elementary grades, middle school, high school, and now university, we focus on preparing young people to take a role in our modern civil society. We are proud that our education is coeducational and brings Muslims and Christians together, learning to respect each other in all diversity, learning to respect our environment as gift and responsibility, learning to respect God who is the divine parent of us all.

We have taught you all civilized methods in which to express yourself—through painting or art, expression or music, film production or communication. And with a healthy word you are equipped to communicate a healthy message: A message that calls for a blessed pluralism and multiculturalism in which we listen to the voice of the other and not only our own voice.

It is with the Word that we will reform our society and offer guidance. It is with the Word that we will build a nation on the principles of peace and love, combating any education toward hatred and violence. It is with the Word that we will reshape our society on the principles of accepting the other and combating the ideas of both superiority and inferiority. It is with the Word that we will teach the world the principle of holding fast to right religion so that all extremism—whether religious or political—is swept away.

Therefore, we ask, as you depart from Dar al-Kalima Evangelical Lutheran College, that you carry with you this Word, the common Word between us all, the Word that is incarnated love in and for you, as well as in and for the other. I do not promise that it will always be an easy Word for you. But in the incarnation of the Word love, peace, and acceptance of the other will find its way in you and in the other—in your neighbor. For truly, I say to you: The Word has become flesh and dwells among us.

Congratulations to you all.

Messages of Reconciliation for a World of Division

Justice, Reconciliation, and Hope
United for God's Mission

LWF General Assembly
Stuttgart, Germany • July 2010

Dear sisters and brothers in Christ:

Salaam and grace from our Lord Jesus Christ!

Can you believe that it was a cup of chocolate milk that first connected me with the Lutheran communion?

Yes, chocolate milk was offered daily to every student, Christian or Muslim, in the Martin Luther School in Jerusalem in the 1950s. On it was written: "A gift from The Lutheran World Federation." This cup of chocolate milk physically nourished us refugees and was an answer to our prayer, "Give us today our daily bread." This cup also nurtured in us knowledge of the theology of the Lutheran communion; it taught us about God's love for us.

My parents were refugees. Our church, the Evangelical Lutheran Church in Jordan and the Holy Land, which grew out of the German mission work in the nineteenth century, embraced our family, educated us, and helped us stand on our feet, while inspiring us to serve others. Another example of this life-giving witness and service is COCOP—the organization made up of ELCJHL and its international church partners, which accompany us by sharing resources and encouragement. Since my childhood, I have asked myself, "How can I ever repay this generous love, though silver and gold have I none?"

A simple cup of chocolate milk sparked in me a love for the Lutheran church, even though I could not differentiate at that time between World Service, Church Cooperation, Lutheran World Relief, or others. The LWF's commitment to provide "daily bread" to those in need deeply impressed on me the truth of those who are justified by grace through faith. Today I believe the LWF's commitment to ensuring life with dignity for all is a powerful invitation to me and every Lutheran to creatively and energetically serve all humanity, regardless of gender, ethnicity, social status, religion, or political affiliation. This commitment emanates from our strong theology of the cross, that God so loved the *world*—not only Lutherans and Christians, but every human being. We are to serve the world as we are sustained by God's love.

It is imperative that the LWF communion remain united and strong, not for its own sake, but for God's mission in the world. Christ desires us to be one as he and the Father are one, and he promises to be with us, especially as we confront issues that threaten to divide us. We trust the Holy Spirit will help us communicate the Triune God among Christians and non-Christians, and serve humanity where God calls us, whether in mission, relief, education, *diakonia*, ecumenism, theological studies, or interfaith dialogue.

We must never lose sight of the fact that our love and our shared apostolic vocation unite us Lutherans with all Christians. Our theology of grace challenges us to be mediators and ecumenists, working and witnessing with one another as the family of God in a broken world. So our communion must strengthen existing dialogues, move forward toward signed agreements, and even dare to dialogue with evangelical churches and communities such as Pentecostals and Baptists, to work cooperatively toward reconciliation and healing in advancing God's kingdom.

As we plan to celebrate of the 500th anniversary of the Reformation in 2017, I pray that we remember *communion semper reformanda est*. Ours is a communion in which the Good News of Christ reforms us again and again in order to respond to the changing needs of the world with God's love and redemption.

As I grew up in Jerusalem among Jews and Muslims, I learned to focus on shared values such as peace, justice, and coexistence. The LWF, in coordination with mission societies and related agencies, must continue to reach across denominational and religious lines to focus on shared values in order to oppose extremism and xenophobia, especially anti-Semitism and Islamophobia. We must develop a common agenda to shape public policies that will effectively address poverty, food insecurity, climate change, illegitimate debt, gender discrimination, governmental corruption, and other contemporary issues. The world may delight in our disagreements, but we are to be boldly prophetic, promoting the Good News, speaking truth to power, and witnessing together in love.

Our agenda is clear: peace based on justice, reconciliation flowing from forgiveness, and hope blossoming from the miracle of resurrection. This is not political. This is about upholding the rights of the poor and oppressed. Since the justice of God culminated on the cross, seeking justice is an integral part of our spirituality and theology of the cross. When our communion speaks up for justice and calls for changes in unjust structures and practices, we carry our pulpit into the street and introduce the God of love to the world.

Surely Burmese pro-democracy activist Aung San Suu Kyi speaks to the hopes of captive people all around the world when she says, "Please use *your* freedom to promote *ours*."

With all our gifts, our communion can promote and protect human rights for all, bringing comfort to refugees, migrants, trafficked people, and disempowered people around the world. We can encourage persecuted Christians in Asia and Africa, advocate for innocent civilians in war-torn countries like Afghanistan and Iraq, stand up for oppressed minorities like Dalits and Romas, and facilitate reconciliation between majority and minority populations in places like Bangladesh, Latin America, Burma, Europe, and Turkey. Of course, the conflict in my own home is never far from my thoughts. It is my hope that God will allow me to see Israelis and Palestinians see God in each other and reach a political settlement. But rather than limiting my agenda, living in the midst of a difficult situation motivates me to work with all churches for justice, peace, and reconciliation in their contexts. It has taught me how to keep hope alive in hopeless situations.

As Dr. Martin Luther King Jr. said,

> As long as there is poverty in the world I can never be rich, even if I have a billion dollars. As long as diseases are rampant and millions of people in this world cannot expect to live more than twenty-eight or thirty years, I can never be totally healthy, even if I just got a good checkup at the Mayo Clinic. I can never be what I ought to be until you are what you ought to be. This is the way our world is made. No individual or nation can stand out boasting of being independent. We are all interdependent. (Address at Morehouse College Commencement, 2 June 1959, Atlanta Georgia.)

I would add that, as long as there is poverty, HIV/AIDS, food insecurity, oppression, and injustice, our Lutheran communion cannot be what it wants to be. Because of the urgency of these issues, we must enable mission societies and aid agencies to know an even deeper sense of ownership in this communion.

Let me close with the Scripture from my ordination and my consecration: "For I am not ashamed of the gospel; it is the power of God for salvation to everyone who has faith" (Romans 1:16). May we in our communion be empowered by the Gospel to faithfully work to create a common strategy for creative mission, prophetic *diakonia*, and genuine accompaniment.

I am honored to be a candidate for president of The Lutheran World Federation. It is a joy to have the opportunity to stand before *this* assembly on *this* occasion to say thank you for all the cups of chocolate milk and for all the ways in which God has acted through the Lutheran communion to bless me, my wife, Suad, our children, our extended family, the ELCJHL, and all people in need throughout God's creation.

Thank you for your prayerful support and love. May God bless you.

Reforming Luther

Toward a Prophetic Interfaith Dialogue for Life among Christians, Jews, and Muslims

The essence of Martin Luther's theology was his experience of justification by grace through faith, of being set free from his bondage to sin by the love of God in Christ so that he could live to serve God and others in joyful freedom. The question that drove him and others of his day was: How do I find a merciful and gracious God? Though this question remains, today there are also other questions.

Where is God in a world torn apart by fear of the other, violence, war, and injustice, with much of it committed in the name of God? What does justification by faith look like to people who live under occupation and oppression? What does justification by faith look like to people whose entire lives are captive to fear in our present age where extremism, terrorism, xenophobia, anti-Semitism, Islamophobia, and Christianophobia are haunting our mindset? How do we live with other faiths? How can we together be stewards of our earth and resources?

The future of global Lutheranism depends on our ability to speak God's liberating Gospel so that it is relevant for today's human condition. It lies in our ability to look theologically at our modern world, interpreting the human condition and the questions of the times, then listening to and giving fresh voice to God's saving activity in the midst of the brokenness. Justification today must go beyond the preoccupation with the freed, forgiven individual. Justification must bring God's healing liberation to communities of different faiths that are trying to live in peace and yet are trapped in oppression, injustice, and fear. Justification today must speak to the millions with HIV/AIDS, the thousands dying daily from starvation, the millions living in ethnic, religious, and political violence. Justification must be less preoccupied with eternal salvation and more attuned to the Gospel's message to set free and restore right relations in this world. Justification today means witnessing to the biblical message of *shalom* and *salaam* that the risen Christ brought to the disciples locked in their upper room behind doors of fear. The biblical message today must speak to us in our locked rooms of dehumanization, xenophobia, oppression, demonization, and perversions of truth, sending us out as ministers of reconciliation and salvation.

The Holy Scriptures have been abused by many to justify violence and oppression, especially in the Middle East conflict. Each religion is good at pointing the finger at the other and blaming the other for extremist behavior. But each religion has its own respective work to do. We Christians are no exception. Hans Küng said, "No peace among nations without peace among religions. And no peace among religions without dialogue."[64] This dialogue must be a prophetic dialogue for life among all faiths. It speaks the truth about reality yet dares to seek the common values for justice, peace, reconciliation, love, forgiveness, mutual respect, and human dignity for all. A study on international affairs in Norway said it well in 2002: "The great world religions have both similarities and fundamental differences. And one of the most important similarities is actually a conviction that it is part of the innermost essence of religion to be a source of peace and reconciliation.[65]

This is the great challenge: "Respect for plurality and diversity is put to the test in a special way in worldviews and beliefs that hold—each independently and in its own respective traditions—that they know the Truth itself. The credibility of religious convictions is put to the test in their desire for peace.[66] Justification by faith—the basis of Lutheran identity—helps us to work with other religions. It takes up the following important questions: How do we evaluate Luther's comments on Judaism and Islam in the modern world? Is it really possible to build a healthy theology that leads to peace and justice among all God's children—regardless of religion, race, or ethnicity—on the foundation of Martin Luther's medieval theology that actually dehumanized others? If we decide that our present task is to work toward mutual understanding and dialogue, then what does it mean to be "evangelical" in today's complicated world of religions? I begin with a discussion of Luther's understanding of Judaism and Islam in his own writings and then provide my own evaluation of Luther's theology of religions for today, followed by a proposal for a dialogue for life among global religions.

Luther and Judaism

Martin Luther's attitude toward Jews changed throughout his life. Until 1536, he expressed concern for their situation and was enthusiastic at the prospect of converting them to Christianity. After 1537, he demonized them and urged their harsh treatment, even persecution.

When Martin Luther began lecturing at the University of Wittenberg in 1513, he had rarely encountered Jews, nor had he ever lived in close proximity to them. He inherited a tradition of both theological and cultural hostility toward them. He was also strongly influenced by the Augustinian tradition, which held that the Jews are sacred because they were given the Old Testament but missed the key revelation of the Messiah. The fact that they could not find the Messiah meant that "God has shown the grace of his mercy to his Church 'in the midst of her enemies,' for, as St. Paul says: 'By their offense salvation has come to the Gentiles.'"[67] Luther's own late-medieval culture viewed Jews "as a rejected people, guilty of the murder of Christ, and capable of murdering Christian children for their own evil purposes."[68]

Although hostility and suspicion characterized the way Christians saw Jews in the Middle Ages, Luther's first treatise on the Jews advocated that they be treated in a friendly manner. Luther published an essay in 1523 entitled, "That Jesus Christ Was Born a Jew."[69] Luther's outlook toward Judaism was positive but called for a missionary stance. Luther hoped that the clarity of Christ's Gospel brought about by the Reformation would inspire Jews to convert to Christianity. He suggested that if Jews were dealt with in a friendly fashion and instructed carefully by the Holy Scriptures, many might become "genuine Christians and turn again to the faith of their fathers, the prophets and the patriarchs."[70] In his commentary, "The Magnificat" (1521), he wrote, "We ought, therefore, not to treat the Jews in so unkindly a spirit, for there are future Christians among them."[71] Luther's strategy was sensible and gradual: "Let them first . . . begin by recognizing this man Jesus as the true Messiah; after that they may . . . learn also that he is true God."[72]

In his later years, Luther's theological view of the Jews remained consistent with his position in 1523, while his practical recommendations for their treatment became very severe. Wilhelm Maurer sees a clear development between 1513 ("Lectures on the Psalms") and 1546 in Luther's pronouncement on Judaism. According to Maurer:

1. Luther regarded Jews as a people suffering under the wrath of God.

2. Without divine intervention they were incorrigible and impossible to convert by human efforts.

3. Their religion remained hostile to Christianity, and they could not cease blaspheming God and Christ.

4. A "solidarity of guilt" existed between Christians and Jews, a common suffering under God's wrath, a common resistance to Christ, a common attempt to gain one's righteousness and salvation apart from Christ, and a common need for grace.[73]

Many theologians ask why Luther proposed to secular authorities such harsh treatment of Jews. Luther writes in "On the Jews and Their Lies" (1543):

> First to set fire to their synagogues and schools and to bury and cover with dirt whatever will not burn. . . . Second, I advise that their houses be destroyed and destroyed. . . . Third, I advise that all their prayer books and Talmudic writing . . . be taken from them. . . . Sixth, I advise that usury be prohibited to them, and all cash and treasure of silver and gold be taken from them. . . . And you, my dear gentlemen friends who are pastors and preachers, I wish to remind faithfully of your official duty, so that you too may warn your parishioners concerning their eternal harm.[74]

This harsh polemic is characteristic of Luther who often appealed to apocalyptic books, such as John's Revelation, when pronouncing judgment on those he disfavored.

Luther tended in stressful situations to demonize his interlocutors, for example Roman Catholics or Jews. Church historian Roland Bainton referenced this polemic in his biography of Luther: "One could wish that Luther had died before ever this treatise was written. Yet one must be clear as to what he was recommending and why. His position was entirely religious and in no respect racial."[75] Dietrich Bonhoeffer wrote in a letter to his parents, "As long as a hundred years ago Kierkegaard said that today Luther would say the opposite of what he said then."[76] Mark Edwards argues that Luther surveyed his own times in the light of this archetype. Luther classified the papacy as the antichrist, the Turks as Gog (Revelation 20:8), the little horn in the Book of Daniel (Daniel 8:9) as contemporary Jewry and the remnant of a rejected people suffering under God's wrath, and his Protestant opponents as the false prophets and apostles who had plagued the true prophets and apostles of old.[77]

Luther contextualized his disagreements with his opponents in terms of a cosmic struggle between God and Satan. When he attacked Jews, Catholics, Turks, or "fanatics," he was not attacking mere humans. Rather, he was attacking Satan, the spirit of the false church motivating these opponents. All of humanity was divided between true and false church. The issues separating the true from the false church were not semantic; they distinguished the saved from the damned. Luther was convinced that he was living on the eve of the last judgment. Richard Marius states:

> Although the Jews for him were only one among many enemies he castigated with equal fervor. Although he did not sink to the horrors of the Spanish Inquisition against Jews, and although he was certainly not to blame for Adolf Hitler, Luther's hatred of the Jews is a sad and dishonorable part of his legacy, and it is not a fringe issue. It lay at the center of his concept of religion. He saw in the Jews a continuing moral depravity he did not see in Catholics.[78]

Contemporary Lutheran Church Responses to Luther on Judaism

The Lutheran church around the world has acknowledged its responsibility for the Holocaust in a spirit of repentance. A number of important documents have been issued by the Lutheran churches. In 1981, the first consultation of The Lutheran World Federation (LWF) and the International Jewish Committee on Interreligious Consultations (IJCIC—a joint agency of five major Jewish organizations) addressed joint questions such as the concept of the human being in Lutheran and Jewish traditions. The LWF met with the Jewish community for a second dialogue 11-13 July 1983, and acknowledged the "openness of views" and "spirit of mutual respect for the integrity of our faith communities," affirmed "the integrity and dignity of our two faith communities and repudiate[d] any organized proselytizing of each other," and committed to "trust replacing suspicion and with reciprocal respect replacing prejudice. To this end, we commit ourselves to periodic consultations and joint activities that will strengthen our common bonds in service to humanity.[79]

In 1988, I attended a consultation in Sigtuna, Sweden, to discuss the document, "Ecumenical Considerations of Jewish–Christian Dialogue." We concluded: "The teachings of contempt for Jews and Judaism in certain Christian traditions proved a spawning ground for the evil of the Nazis and the Holocaust. The church must learn to preach and teach the gospel so that it cannot be used toward contempt."[80]

The LWF document, "A Shift in Jewish–Lutheran Relations?" decisively claims that a theology of justification by faith does not support anti-Semitism.[81] The Evangelical Church in Germany (EKD) published a statement in 1950: "We confess that we have become guilty before the God of compassion by our omission and silence and then share the blame for the terrible crimes committed against the Jews by members of our nation."[82] Studies in 1975, 1991, and 2000 examined the theological issues at stake in Jewish–

Christian relations. Discussions focused on common uses of terms, for example, "covenant, and explosive issues, such as the evangelization of the Jews, the interpretation of Old Testament promises referring to the Holy Land and the Palestinian–Israeli conflict, and common moral responsibilities of synagogue and church in the modern world."

Numerous other churches, such as the Lutheran Church–Missouri Synod,[83] the Lutheran Church of Bavaria,[84] and the Evangelical Lutheran Church in America (ELCA), have formulated statements addressing anti-Semitism. In its 1994 "Declaration to the Jewish Community," the ELCA publicly repudiated the anti-Jewish views of Martin Luther, expressed repentance for Christian complicity in hatred and violence against the Jews through the centuries, and committed itself to building a relationship with the Jewish people based on love and respect.[85] This document is the basis for any Lutheran understanding concerning its relation to the Jewish community.

In September 2004, our church, the Evangelical Lutheran Church of Jordan and the Holy Land (ELCJHL), initiated a statement that condemns anti-Semitism. I stated that, "as a Palestinian Christian living under Israeli occupation, our church is concerned about the reemergence of anti-Semitism around the world, particularly in Europe. There is a clear distinction between the politics of the state of Israel and the attitudes of the Jewish people." I called on the LWF to reiterate its clear statements from the past by insisting, "We must fight anti-Semitism." The statement was unanimously accepted by the Council of the LWF. "The LWF Council voted to express its grave concern at the growth of anti-Semitism around the world and to restate its rejection and abhorrence of anti-Semitism."[86]

In 1987, Jewish and Christian laity and clergy formed an interfaith coalition, the Institute for Christian and Jewish Studies (*Dabru Emet*). They were concerned that ignorance, fear, and hostility all too often define the Christian–Jewish encounter. They were committed to in-depth studies of sacred writings and traditions in order to "reexamine the meaning of [respective] religious assumptions," "question the theological distortions and misconceptions that have contributed to the historical conflict between Christians and Jews," and "develop resources within our respective communities that inspire both Christians and Jews to appreciate the legitimacy and distinctiveness of one another."[87]

Luther and Islam

Luther and Islam,[88] like Luther and Judaism, must be contextualized in the Middle Ages and not appropriated as a guideline for the future. Luther lived during a time when fear of Islam was dominant. The Turks had extended their military power into Europe and were at Vienna's doorstep in 1529. Gregory Miller explains it succinctly: "To a large degree, the Turkish threat was so terrifying because many Germans understood the conflict between the Hapsburg and Ottoman Empires to be a struggle not between political powers but between the face of Christendom and that of its archenemy, Islam."[89] In this respect, Martin Luther was a man of his times.

Luther, like others, read this event through apocalyptic lenses. As early as 1518, Luther identified the Islamic faith (inseparable from "the Turks") as the "scourge of God." He believed that Muslims were God's punishment upon a sinful Christendom which had, among other sins, tolerated the papal abomination. The Turks would function as a German schoolmaster who must correct and teach the German people to repent of their sins and to fear God.

Sarah Heinrich and James L. Boyce explain that Luther's position was framed throughout this period by his perspective of the two realities, civil and spiritual, and the duties appropriate to each.[90] Luther repeatedly argued on the basis of Romans 13 for the obligation of obedience to all secular authority. According to Luther, they had instituted secular authorities, even the Turkish captors, for the preservation of order. His position was often charged for representing the Reformation's reluctance to fight against the Turkish invaders and thus hinder good morale on the part of Europe's defenders.

Luther was more concerned with Christians at home than with the Turks. He used the occasion of Europe's war with the Turks to articulate a theodicy; the present catastrophe was God's punishment for Christians. Luther issued to Christians a call for contrition and mandate for inner preparation. It was clear in "Explanations of the Ninety-Five Theses" (1518) that "to fight against the Turk is the same as resisting God, who visits our sin upon us with this rod."[91] In his "On War against the Turk" (1529), Luther uses the same language, describing the Turk as "the rod of God's wrath" by which "God is punishing the world." This conviction led him to call for leaders who would exhort the people "to repentance and prayer" because "we have earned God's wrath and disfavor, so that he justly gives us into the hands of the devil and the Turk."[92]

In his "Preface to the Tract on the Religion and Customs of the Turks" (1530), Luther writes, "We see that the religion of the Turks or Mohammad is far more splendid in ceremonies—and, I might almost say, in customs—than ours, even including that of the religious or all the clerics. The modesty and simplicity of their food, clothing, dwellings, and everything else, as well as the fasts, prayers, and common gatherings of the people that this book reveals are nowhere seen among us—or rather it is impossible for our people to be persuaded to them."[93] Luther expresses admiration for the Turk's way of life and then ridicules the religious customs of his own day. He writes in the same text: "Our religious are mere shadows when compared to them [Muslims], and our people clearly profane when compared to theirs."[94]

Martin Luther thought that the religion and customs of "Mohammadism" should be published and publicized. In 1542, he was delighted to own a translation of the *Qur'an* in Latin. He read it firsthand in order to understand Islam properly. Luther also—and to our amazement—convinced the Council of Basel in December 1542 to lift the ban on the Latin translation of the *Qur'an* undertaken by the printer Oporinus. The ban was lifted provided that the *Qur'an* be published and distributed outside of Basel. Both Martin Luther and Philip Melanchthon wrote prefaces to the Bibliander translation, published in 1543.[95] As Heinrich and Boyce write, Luther's "actions in support of the publications of the *Qur'an* and his written remarks argued repeatedly for a clear and honest presentation of matters of religion so that the truth might be pursued and the false refuted through consideration of what is, not of some perversion or monstrosity."[96]

Nevertheless, Luther's views did not originate in the context of open dialogue. His intention was to equip Christians against the teachings of Islam that he thought contradicted the Christian doctrines of salvation and justification.[97] Luther believed that Islam was a faith patched together from the faith of Jews, Christians, and heathens. He saw the chief theological differences between Christianity and Islam manifested in the following two ways:

1. The Muslim faith is a faith of justification by works. Luther summarized it like this: "If you are pious and just, and if you perform good works, you are saved."[98] According to Luther, the prayer of the Muslim is, "May God spare my life, that I may atone for my sin."[99] Thus, for Luther, the Muslim possesses a false righteousness that strives to be holy, not through faith in the merits of Christ but through his own self-chosen works.[100] The Muslim strives to "do good according to the light and understanding of reason and to be saved in this way."[101]

2. According to Luther, the Muslims believe, like their ancestor Nestorius, "that only Mary's Son, not God's Son died for us."[102] The Muslims hold Christ to be "an excellent prophet and a great man"[103] who preached

to his own line and completed his work before his death just like any other prophet. Christ, however, is not as great a prophet as Muhammad, who is to be "worshipped and adored in Christ's stead."[104] Thus, the Muslims storm against the teaching of Christ as true God[105] and refuse to accept the testimony of Jesus that he is true God and true man.[106] The doctrinal disagreement is about the two natures of Christ, which is the central doctrine for Christianity.

Luther's eschatology was crucial to his view of Islam. As Gregory Miller succinctly puts it, "In place of the crusade, Luther saw a spiritual eschatological battle."[107] Luther derived his understanding of Islam from Daniel's dream concerning the four beasts in Daniel 7. In Daniel's vision each beast represented, according to Luther, the kingdoms of Egypt, Greece, and Assyria, with the last beast signifying the Roman Empire. Luther identified the small horn, which had displaced the above-mentioned kingdoms (Daniel 7:20), with the origin of Islam. Finally, Luther ends his eschatological predictions with these words, "But just as the pope is the antichrist, so the Turk is the very devil incarnate. The prayer of Christendom against both is that they shall go down to hell, even though it may take the Last Day to send them there; and I hope that day will not be far off."[108]

One may ask, "Doesn't Martin Luther identify non-Christian religions with specific eschatological events?" In his article, "Luther, the Turks, and Islam," Robert O. Smith writes, "Luther was not a modern dispensationalist looking for a scientific system of biblical interpretation. When read into the Bible, such schemes are allegorical. . . . In his preface to the Book of Revelation. . . Luther states that . . . [t]he second woe is 'the sixth [evil] angel, the shameful Muhammad with his companions, the Saracens, who inflicted great plagues on Christendom, with his doctrines and with the sword.' . . . Finally, when 'these last woes combine [Islam and the papacy] and make a final concerted attack on Christendom. . . all hell is loose.'"[109] Martin Luther was not an extremist in his time, but when he read his own context through the lenses of biblical prophecy, he was driven to such a view.

Contemporary Lutheran Church Responses to Luther on Islam

Luther was remarkable for his time in that he advocated the importance of understanding Islam and the *Qur'an*. He taught that it is only by understanding Islamic faith on its own terms that Christians could effectively witness to their faith. He thereby set an historic example.

As Luther taught, we must try to understand the other and the other's religion. Going beyond Luther, we must apologize and make it our responsibility to rehumanize where our religions have dehumanized. We should apologize to one another for the harm we have caused one another.

I ask a serious and principled question: Had Martin Luther known that there would be Palestinian Lutherans carrying the message of his teaching of justification by faith in an Arab and Muslim context, would he have written differently? Luther was a person of his time, and his language expresses the roughness of his time. I am, however, surprised that this burdensome past has not been taken seriously enough. For this reason, as a Palestinian Christian, I urge the LWF and its member churches to make a shift in the Lutheran–Muslim dialogue. I call the followers of Luther to repent as well as to apologize to Muslims for any offense that Lutherans have issued against them and their religion. This recommendation follows the lead of an LWF Council in September 2004 that voted to "express its grave concern at the growth of anti-Muslim feeling around the world, particularly in the context of the 'war on terror.'"[110]

Especially in a time of growing Islamophobia, we must not read every doctrine of other religions from the correctness of our own doctrines. Although our church father Luther brought us the freshness of the gospel, today's Lutherans can learn from Palestinian Christianity how to live with Muslims. What would Dr. Luther say today to Palestinian Lutherans who are witnessing to the Muslims in the Arab world through education and *diakonia*? We might be surprised. Luther was far ahead of his time. He reminded us of the importance of the Muslim reality. We share his regret that scholars do not seek to understand Islam as it understands itself. Luther was right when he encouraged his followers to understand the *Qur'an* in order to understand the Muslim faith. The time has come to invest more in understanding Islam rather than fearing it.[111]

Luther, the Doctrine of Creation, and a Prophetic Interfaith Dialogue

The Lutheran World Federation has been engaged in developing what it calls "diapraxis." Danish Lutheran theologian Lissi Rasmussen[112] proposed this term to signal the new kind of prophetic interfaith dialogue that we need to cultivate: "I see dialogue as a living process, a way of living in coexistence and pro-existence. Therefore, I want to introduce the term 'diapraxis.' . . . By diapraxis I do not mean the actual application of dialogue but rather dialogue as action. We need a more anthropological contextual approach to dialogue where we see a meeting between people who try to reveal and transform the reality they share."[113] By adopting this kind of prophetic dialogue for life, we stand for abundant life for every human being and for the love and freedom Christ brings to all of God's creation. We are set free from the slavery of a system of exclusive doctrinal truth claims as the basis for living with one another as well as the many historical corruptions of the Christian faith.

Being justified by faith returns us to the real meaning of biblical justice. Justification describes the ambiguous situation in which we human beings find ourselves. We are at the same time sinners and saints, always in need of the justice and liberation that God graciously gives us. Justification means being simultaneously judged and freed. Those of us experiencing injustice in the world are promised the wonderful hope of justice through Christ's cross and resurrection. Yes, we are victims of injustice, but as we are saved by God's grace, we never allow injustice to have the final word.

The central tenet of Lutheranism has shifted from an individualistic understanding of justification to the reconciliation of people with each other in community and a life of justice, peace, compassion, and healing. The important question now is: What will it take to bring healing and wholeness? Although the law must continue to be respected, the motives and initiatives shift toward mercy and healing for the future rather than remaining fixed on the punishment and pain for the past.

We who live in the world of religion must also restore what we have destroyed. We must commit ourselves to rehumanize together where our religions have dehumanized. We must work together to forge a prophetic dialogue for life that urgently confronts the very real human rights violations of our day, and we must dare to work together to forge common values of peace with justice, compassion, and reconciliation. This call arises from Luther's theology of the cross.

The doctrine of creation is expressed in the worth and human rights of every human being. Lutheran theology emphasizes both creation and redemption. For centuries, we emphasized the theology of redemption more than the theology of creation. This overemphasis on "justification by faith" got Luther into trouble with Jews and Muslims. We are to correct this imbalance and take the theology of creation very seriously in living with other faiths. The intention of Genesis 1:27 is that we all—male and female, Jews, Muslims, Christians, and others—are created in God's own image. This means that we share equal humanity. We are all children of God, equally worthy of love and dignity. Every human being should enjoy the freedom of religion and one's own convictions.

As Luther pointed out, God works in the world through law and gospel. The gospel is God's saving word, incarnate in Jesus. The law, according to Luther, is the word by which God preserves creation through demands that we care for the earth and its people. While other religions generally disagree with the Christian understanding of the Gospel, there tends to be a lot of agreement about God's expectations for human life on this earth and about our responsibilities for meeting them. Lutherans must be concerned with human actions in the world. Lutheranism cannot adopt Luther's own criticism that non-Christian religions are much too concerned with human actions in the world.

We as Lutherans must never give up our theological conviction that human actions in this world cannot bring us salvation. Nevertheless, we could stress more that we have been placed on this earth together with all humans precisely to be stewards of the earth and of each other. When we emphasize this point, we fulfill God's basic expectations without deemphasizing the gospel. We can care for this earth although this stewardship does not draw us, as faith in Christ does, into the life of God. Yet we can stress stewardship all the more when we have been incorporated into God's saving word in Jesus, when we begin to have "the mind of Christ" (Philippians 2:8), through whom we know that God has "loved the world" (John 3:16). While we may have different motivations to engage in a dialogue for life, Christians can participate actively with people of other religions to serve the world as part of the common human vocation.

Living and Serving with Other Religions

Martin Luther's concern was to convert Jews and Muslims to Christianity. As an Arab Palestinian Christian Evangelical Lutheran, I have had to learn what it means to live my faith in Christ among three strong monotheistic religions. Muslims in Palestine call me their bishop. They come to me with problems; we share feasts together. We have similar relations with many Jewish friends. We have established a dialogue group for Jewish and Christians leaders called the Jonah Group. Together, we are enriched by one another's faiths, and we challenge one another about how our respective faiths compel us to treat our neighbor. Together we engage the world, seeking common values of justice, love of neighbor, forgiveness, and reconciliation. In our world of extremism and violence, we work toward nonviolence and moderation by living out a prophetic dialogue for life.

This dialogue for life has six key points. First, this dialogue must engage urgently the immediate suffering of people. Dialogue can never succeed until the dialogue partner understands the pain of the other. Just as Palestinians—and all humans—must understand the deep trauma of the Holocaust, Israelis—and all humans—must understand the pain of the Nakba and the continuing occupation. Though we should not compare our sufferings, we must understand each other. Only when we understand the pain of the other will we truly accept our common humanity.

Second, this dialogue must challenge the structures and realities of injustice, just as Jesus did. Like the incarnation, dialogue must be embodied in the flesh and the truth. We cannot afford to gesture toward dialogue without ever breaking through to the realities on the ground. In the Palestinian–Israeli conflict, Jews, Christians, and Muslims discuss the root cause of the conflict. Israeli Jews attribute the conflict to violence and the denial of their existence. Palestinian Christians and Muslims say that it is occupation. We must come together to discuss the holy writings and traditions of the three religions. Do any of our religions promote violence, the denial of the other, or occupation?

Third, this dialogue should be a catalyst for reconciliation through rigorous self-examination. In my book, *Witnessing for Peace,* [114] I challenge each of us to look at our own respective religions: Are we a source of conflict and disagreement or a catalyst for reconciliation? Have we built bridges or widened the gap between the people? It is always easy to blame another's religion without examining one's own. It is very tempting to use religion for narrow, selfish purposes—especially for justifying political interests. The key to a robust Lutheran theology of justification is the call to be brokers of justice, instruments of peace, and ministers of reconciliation.

Fourth, the dialogue for life cannot be merely an intellectual exercise but must have a spiritual dimension in order to be deep and enduring. We must submit ourselves to God's will. In this way, God helps us to be self-critical, while at the same time transforming us so that we can walk on the path to justice and security. We are to learn about the other's spirituality in order to stand together before God.

Fifth, this dialogue for life also calls us to work toward democracy and to build modern civil society. Dialogue for life invites us to explore how our religions view citizenship. As a Palestinian Christian, I am not a *dhimmi* or a minority but an integral part of Arab Palestinian society. Modern societies must wrestle with the tension between loyalty to religion and country and the task to uphold fully equal rights and responsibilities among all.

Sixth, a prophetic dialogue for life means that we all share in a common responsibility to seek social justice in the whole world and to promote abundant life for all. We must use our shared biblical traditions and sacred scriptures to seek common values of compassion, justice, peace, forgiveness, and nonviolence. We must stand against war and militarization and must work for freedom, equality, tolerance, and democracy. We must work together for the healing of the world by eradicating poverty, HIV/AIDS, and other illnesses by caring for our globe's ecological health. We must also work together to fight against any kind of extremism as well as to uphold religious freedom and minority rights. Dialogue for life calls us together as stewards.

If Luther was a man of his time, we are to be people of our times, envisioning anew "what conveys Christ" (*was Christum treibet*) in this day and age. If justification by faith drives us to understand that the essence of religion is the love of God and thus the love of neighbor, then justification by faith helps us see that religion is no longer part of the problem. Religion becomes part of the solution in this theology of love. "For freedom Christ has set us free. Stand firm, therefore, and do not submit again to a yoke of slavery" (Galatians 5:1).

We are to see God in the other and to accept the otherness of the other. We are set free from being right in doctrine and freed to love each other in relationship. We are set free from earning our way by theology to experiencing and sharing the grace of God we have been given in Christ. Because of this, we can stand firm against extremism, violence, and hate, becoming the people of faith that God meant us to be, striving in God's mysterious vineyard for the peace we are meant to share.

Give Us Today Our Daily Bread

Asia Pre-Assembly Consultation (APAC) &
Asia Church Leadership Conference (ACLC)

Bangkok • December 2009

Dear sisters and brothers in Christ:

It is a great privilege to deliver the keynote address on "Give us today our daily bread," the fourth petition of the Lord's Prayer and the theme of the LWF Eleventh Assembly in Stuttgart, Germany, next July. I know that most of you are bishops, pastors, catechists, and teachers, and you have taught on this text many times, especially in confirmation class. I don't know that I can add to your hermeneutic wisdom, but I will try to offer some biblical-theological reflection on the fourth petition, apply it to the diverse Asian context, and draw some conclusions for our understanding of the church's call.

In good Lutheran fashion, let us begin with Luther's explanation of the fourth petition, as found in his Small Catechism.

> Give us today our daily bread. What is this?
>
> **Answer**: In fact, God gives daily bread without our prayer, even to all evil people, but we ask in this prayer that God cause us to recognize what our daily bread is and to receive it with thanksgiving.
>
> What then does "daily bread" mean?
>
> **Answer**: Everything included in the necessities and nourishment for our bodies, such as food, drink, clothing, shoes, house, farm, fields, livestock, money, property, an upright spouse, upright children, upright members of the household, upright and faithful rulers, good government, good weather, peace, health, decency, honor, good friends, faithful neighbors, and the like.

One of Luther's main contributions to the interpretation of the fourth petition was that "bread" did not mean sacramental bread but ordinary bread—that is, that which is needed to meet people's physical needs. As Luther's was an agricultural world, entirely dependent on weather, it meant that a vast majority of people lived on the edge of poverty. The same is true throughout Asia as well as the rest of the world, where "bread" may be rice, maize, legumes, plantains, millet, pasta, potatoes, bananas, or anything else that is a dietary staple.

At the same time, Luther did not mean to exclude a spiritual understanding of daily bread. He saw God as provider of *all* that is needed for this life, both physical and spiritual.

In my Palestinian culture, bread is the focal point of life. It is our tradition that, if we find a dry piece of bread in the street, we pick it up, kiss it, and touch it to our forehead in thanksgiving for God's gifts. When my late mother made bread, she followed a Palestinian Christian tradition: She drew the sign of the cross on the ball of dough, asking God to bless it to us and to use it as a reminder of God's grace.

When humans trust God to meet their needs, daily bread "ceases to be our god and becomes a lifeless thing, a gift of God given to us," he wrote. Further, daily bread is not given as a reward for prayer. Rather, God gives daily bread to all, even evil people, without prayer. This is an important message in a time when some preachers promote works righteousness or prosperity gospel.

Thus, in this petition we acknowledge and thank God for our daily bread and express trust in God's all-inclusive provision. This understanding reflects Jesus' words in Matthew 6:26: "Look at the birds of the air. They neither sow nor reap nor gather into barns, and yet your heavenly Father feeds them. Are you not of more value than they?"

Biblical Insights

Let us look more closely at the biblical text. The Lord's Prayer appears in two places, Matthew 6:11 and Luke 11:3. These are the only occurrences in the Bible of *epiousios*, the Greek word for "daily."

In his commentary on Matthew, New Testament scholar Ulrich Luz argues that the passages should be translated: "Give us today our daily bread for tomorrow." This translation better reflects the social reality of the text in which people were in dire need of securing bread today to feed their families tomorrow. As day laborers, their future was unsure. This prayer speaks to a deep existential fear that still plagues humanity today, as millions of mothers and fathers do not know how they will feed their children tomorrow. It is a fear confirmed by the fact that 16,000 children die of hunger every day.

Another noteworthy feature of the phrase is its communal setting and language. Jesus taught the prayer to a group of itinerant disciples and instructed them to pray for daily bread as a *koinonia*, as a community. The very language of the prayer is communal, using "we," "us," and "our" rather than "I," "me," and "mine." Thus it is intended as the prayer of a group and not of an individual.

Further, God's very nature as creator and sustainer of all demands that our prayer is not just for me or my social, ethnic, or national group. We pray to a God who clearly cares for the whole creation, who "makes his sun rise on the evil and on the good, and sends rain on the righteous and the unrighteous" (Matthew 5:45). A sincere prayer will seek daily bread for all and will be lived out in ministry to the poor and needy. Those who are nurtured by God's mercy, forgiveness, and provision will naturally share God's compassion for creation and participate in the sharing of bread.

I am also convinced that the literary context of the Lord's Prayer is theologically significant. Matthew places the Lord's Prayer in the very center—the heart—of the Sermon on the Mount (Matthew 5–7). Surely this is no accident, for it serves to emphasize the centrality of the need for trust in God as the ultimate giver of all things.

If trust is the heart, righteousness is the body. The Sermon on the Mount is very much concerned about righteousness. It stresses the intimate relationship between God's grace and God's *torah* (that is, instruction). Matthew 5:20 says, "For I tell you, unless your righteousness exceeds that of the scribes and Pharisees, you will never enter the kingdom of heaven." Matthew 6:33 says, "But strive first for the kingdom of God and his righteousness, and all these things will be given to you as well." It is often observed that "God is close to those who are committed to righteousness."

It is worth noting that Jesus in Matthew is not so much concerned about orthodox faith as about *orthopraxis* (cf. Matthew 7:21). Righteousness as "right practice" is a key theme in Jesus' preaching, teaching, and ministering. Jesus dreamed of an eschatological kingdom where the hungry are fed, the crying laugh, and the marginalized are included. (See Luke 4:18: "The Spirit of the Lord is upon me, because he has anointed me to bring good news to the poor. He has sent me to proclaim release to the captives and recovery of sight to the blind, to let the oppressed go free.") In the Sermon on the Mount,

Jesus taught a *"Kontrastethik"*—a different ethic that challenged the rules of *Pax Romana.* Justice is the distinguishing mark of the new order, as described in kingdom of God parables.

As the human heart pumps blood throughout the body, the Lord's Prayer moves those who pray it out into the world to enact God's righteousness. As we return to the "Our Father" for sustenance, we are enlivened for the bringing of God's kingdom.

Jesus' teachings in the Sermon on the Mount are in continuity with the Hebrew prophets. Again and again they speak of God's justice, or *zedekah.* For the Hebrew prophets, righteousness and justice were inseparable, almost synonymous—a sense that, sadly, is often lost in contemporary Christian doctrine and life. Isaiah 1:27 says, "Zion shall be redeemed by justice." Isaiah 30:18 says, "The Lord is a God of justice; blessed are all those who wait for him."

Not only Isaiah, but Amos, Hosea, Micah, and others also impatiently confronted political leaders for their injustice and accused religious leaders of valuing religious practice above justice. Prophets repeatedly criticized selfishness:

Isaiah 58:6-7, 10 says, "Is not this the fast that I choose: to loose the bonds of injustice, to undo the thongs of the yoke, to let the oppressed go free, and to break every yoke? Is it not to share your bread with the hungry, and bring the homeless poor into your house; when you see the naked, to cover them, and not to hide yourself from your own kin? . . . If you offer your food to the hungry and satisfy the needs of the afflicted, then your light shall rise in the darkness and your gloom be like the noonday."

Hosea 6:6 says, "For I desire steadfast love and not sacrifice, the knowledge of God rather than burnt offerings."

Amos 5:21, 24 says, "I hate, I despise your festivals, and I take no delight in your solemn assemblies. . . . But let justice roll down like waters, and righteousness like an ever-flowing stream."

Nor was the prophetic understanding of justice like that of our day, as represented by the blindfolded *justitia* with her balanced scale in hand. By today's standard, prophetic justice was radical. It was redistributive sharing, restoring social relationships, and correcting systemic failings in society. To be blunt, justice for the prophets was biased—biased in favor of the poor and critical of the egocentrism of the rich. The prophets were eccentric disturbers who would have never been invited to the White House prayer breakfast—a meeting of high-level government officials and faith leaders held every year in Washington, D.C. The prophets were highly inconvenient voices that focused on a ruler's duty to "know justice" (Micah 3:1). The prophets were agents of *zedekah*, midwifes of a new consciousness, and enemies of the *status quo*, proclaiming an alternative socioeconomic reality that gave priority to justice.

Was Jesus any different? Listen to his words in Matthew 25:40: "Whatever you did for one of the least of these brothers [and sisters] of mine, you did for me" (NIV). Those who give food to the hungry or water to the thirsty are blessed by God. They are manifestations of the in-breaking kingdom of God, practicing a righteousness that exceeds that of the scribes and the Pharisees.

Kingdom of God

As this passage in Matthew illustrates, food is often a symbol as well as an instrument of justice. Throughout the synoptic Gospels, eating and drinking function eschatologically as an image of the kingdom of God

Theologian Ernst Lohmeyer points out, "The glory of the coming kingdom is portrayed in a large number of figures: in the picture of the marriage feast, the royal supper, eating and drinking or sitting down at table with the patriarchs in Jesus' kingdom." (Cf. Matthew 8:11: "I tell you, many will come from east and west and will eat with Abraham and Isaac and Jacob in the kingdom of heaven.") One could argue that such table communion is *the* central image and prophetic action of Jesus' earthly ministry. It is perhaps the most evocative and concrete symbol of the Good News, of the advent of the kingdom of God Jesus proclaimed. Theologian Marcus Borg writes that "God's Kingdom (in contrast to the other kingdoms [Jesus' hearers] knew) is about enough bread." That Jesus ate and drank with marginalized, poor people is "a sign and actualization of the fact that they have been called and belong to the kingdom," according to theologian Herbert Girgensohn.

This imagery is echoed in the table communion—the Lord's Supper—that is central both as image and action to the Christian relationship with God. How much deeper and richer our experience of Holy Communion would be if we kept in mind our responsibility to provide both figurative and literal bread for the world as we participate in this tradition.

There is a story that invites you to imagine the world as a village of 100 people and describes the village on the basis of world population statistics. I would like you to imagine the world's population as guests at a banquet,

100 people seated around a long, narrow table. Look around you. Who do you see? You see that fifty-two of the guests are female and forty-eight are male. You see that we Asians are in the majority, with sixty guests at the table. Other guests include thirteen Africans, twelve Europeans, nine from Latin America and the Caribbean, five from North America, and one from Oceania.

As you lift a bite of food to your mouth, you notice that the person across the table from you has no food. You begin to feel embarrassed as you scan the room and see that fifteen people have no food in front of them. Of these fifteen, ten are Asian, nine are female, four are children.

You stare down at a full plate of food, shifting in your chair. How can you enjoy this meal when many have no food?

Daily Bread in Asia

This story, of course, is an oversimplification of the world situation. But the statistics are real. The fifteen people at the table without food represent the estimated 1.02 billion people in the world who go hungry. The ten Asian guests without food represent the 642 million people in Asia and the Pacific who go hungry, according to the United Nations Food and Agriculture Organization. This is the largest number of hungry people in the world.

As the story illustrates, females disproportionately suffer from hunger, accounting for about sixty percent of hungry people. This is ironic, if not tragic, considering the fact that females are the world's primary food producers. According to the World Food Program, "Cultural traditions and social structures often mean women are much more affected by hunger and poverty than men. A mother who is stunted or underweight due to an inadequate diet often gives birth to low birth-weight children."

One quarter of all hungry people are children. In addition to the 16,000 children who die every day from starvation, still others die from related causes. For instance, chronic hunger makes children more vulnerable to disease. More than two million children die every year from dehydration caused by diarrhea. Malnourished children are at increased risk of infection. They are deprived of nutrients needed to grow and develop so that, even if they survive childhood, they often lack the ability to be self-sufficient later in life.

The picture in Asia is further complicated by the fact that life has improved for many Asians, with significant gains made in the past three years in per capita income and calorie consumption. These increasingly affluent Asians are able to diversify their diets and create an explosion in the demand for livestock, products, fruits, vegetables, and feed grains.

At the same time, some 800 million Asians still live in poverty. Ninety million preschool children remain malnourished. India, for example, has the world's second-fastest growing economy—as well as a child malnutrition rate of forty-six percent, according to a 2006 National Family Health survey. Its proposed Right to Food Act would ensure that its citizens at all times have access to or the means to acquire adequate, nutritious food.

The vast majority of those who are hungry still rely directly or indirectly on the agricultural sector both for their food and livelihoods, a dependency that places enormous pressure on natural resources. Further, agricultural growth is needed to complete the economic transformation of rural Asia, but it must be more equitable and environmentally sustainable than it has been in the past. It must support small farmers. It must also capitalize on changing food consumption patterns in the region and a growing global demand for diverse products. These factors make it doubly challenging to create effective and long-term strategies for alleviating poverty and malnutrition in Asia.

Obstacles to Daily Bread in Asia

Does God hear the cry of the woman who struggles to feed her children? Is God present when famine wipes out entire villages? Is heaven indifferent to the anguish of the father who buries yet another child killed by chronic hunger?

Sisters and brothers, it is natural—and maybe even healthy—to ask our heavenly Father, who promises us daily bread, these questions. But we must be prepared to accept the honest answer. The ancient prophets' words are as true today as ever:

Ezekiel 16:49 says, "This was the guilt of your sister Sodom: she and her daughters had pride, excess of food, and prosperous ease, but did not aid the poor and needy."

Jeremiah 22:13, 17 says, "Woe to him who builds his house by unrighteousness, and his upper rooms by injustice; who makes his neighbors work for nothing, and does not give them their wages. . . . But your eyes and heart are only on your dishonest gain, for shedding innocent blood and for practicing oppression and violence."

According to Bread for the World, just one of many organizations working to overcome worldwide hunger, "Hunger is a political condition. . . . Hunger does not exist because the world does not produce enough food. We have the experience and the technology right now to end the problem. The challenge we face is not production of food and wealth, but more equitable distribution."

According to the new book *Waste: Uncovering the Global Food Scandal,* "Rich countries waste around half of their food supplies."

According to the World Hunger Education Service, world agriculture produces seventeen percent more calories per person today than it did thirty years ago, despite a seven percent population increase. This is, according to the UN Food and Agriculture Organization, enough to provide everyone in the world with at least 2,720 calories per person per day. Production is clearly not the problem.

God hears. God accompanies. God weeps. And God provides. It is we humans who allow our sisters and brothers to starve. Let us briefly discuss a few of the things human beings do that create the conditions for widespread hunger.

Colonialism: From the vantage point of history, we observe that most poor countries today were once vassals of the great colonial powers of the nineteenth and twentieth centuries. Even when the colonists exited these countries, they did so in a way that advantaged the empires, leaving the newly-independent countries disempowered and dysfunctional, fighting with their neighbors over things like ports and borders.

Sri Lanka provides an example. Tamils were able to advance above the native Sinhalese during colonial rule. When they gained independence, the majority Sinhalese implemented policies that gave them advantages, inflaming the distrust and conflict that was planted during the colonial period, resulting in a bloody, twenty-six-year civil war.

A sort of "invisible" colonialism continues in the form of global trade rules that advantage farmers in wealthy countries, such as massive subsidies available to U.S. and European farmers. Consequently, poor countries are unable to break the shackles of the colonial economic model, which depends largely on the export of natural resources.

Debt: Whether by design or by accident, global finance institutions keep poor countries locked in an inescapable cycle of debt. Organizations like the World Bank and the International Monetary Fund, ostensibly created to foster global macroeconomic stability, impose conditions that prevent the poorer of the borrower countries from providing education, health, social safety nets, and opportunities for work—the very things necessary for these countries to pay back their loans and become self-sufficient. The unbearable levels of debt, coupled with corruption, weak democracies, and clientele politics, hinders delivery of aid and business investment, making the escape from poverty all but impossible.

Militarization: The United Nations Development Program estimates that the basic health and nutrition needs of the world's poorest people could be met for an additional $13 billion a year. The United States spends more than that—about $16 billion—on its wars in Iraq and Afghanistan in a *single month*. According to the NATO website, India increased its military spending for 2009-2010 by twenty-four percent compared to the year before.

In a world that cries out for plowshares, global powers build swords. It is a double tragedy. Some countries spend their resources making war against poor countries, which are forced to abandon social needs, education, and infrastructure in order to defend themselves against sophisticated, well-funded armies. They are forced to abandon affirming life *(creatio continua)* in favor of staving off death. Let me be clear: I do not defend the approach of either side, for what results is as good a definition of "evil" as has ever been proposed.

Climate change: Poor countries do not have the luxury of debating the reality of global climate change. They are already suffering the consequences. According to the UN's Intergovernmental Panel on Climate Change, "Wheat production in India is already in decline, for no other reason than climate change." An Oxfam briefing states that "hundreds of millions of people are already suffering damage from a rapidly changing climate, which is frustrating their efforts to escape poverty."

Experts attribute an increase in extreme weather, such as droughts, heavy precipitation, heat waves, and intense cyclones to climate change. Extreme weather disproportionally impacts Asians, according to the Asian Development Bank, which says that Asia is the most disaster-afflicted region in the world, accounting for about eighty-nine percent of people affected by disasters worldwide.

Similarly, the poorest countries suffer the greatest impact while being the smallest contributors. Research by the International Institute for Environment and Development shows that the 100 countries most vulnerable to climate change produce just 3.2 percent of global carbon dioxide emissions. Dr. Per Prestrud, director of the Center for Climate and Environmental Research in Oslo, said that the 2003 heat wave in Europe resulted in a drop in food production of twenty to twenty-five percent, and natural vegetation productivity dropped by thirty percent in just one summer.

Climate change is, in a sense, a gender issue as well. The 2007 UN Human Development Report predicts climate change will "magnify existing patterns of gender inequalities." Women are disproportionately affected by access to water, firewood, medicine, and livelihood. A recent LWF Mission and Development Program publication quoted 2004 Nobel Peace Prize laureate Wangari Maathai on this subject: "Climate change is harder on women in poor countries where mothers stay in areas hit by drought, deforestation or crop failures as men move to literally greener pastures.... Many destructive activities against the environment disproportionally affect women, because most women in the world, and especially in the developing world, are very dependent on primary natural resources: land, forest and water. Women are very immediately affected, and usually women and children can't run away."

Occupation: I need not look any further than my own country to see how occupation impacts daily bread. In Palestine's West Bank, one in four people is hungry, according to the UN Food and Agriculture Organization (FAO). This is largely due to transportation restrictions, which hinder people from getting to work and goods from getting to markets. FAO estimates that sixty-five percent of my people in Gaza are hungry. Israeli naval vessels fire at Gazan fishermen. Fertile fields have been turned into military "buffer zones." Half as many truckloads of humanitarian goods as needed are allowed to enter the territory. Bread bakeries are closing because they cannot get gas to fire the ovens. In a recent week, two percent of the cooking gas needed was allowed into Gaza. I heard of one father in Gaza who burned his child's shoes in order to cook food for the child.

Implications of Daily Bread on the Church and Its Mission

Let's return to the banquet table for a moment. While your plate is full, one in six of the 100 guests have no food at all. You want to eat, but you feel guilty.

Suddenly the solution to the situation is obvious, and you begin sharing your food with those who have none. Others follow suit, and soon the banquet hall is buzzing with the chatter of 100 people enjoying food and fellowship. You can leave the banquet knowing you did your part to share your food with those who had none.

In the same way, churches hold food drives, raise funds for hunger-prevention programs, and give generously to local charities. We go home to our full refrigerators and overflowing pantries, feeling satisfied we have done our part. After all, hunger is a complicated problem. What more can we do? And didn't Jesus say the poor will always be with us?

Indeed, he did—because he knew we would continue to feast while expecting others to be satisfied with our crumbs. Jesus did not teach us to pray, "Give us our daily crumbs." The work of feeding the hungry is not finished after we have thrown them our crumbs. The work of feeding the hungry is done when there are no more hungry to feed! I am not content that my neighbor has only crumbs. Nor was Jesus, who, in the tradition of the prophets, preached a radical justice. If we are to follow in Christ's footsteps, we too must return to the prophetic tradition and address the causes of hunger. What's needed is prophetic *diakonia*. The prophets listened to the cries of the people and criticized their oppressors. They championed the cause of those in need of justice. According to the LWF publication, "Diakonia in Context: Transformation, Reconciliation, Empowerment," diaconal work "by its very nature includes the task of unmasking especially systemic forms of injustice and of promoting justice."

Allow me to give an example from my own context. I never miss an opportunity to speak openly about Israel's illegal occupation of Palestinian land. I speak about the hardships created for my people by the separation wall and other Israeli policies that restrict our movement. I tell about families made destitute by home demolitions. I describe how Palestinian land is confiscated for illegal Israeli settlements. I speak about the fear Israelis face because of on-going violence. But I also speak of my hopes for a two-state solution. I offer my vision for Palestinian and Israeli states, laid out along 1967 borders, coexisting in peace, justice, and reconciliation. I explain that a just solution includes a settlement freeze, a political solution for refugees, fair distribution of natural resources, and a Jerusalem shared equally by Israelis, Palestinians, Jews, Muslims, and Christians alike. I point out that security for Israel depends on freedom and justice for Palestine, and freedom and justice for Palestine depend on security for Israel. It is a symbiotic relationship. I am giving this example not to brag or because I think it is a great example of prophetic *diakonia*, but because it illustrates some important elements.

Prophetic *diakonia*:
- names the injustice and the impact on its victims
- speaks for justice despite personal inconvenience or cost
- opposes entrenched means of exploiting others such as class or caste
- openly criticizes any violation of human rights
- resists blaming the victim and exposes underlying systemic causes

But just as important, prophetic *diakonia* dares to dream the dream of a better world. It refuses to accept simply minimizing hunger when eradicating hunger is the goal. It envisions a time in which the economy serves not possessive individualism but instead is replaced with the biblical vision of economy as the *oikos*—the household—in which all of creation is interrelated and committed to helping all to flourish. It is, in a sense, "prophetic daydreaming," which, rather than being a pastime of the idle, is a source of life. "Where there is no vision, the people perish" (Proverbs 29:18, KJV).

Just as ruling leaders in ancient Israel tried to silence prophetic voices, we should not expect that today's world leaders and the minority profiting from the present system will welcome the criticism. But the church is called to walk in the footsteps of Christ, who was crucified because he dared to challenge the unjust religious and social structures of his day. Are we prepared to accept this role?

Before you answer, consider this: Is the church today qualified to critique the world? Or has the church conformed to the world, adopting practices of religious consumerism and ethical indifference? A 2003 study of North American churches showed that eighty-five cents of every dollar donated to the church benefits its own members. That leaves just fifteen percent for people and programs outside its walls. Is this a tithe given to God—or given back to oneself?

Let's return to our banquet table once more. It's good for those who have food to share with those who do not. This is *diakonia*, and as long as there are tsunamis, earthquakes, and other such disasters, there will always be a need for charity. But treating systemic injustice with charity is like pulling victims out of a river and ignoring who's pushing them in. Prophetic *diakonia* calls us to get up from the banquet table and find out why some get no food.

Daily Bread Is a Holy, Communal Call to Action

Let's move from the fictitious banquet back to the real world. Allow me to suggest ways in which Asian churches can engage in prophetic *diakonia* and join in God's work in the world.

• In light of the fact that twenty percent of the world's population uses eighty percent of its resources, the church must demand that world leaders ensure equal bread for all, not bread for some and crumbs for the rest. In a world with finite resources, raising everyone to a lavish living standard is not an option. Resources must be equitably shared.

- The church must support the efforts of people around the world seeking freedom. This means rejecting uncritical allegiance to "democracy" in favor of self-determination and systems that protect the rights of all residents.

- We in the Asian church should learn from and emulate northern churches in their emphasis on fair trade products, which ensure the dignity of their producers. Together, southern and northern churches should work to make fairly-traded products the norm.

- Asian churches should demand that the money used for armaments be used instead for education and eradicating poverty. We know that total disarmament will not take place. But if even five percent of the money spent each year on arms purchases could be diverted to helping the poor, I can assure you that within ten years we would have no poor among us. Further, Asian churches must demand a halt to the production of nuclear arms, with those funds reallocated for assuring food security in the respective countries. Sharing of resources and solidarity with the poor is a precondition to "Give us our daily bread."

- Recent news reports say that U.S. President Barack Obama gave provisional approval for reducing greenhouse gas emissions in his country. Asian churches should press for a firm commitment and hold the president accountable for whatever promises are made. World leaders meeting for the U.N. Climate Change Conference should be reminded of their responsibility to consider those who may not be well represented at the meeting—the poor who will be among the first to be harmed by climate change and who have no resources to counter the effects.

- Asian churches should join climate campaigners to advocate a transfer from rich to poor countries to fund adaptation and clean energy technologies, additional and comparable in value to existing flows of foreign aid. This implies commitments in excess of $100 billion per year, a figure not yet remotely accepted by richer countries. Also, Asian churches can ring their bells 350 times on December 13 as part of the World Council of Church's climate justice campaign.

- When I was in Bangladesh recently, I saw beautiful textiles produced for multinational companies. The skilled laborers making them receive less than livable wages for their work. The church must confront such enterprises and demand wages that are fair and allow people to live in dignity. Further, international trade practices should be rewritten so as to not unfairly advantage rich countries, practices that currently trap poor nations in perpetual debt.

- In 1970, leaders of industrialized nations agreed to donate an amount equal to 0.7 percent of their GDP to developmental assistance. Considering the challenges that have arisen since then, might Asian churches call for countries to raise this level to five percent instead? The funds should be used, to paraphrase an Asian proverb, not to provide fish but to teach people to fish so they will be fed for a lifetime.

- Last February, I visited Gaza after Israel's bombardment of the area. The devastation was horrific. But what shocked me more than anything was to see children eating from garbage bins. To think that in this land, formerly described as a land flowing with milk and honey, children are now forced to eat garbage is intolerable. The church must demand an end to the siege of Gaza. Humanitarian aid and reconstruction material must be allowed to enter freely.

- We in the Middle East ask the church to call for a single standard of justice for our region. All violence must be condemned. All national aspirations should be honored. All claims to dignity must be upheld. As long as the claims of one people are given priority over the other, there will not be peace and security for either. The church must demand that a uniform, biblical standard of justice is applied to resolving the Israeli–Palestine conflict.

- According to the recent LWF report, "It Will Not Be So Among You," rigidly ascribed gender roles limit women's access to power structures, education, training and productive resources. Therefore, the church must take a stand against the feminization of hunger by educating, empowering and enabling women for full membership in all spheres of society.

- Asian churches must expose and denounce aid programs that ultimately create or perpetuate dependency. In particular, we must demand that church aid and development agencies adhere to two principles: 1) that their involvement empowers churches in the south to be self-reliant, and 2) that they recognize the significant contribution to development churches make in providing health care and education, which is vital for eradicating poverty and building civil society.

- Churches are not above needing some prophetic words themselves. As we are called to share Holy Communion with each other, so we must pool our resources to confront the world's challenges, like HIV/AIDs and refugee assistance. Table communion should remind us that all that exists is God's and should be shared equitably. Perhaps it is this resistance to join hands across denominations that has prevented us from, for example, eradicating poverty once and for all. Action by Churches Together (ACT) is a step in the right direction.

Conclusion

Let me tell you another story, one I learned from a Bangladeshi Muslim leader:

Leaders from all religious groups were sent to hell and heaven for an exploration trip. When they landed in hell, they saw tables filled with food. Nevertheless, the people they met were all very thin. The visiting leaders asked why they were are all very thin even though there was plenty of food on the tables.

"Yes, you are right," the people answered. "We have plenty of food. The problem is that we are only allowed to eat it with spoons with handles so long that we are unable to feed ourselves."

The group went on to heaven and found the same scene: tables filled with plenty of food to eat. Unlike in hell, the people in heaven were well fed and enjoyed their lives. When they asked why they were all so well fed and enjoying life, the people answered: "Even though we have only these long spoons to eat with, we have discovered that we just have to feed each other in order to be fed!"

We just had a delicious lunch. Maybe some of us feel sleepy from such a big meal. So when we hear this story, we imagine ourselves as the people in heaven, well fed and content. But I'm sorry to tell you, dear sisters and brothers in Christ, that as long as there are hungry people in this world, we *all* are the people in hell.

Martin Luther King put it this way:

> As long as there is poverty in the world I can never be rich, even if I have a billion dollars. As long as diseases are rampant and millions of people in this world cannot expect to live more than twenty-eight or thirty years, I can never be totally healthy, even if I just got a good checkup at the Mayo Clinic. I can never be what I ought to be until you are what you ought to be. This is the way our world is made. No individual or nation can stand out boasting of being independent. We are all interdependent.

The first thing we must do as a church is to repent—repent for assuming that if I am well fed and content, everyone else is too.

Someone once said, "Ethics begins at the point of pain." We must recognize that these changes will not come easily or painlessly. Justice requires painful sacrifices. It will require great courage to pursue this path of prophetic *diakonia*. We must ask ourselves if we as churches are willing to take this narrow path.

Finally, we are in urgent need of prayer. We must pray for a greater vulnerability, a greater awareness, and a greater compassion for those who are still in need of daily bread. Then we can truly pray, "Give *us* today our daily bread."

What's Lutheran About Health Care?

Insights from Martin Luther

Faith Based Health Care Conference
Jerusalem • 13 November 2011

"To endow hospitals and help poor people is, indeed, a precious good work."[115] So wrote Martin Luther in his *Commentary on Psalm 82*. It should not be surprising therefore that Lutherans place a great emphasis on health care or that Augusta Victoria Hospital is one of many Lutheran hospitals throughout the world.

Martin Luther lived in a context totally different from ours today. Germany in the sixteenth century clearly did not have our scientific understanding of disease nor did they have the understanding or technology to treat illness as we do today. Child mortality was high and life expectancy was low. This was an era of great pandemics. The Black Plague was responsible for twenty to thirty million deaths over several centuries, coming in various waves. It was common for people to take fatalistic attitudes or to interpret illness as judgment from God. Oftentimes people responded by passively accepting this suffering and death, though rulers and people who saw themselves as belonging to higher classes sought ways of escape from exposure to such diseases.

So during the summer of 1527—ten years after Luther had posted the ninety-five theses, yet three years before the Lutherans were able to present their theological case before the emperor in the Augsburg Confession—the plague arrived in Germany, including the town of Breslau. The Lutherans in that town were uncertain what to do. In view of Luther's teaching of a merciful God, who offered salvation by faith through grace, how were they to respond? They wrote Luther asking him to respond to a single question, "Was it all right for a Christian to flee a deadly plague?" It was a theoretical question for Luther and he was a theologian, but he was unable to answer the question for over six months until in November 1527 he wrote a thirty-five page response, "Whether One May Flee from a Deadly Plague."[116]

A Theology of Neighborliness

In the meantime, the issue was no longer theoretical for Luther. On August 2, 1527, the plague hit the city of Wittenberg. The entire university, professors and students, were relocated to the city of Jena to spare their lives. On August 10, the regional governor (Elector John) ordered Luther to leave town for his own safety. His health and his life were too important to put himself at risk. Should Luther flee from the plague? The question was not theoretical. It was real. And how did he respond? He stayed. Yet more than that, he established a hospital in his own house with his own pregnant wife, Katie Luther, and Pastor John Bugenhagen. Within a week, there were eighteen dead, including the pregnant wife of a town pastor, George Roerer.

Why did Luther choose to stay? Why in a real sense did he risk not only his own life but also the lives of his family and friends? We, of course, learn his reasoning from his later book. He said that no one in church should compel another, they could make up their own minds, but, as St. Paul said in 1 Corinthians, they should respect the decisions of one another. As far as pastors, however, he calls upon them to be as shepherds who are willing to lay down their lives for their sheep (John 10:11).

Luther's view could be called a theology of neighborliness. Just as the Good Samaritan took care of the stranger he found beaten on the Jericho road and made sure he would be nursed back to health, this is the expectation of every neighbor. So in his pamphlet on "Whether One May Flee from a Deadly Plague," Luther wrote, "Yes, no one should dare leave his neighbor unless there are others who will take care of the sick and nurse them."[117]

Jesus' words, "I was sick and you did not visit me" (Matthew 25), are a reminder of this basic responsibility of being a neighbor. Luther even went so far as to suggest that such neglect was equivalent to murder (on the basis of 1 John 3:15), "Whoever does not love his brother or sister is a murderer." Health care begins with this understanding of neighborliness.

Health Care As a Justice Issue

As an extension of this focus on the neighbor, Luther saw the role of both church and government in providing health care. Thus the quotation at the beginning of this talk spoke of endowing hospitals as an admirable, good work. Here Luther was speaking about the role of government. His commentary on Psalm 82 is a discussion about what makes a good prince. In verses three and four of this psalm he shows the parallel functions of providing services like health care—"Rescue the small and the poor man" (verse 4)—and in working for justice—"Judge the poor and the orphan and help the wretched and needy to justice" (verse 3). So the underlying task for government is to provide just laws and conditions for its people. As an example of this, he cites the good work of endowing hospitals.

Actually we can divide his thoughts on hospitals into three parts.

1. The highest ideal is to provide a kind of preventative health care. Before mentioning the actual endowment of hospitals made of brick and mortar, Luther writes: "See now what a hospital such a prince can build! He needs no stone, no wood, no builders; and he need give neither endowment nor income."[118] Luther had just discussed what happens when a ruler has provided justice and equality for all his subjects. It seems that Luther understands that many health care issues are created when people do not have good nutrition, clean water, living space that is not crowded or occupied by insects and rats. When a ruler rules justly and provides for the well-being of the people, the ruler is in a sense building the finest hospital for society.

2. Such a utopian ideal is still far from reality, so Luther is very practical in calling for government to provide such hospitals that can provide care beyond the means of basic, neighborly care. So here is where he says, "To endow hospitals and help poor people is, indeed, a precious good work in itself."[119] Again this is a justice issue and not merely an act of charity. It would seem that in Luther's day, as is sometimes the case today, rulers endowed hospitals which would care for members of the elite and not for all people equally. So he writes:

> But when such a hospital becomes so great that a whole land, and especially the really poor people of that land, enjoy it, then it is a general, true, princely, indeed, a heavenly and divine hospital. For only a few enjoy the first kind of hospital, and sometimes they are false knaves masquerading as beggars. But the second kind of hospital comes to the aid only of the really poor, widows, orphans, travelers, and other forlorn folk.[120]

Health should neither be restricted to the wealthy, nor should it force people to be reduced to beggars in order to receive it. It should be available for all people equally.

3. A good ruler knows how to delegate authority and to find talented people to administer and staff hospitals. The Holy Spirit endows each of us

with different gifts, and the wise use of such gifts benefits all of us, including those needing health care. Yet in his discussion of Psalm 82, he offers a suggestion that would ensure that the government understood the needs of hospitals and appreciated the work of all serving in health care. Luther recommends that government officials should give of their own time in volunteer service. When rulers come for a visit or an inspection of a hospital, they should do so in humility, not with glitzy show. He actually cites the example of Elizabeth of Hungary and Thuringia, who through her marriage lived at the Wartburg Castle in Germany in the early thirteenth century (where Luther himself had lived translating the Bible into German when he had been declared an outlaw). Elizabeth was said to have built a hospital at the base of the hill for the common people of that area, and she often secretly went there to attend to the patients herself. So Luther writes:

> It does not make a glittering show. Therefore it counts for nothing. But if a prince or a princess were to go to a hospital sometime and there wait on the poor and wash their feet—as we read that St. Elizabeth did, and as some great folk in foreign lands still do—that would be a great thing! That glitters! It opens people's eyes and gives them a greater reputation than all the virtues give! And it is true! We have to praise it and we ought to praise it as a great and beautiful, though human, act of virtue.[121]

So these ideas about health care by Martin Luther are really an extension of his theology of neighborliness, built also on views of justice. While the good will of individuals is admirable and the church can and does play an important role, in the end a just and fair government will enable us all to be good neighbors in providing for the health care needs of all.

A Wholistic View: Health Care, Education, and the Sciences

Finally, it is important to make a connection between Lutheran emphases on health care and education. In 1851, four Lutheran deaconesses came to Jerusalem from Kaiserswerth, Germany to begin a school for young girls named Talitha Kumi. This is an Aramaic phrase from the gospels when Jesus brought healing to a young twelve-year old girl. For these deaconesses, education and health care went hand in hand. The deaconess educated these young girls primarily for the purpose of becoming nurses in a deaconess hospital in Jerusalem, and eventually for the establishment of Augusta Victoria Hospital. These young girls needed the education and skills necessary to provide the right kind of neighborly care for the sick and the suffering. It is not enough that one has that sense of compassion—though that is the starting point—one also needs the skills and understanding to provide high quality health care.

In his explanation of the first article of the Apostles Creed, Luther wrote: "I believe that God has created me together with all that exists. God has given me and still preserves my body and soul: eyes, ears, and all limbs and senses; reason and all mental faculties."[122] This is a wholistic view of creation. God has created us body and soul, and we therefore care for the whole person; we provide physical, mental, and spiritual care together. Augusta Victoria Hospital reaches out to the broader community, offering excellent specialty care to Palestinians regardless of financial status, religion, or social status. There is a special social dimension to health care at Augusta Victoria Hospital, treating patients in a way that does not isolate them or alienate them from family or culture. Instead, the staff assists family members so that they can stay with patients who are in need of long-term care for chronic or terminal illness.

At the same time, because of this wholistic view of creation, we use the resources of all creation to provide the best possible care for individuals. The emphasis here on the person's senses, on our reason and all mental faculties, is the source of our emphasis on education for all. Education then becomes a kind of preventative health care when people understand how to take care of themselves, but education also prepares individuals for special roles in health care. Education also encourages research and discovery, to better understand our world and to seek scientific developments that improve our quality of care which means a higher level of life for all. This is the highest form of praise to the God who has created us.

Our goal is to create on the Mount of Olives a mountain of healing, not because we seek prestige or reputation or fame, but because it is an integral part of our calling as a church. We are called to continue the healing ministry of Jesus that has provided for the needs of people in this place for nearly 2000 years. We are called to help people no matter what their nationality, ethnicity, social class, political persuasion, or religion. We are called to be faithful and responsible citizens as we work together to build a modern civil society. This is our duty and role as Palestinian Christians. May the Lord continue to give us wisdom and strength to serve in order that we may be an integral part of the Palestinian strategic plan for health.

Ecumenism Is Reconciliation
in the Middle East and in the World

Ekumeniskt Idéforum
Sigtuna, Sweden • 11 April 2011

The topic of my address is the meaning of ecumenism in connection with reconciliation, particularly in the context of the Middle East. I shall first share with you some thoughts about ecumenism, both with regard to the Middle East and globally. I will then expand the perspective and share with you some developments in and reflections on interfaith relations.

One note: There are those who would like to extend the notion of ecumenism itself to include interfaith relations. I do not recommend this, for the motivation behind ecumenism in the Christian context is inseparably connected with the Gospel of God's work in Christ by the Holy Spirit. But we are bold enough to believe, at the same time, that the meaning and values we see in ecumenism can also stimulate and guide our engagements in interfaith relationships.

Ecumenism As Integration of Faith and Life

Ecumenism comes from the Greek term *oikoumene*, which refers to the inhabited land of the earth, where people have their houses (*oikoi*)—their homes—and where, by implication, they seek to fulfill their needs and their aspirations. It is a comprehensive term, which provides a holistic perspective on human nature, human living conditions, and human society. As a Christian concept, it is used especially with regard to the universal Christian church and the search for its unity. But even in this Christian meaning, we maintain also the broader understanding of ecumenism.

We consider the life of the church in relation to our common human life in the perspective of the inner unity of the Holy Trinity, into which we are included by grace and faith. Just as the Triune God is the all encompassing one—a differentiated, divine unity—human life is shared life in the setting of divine reconciliation. The community of the church, which is human life in a complex, God-given unity, is not only a unity in diversity, but a unity in *reconciled* diversity.[123]

What do I mean by saying that "ecumenism *is* reconciliation"? The answer is as simple as it is true: Ecumenism happens when, and only when, there are partners who intentionally seek to establish or further pursue relationships aimed at increased mutual communication and understanding. Such processes presuppose (a) a certain level of commonality between the partners. They also presuppose (b) the existence of differences. These differences normally constitute the focus of dialogue and the challenges in relations. An important third factor is (c) the motivation to pursue an ecumenical process with a view to overcoming divisive factors, i.e. with a view to reconciliation. Then, (d) ecumenical dialogue is led by the Holy Spirit, who works in us to see Christ in the other and to achieve convergences. Finally, as always, (e) there is a blend of theological and historical factors at work in the development of ecumenical relations.

In the history of the ecumenical movement, we have continuously struggled with the relationship between the spiritual and the human dimensions of the church. Take the two movements that developed during the early part of the twentieth century: Life and Work, and Faith and Order.

The Life and Work unit was established first in 1925 under the theme "Doctrine divides but service unites." When the Faith and Order unit was established in 1927, it was done so in order that it might complement the Life and Work unit, providing a platform for joint theological discussions and efforts within the church on matters of faith, order, and worship for the sake of common mission. Because of their complementary work and mission, these two units merged in 1948 to become the World Council of Churches (WCC). In 1961, the WCC once again expanded in its ecumenical work when the International Missionary Council merged with it.

Ecumenism As the Image of Rings Expanding in Water

Ecumenism is an essential part of the nature and mission of the church itself. The unity for which ecumenism strives is not apart from the unity that is sought by the church—the unity by which the church wishes to be recognized. The unity established in Word and Sacrament within a single congregation is the same as that which unites the congregations of a church body, and the same as that which drives the pursuit of unity among churches of differing traditions and confessions.

As such, ecumenism can be likened to the image of ever-expanding rings in water. Ecumenism on the local level is a God-given gift in Christ by the Holy Spirit. More often than not, it grows naturally between the churches of a community. It is neither a result of dialogue nor negotiation, but the result of lives lived together in community, overlapping and interconnected.

Ecumenism on a broader level necessarily enters deeper into issues of theology and doctrine. We praise God for the ecumenical work and agreements of church bodies, especially in the reciprocal recognition of Baptism in the name of the Triune God. Baptism is an expression of God's pure grace, received in faith. It is not a product of human theological endeavor. But Baptism is, certainly, an appropriate subject for ecumenical theological reflection.

I am very pleased, therefore, that the current phase of the Roman Catholic–Lutheran dialogue, "The Lutheran–Roman Catholic Commission on Unity," seeks precisely to clarify what mutually recognized Baptism means in regard to ecumenism. This is a crucial matter, not only within the professional ecumenical sphere, but also within the pastoral sphere. For families in which more than one denomination is represented, the Sacrament of Holy Communion becomes a source of pain when members of the same family are not welcomed to the table, even though their Baptism is recognized. This sacramental discrimination is in opposition to the source of life and hope that is essential to the sacrament.

Because of the significance of this issue, an issue that is close to the heart of many Christian families, I raised the issue of eucharistic hospitality in my address to Pope Benedict XVI when he received the Rev. Martin Junge, general secretary of the LWF, and me as part of a small LWF delegation in December 2010. And I again raised the issue with the ecumenical patriarch of the Orthodox church in March 2011.

It is my sincere hope that, out of our ecumenical relationship with both the Roman Catholic and Orthodox churches, we will achieve increased openness for mutual eucharistic hospitality for the baptized who have been incorporated into Christ, as stated by the Congregation for the Doctrine of the Faith in the declaration *Dominus Iesus* (2000):

> [T]hose who are baptized in [the ecclesial] communities are, by Baptism, incorporated in Christ and thus are in a certain communion, albeit imperfect, with the Church. Baptism in fact tends per se toward the full development of life in Christ, through

the integral profession of faith, the Eucharist, and full communion in the Church.

If we are already incorporated into Christ through Baptism, what more can be required for eucharistic hospitality, on occasion, as we await the fullness of Christian unity?

Ecumenism As Reconciliation

I believe it is vital that we, as Lutherans, maintain a clear focus on the theological core of ecumenism, that is, unity in Christ. For it is only with our unity in Christ at our core that we can properly base our commitment to the ministry of reconciliation, transcend our own boundaries, and engage in mutual acceptance and affirmation.

In his treatise, "The Blessed Sacrament of the Holy and True Body of Christ, and the Brotherhoods," Luther criticizes the "brotherhoods" of his time for being guild-like societies Luther considered exclusivist and self-indulgent. Over and against these so-called "brotherhoods," Luther describes the sacramental community of the church, which Luther calls the "one spiritual body":

> The significance or effect of this sacrament is fellowship of all the saints. . . . Hence it is that all saints are one spiritual body, just as the inhabitants of a city are one community and body, each citizen being a member of the other and of the entire city. . . . This fellowship consists in this, that all the spiritual possessions of Christ and his saints are shared with and become the common property of him [or her] who receives this sacrament. Again, all suffering and sins also become common property; and thus love engenders love in return and [mutual love] unites.[124]

Luther further develops the perspective of the unity that follows from offering ourselves with Christ. Such is a real unity of human beings, which emerges from our identification with Christ and Christ's sacrifice:

> When Christ instituted the sacrament, he said, "This is my body which is given for you, this is my blood which is poured out for you. As often as you do this, remember me." It is as if Christ were saying, "I am the Head, I will be the first to give myself for you. I will make your suffering and misfortune my own and will bear it for you, so that you in turn may do the same for me and for one another, allowing all things to be common property, in me and with me." [We] must make the evil of others our own, if we desire Christ and Christ's saints to make our evil their own. Then will

the fellowship be complete, and justice be done to the sacrament. For the sacrament has no blessing and significance unless love grows daily and so changes a person that he [or she] is made one with all others.[125]

By this interpretation of the sacrament of Holy Communion, an essential link is realized between Christ's sacrifice, faith in the forgiveness of sins, and the commitment of believers to each other.

In light of this essential link, it is important to mention the significance of forgiveness where our own relational history has included condemnations that have inflicted long-standing pain. In an action taken by the LWF Eleventh Assembly in Stuttgart in July 2010, the Lutheran communion formally presented a petition to the Anabaptists repealing the condemnations spoken and written by Lutherans in the time of the Reformation and asking for forgiveness for the persecution and killing by Lutherans at that time. Set amidst worship, this significant moment of confession and forgiveness was not only a very emotional moment for those present at the assembly, but also a moment of great significance for the present and future relations between Lutherans and Mennonites/Anabaptists.

Recall also the actions taken by The Lutheran World Federation and the Roman Catholic Church in Augsburg in 1999, when, as part of the signing of the "Joint Declaration on the Doctrine of Justification" (JDDJ), the two parties declared that their historical mutual condemnations in the area of justification were now refuted in the shared understanding expressed in the JDDJ.

And finally, we recall the Leunberg Agreement of 1973. Signed by the Lutheran, Reformed, and United churches in Europe, it was the first ecumenical agreement that formally dealt with mutual condemnations from the time of the Reformation. In its signing, the Leunberg Agreement opened the way for ecumenical relationships among Protestants in Europe and beyond.

In true confession and honest repentance the way of reconciliation is made possible, and in the journey toward forgiveness our community in Christ is deepened. And when our ecumenical community in Christ is reconciled through confession and forgiveness, ecumenism truly becomes synonymous with reconciliation.

The Real Presence and the Rings in the Water

Let me, however, return briefly to the image of expanding rings in water. What is at the center? Who or what is the drop that is the impetus for the ripples? The drop can be none other than the very presence of God incarnate among us in the Word become flesh, Jesus Christ, in whom we are united by the Holy Spirit through faith. In the same way, within our Lutheran tradition, we proclaim the real presence of Christ's body and blood "in, with, and under" the visible elements of bread and wine in the sacrament of Holy Communion by the power of the Word.

In the true presence of Christ received in Holy Communion we are joined with Christ and with the whole communion of saints across time and space. And just as the means of grace effected in Holy Communion are not only proclaimed, but also visible, so must our own proclamation of the Word of God be tangible in deed. It is this very dichotomy that plays a central role in the Apostle Paul's first letter to the congregation in Corinth, where the diaconal practice of the congregation undermined the unity of the Lord's Supper and, in turn, the unity of the church:

> Now in the following instructions I do not commend you, because when you come together it is not for the better but for the worse. For, to begin with, when you come together as a church, I hear that there are divisions among you; and to some extent I believe it. . . . When you come together, it is not really to eat the Lord's supper. For when the time comes to eat, each of you goes ahead with your own supper, and one goes hungry and another becomes drunk. What! Do you not have homes to eat and drink in? Or do you show contempt for the church of God and humiliate those who have nothing? What should I say to you? Should I commend you? In this matter I do not commend you! (1 Corinthians 11:17-22).

And let us also not forget Luther's words quoted earlier: "For the sacrament has no blessing and significance unless love grows daily and so changes a person that he [or she] is made one with all others." In both Paul and Luther, the absolute inseparability of faith from service in the life and mission of the church is reiterated.

And yet there are some who wish to separate these two dimensions of the Christian life, asserting that one (the means of grace) is necessary to the church, whereas the other (*diakonia*) is good, but not necessary. Conversely, there are those who will readily affirm and promote the necessity of *diakonia* and the work of specialized ministries, but are very reluctant to affirm the vital need for Word and Sacrament in the mission of the church. Truly I tell you, both faith and service are necessary and, indeed, essentially interrelated to the mission of the church.

Testing Faith by Its Fruits

Let us now turn for a moment to Christ's words about the tree and its fruits:

> Beware of false prophets, who come to you in sheep's clothing but inwardly are ravenous wolves. You will know them by their fruits. Are grapes gathered from thorns, or figs from thistles? In the same way, every good tree bears good fruit, but the bad tree bears bad fruit. A good tree cannot bear bad fruit, nor can a bad tree bear good fruit. . . . Thus you will know them by their fruits (Matthew 7:15-20).

With these words, Christ encourages his disciples to beware of those who claim to represent that which is good. And the judge shall be their fruits: Is that which is proclaimed in word made present in practice, so that life is promoted in hope, in love, and in community. As with Word and Sacrament, it is only in conjunction with the visible embodiment of the proclaimed Word that the message is judged "good."

Once again, the unity of faith with *diakonia* and *diakonia* with faith is necessitated. And in this lies the essential relationship between the drop of water and the expanding rings, not only in application to the beliefs and values of individual church bodies, but also to ecumenical relationships, interfaith relationships, to human life and community. Indeed, the rings expand ever outward to country, to government, to culture, and throughout the world. "You will know them by their fruits."

The true realization of this perspective is essential in the Middle East, even as it is essential everywhere. We have no use for faith without service. We have no use for a tree that fails to produce good fruit. We have had enough of impressive-sounding plans and rationales that fail to bring forth constructive fruit. It is constructive fruit for which we now wait, and by which we continue in hope. And I truly believe that much constructive and "good" fruit is found in the ecumenical movements of the Middle East.

Churches As Instruments of Peace in the Arab World

The Ottoman *Firman*, 1852. The beginnings of the modern ecumenical movement in the Middle East can be traced back to the Ottoman *Firman* of 1852. In this regulation, the Ottoman Sultan defined the rights of preeminence to the holy places of Jerusalem and Bethlehem. Confirmed by the Treaty of Berlin of 1878, this regulation established the *Status Quo* agreement guaranteeing the rights and freedoms of all Christian church bodies with regard to access and worship within the Church of the Nativity in Bethlehem and the Holy Sepulchre in Jerusalem.

Common dates for ecumenical celebration of Christmas and Easter. These holy places offer for Christians living here and those visiting as pilgrims the opportunity to gather with the great cloud of witnesses who have worshipped in these places for 2,000 years. Yet, long-standing traditions can be a source of tension, making everyday ecumenical life difficult. It is therefore significant that, while I was still a parish pastor in Ramallah in 1993, the local Christians came together and agreed to celebrate Christmas and Easter ecumenically on a common date. But in Jerusalem, in Bethlehem, in Nazareth, and in much of the world, we continue our celebrations not only separated by our traditions, but also by the way in which we each determine the date our celebrations. Conversation as to how we might determine common dates for the celebration of Christmas and Easter have been on the table for a long time now, and helpful proposals have been presented. But a mutually agreeable solution has yet to be found.

It is my vision that the Christians in the Middle East, along with the WCC, the Vatican, the LWF, and other world church communions work together to assign Christmas according to the Gregorian calendar and Easter according to the Julian calendar, following the decisions of the Council of Nicea that called to follow Jerusalem time, so that our common celebration of Christmas and Easter may become a sign of our common witness in a multireligious and multicultural world.

Patriarchs and heads of local Christian churches in Jerusalem. And yet we have found significant ways in which to work together as the patriarchs and heads of local Christian churches in Jerusalem. Since soon after the beginning of the first Intifada in 1987 we have come together often to discuss issues of common concern, such as the emigration of Christians, the rise of Christian Zionism, and the relationship between church and state. We have also come together in order that we might, as one, issue joint statements and pastoral letters. Between 1988 and 2008 (the siege of Gaza), sixty-eight joint public statements were issued on the situation of Christians in the Holy Land and especially in Jerusalem. Among the significant statements made have been the 1994 statement on "The Significance of Jerusalem" and the 2006 statement on "The Status of Jerusalem," a statement on the emigration of Christians, the endorsement of the Ecumenical Accompaniment Program in Palestine and Israel, and the endorsement of the "Kairos Palestine Document."

We are in a very difficult phase of our lives in the region generally. And, at times, we struggle as heads of churches to achieve results. And yet, the communication and fellowship that exist among us is an important instrument for unity in Jerusalem. Our relationships are ones of trust. And so I want to stress that, even if our fruits are not bountiful or prominent, and even though our common tree is small, I know that tree is good, because our fruits, small though they are, are good. And we hope and pray that growing conditions will improve, and our tree will blossom and grow ever greater.

The issue of Palestinian Christian emigration. The most pressing issue facing the Palestinian church today is Christian emigration, with Christians now numbering less than 1.7 percent of the population, a vast decrease from the ten percent prior to the events of 1948. Surveys about this phenomenon have shown the three reasons most commonly given for emigration to be:

• The continued unsettled political situation and the absence of a horizon of peace and justice[126]

• Lack of jobs

• The growth of extremism among both Palestinians and Israelis

We as the church are stressing a number of essential programs in order to face the problems of emigration, such as:

• Community-based education

• Assistance in finding jobs

• The building of affordable and secure housing, such as the Mount of Olives Housing Project

• The strengthening of Christian institutions serving every human being regardless of ethnicity, religion, or nationality.

In response to the problem of emigration, my church also has initiated a program to develop leadership skills in young people and to meet the spiritual as well as material needs of its people and its communities in this Holy Land context, as it has done throughout its history. At the same time we appeal to all of our accompanying churches to walk with us to encourage our people not to emigrate.

For Arab Christians the guarantee of a democratic, modern, civil society that respects human rights, gender issues, freedom of religion, and freedom of minorities in the Middle East is crucial, as is the guarantee that the Middle East conflict will not become a conflict of religion, but remain a political conflict working for peace and justice for all. Truly I ask: What would the Middle East be without a Christian presence?

We are very thankful for the special Vatican Synod held in October 2010 on the subject of Christians in the Middle East and for the recommendations that have come from this synod. My vision, which I shared with Pope Benedict XVI in December when we met, is that out of ecumenical dialogue the Vatican together with the World Council of Churches and other world church communions will come together in developing a strategy for a concerted effort for Christians in the Middle East.

The Ecumenical Accompaniment Programme in Palestine and Israel (EAPPI). During the second Intifada and incursion into Palestinian lands by the Israeli army, with an extreme escalation of violence, we as leaders of local churches called upon the world to "come and see" (John 1:46). By September 2001, the WCC executive committee recommended that we "develop an accompaniment programme that would include an international ecumenical presence," would build upon the experiences of the Christian peacemaker teams, and would be closely linked to and owned by the local churches while being administered by the WCC.

In February 2002, the EAPPI was officially launched. We had searched for words and actions to embody this call, which would be more than "monitoring." What we called for in the end was "accompaniment," which has a broad biblical and theological background—walking together and breaking bread together as did Jesus and the Emmaus disciples in Luke 24. Accompaniment seeks justice, shows compassion, and calls for truth-telling that transcends public political rhetoric and rationales.

Now after nine years we have been blessed with thirty-nine groups comprised of nearly 1000 accompaniers. These EAPPI members, divided into teams of four or five, have each spent three months living, experiencing occupation, observing, and bearing witness in Hebron, Bethlehem, Jerusalem, Jayyous, Tulkarm, and Yanoun. They provide a protective presence to vulnerable communities, monitor and report human rights abuses, and support Palestinians and Israelis working together for peace. When they return home, they campaign for a just and peaceful resolution to the Israeli/Palestinian conflict through an end to the occupation, respect for international law, and implementation of UN resolutions. As such, they become an ecumenical human chain working for justice, peace, and reconciliation.

The "Kairos Palestine Document": A Moment of Truth—A word of faith, hope, and love from the heart of the Palestinian suffering. The "Kairos Palestine Document" was presented to the world community on December

11, 2009. Kairos is a movement of grassroots Christians, not a document of the heads of churches. At the request of our members the leaders have endorsed this statement because it promotes faith, hope, and love, and it answers the queries of many Palestinian Christians in their reading and interpretation of biblical texts. Its importance stems from the sincere expression of the concerns of the people and their view of this moment in history in which we are living. It seeks to be prophetic in addressing things as they are without equivocation and with boldness. In addition, it puts forward an end to the Israeli occupation of Palestinian land and all forms of discrimination as the solution that will lead to a just and lasting peace. This document is the first of its kind daring to speak publicly on nonviolence and teaching the Palestinian people to see the image of God in the Israeli people.

Week of Prayer for Christian Unity. One of the highlights of our life together in Jerusalem is the celebration of the Week of Prayer for Christian Unity. I know that this is a worldwide initiative, but in Jerusalem and in the Middle East it is truly an ecumenical week with great energy and intention behind it. Each afternoon during the week in January, hundreds of our members of all denominations crowd into a different church to pray and sing, to hear God's word, and to share in fellowship. This year the World Council of Churches and the Vatican Pontifical Council for Promoting Christian Unity requested that the worship materials for the worldwide celebration be prepared by Palestinian Christians in Jerusalem. Remembering the first Pentecost, the focus of the week was on unity through "the Apostles' teaching, the breaking of break, fellowship, and prayer" (Acts 2:42).

World Day of Prayer. Similarly, women of all denominations take the lead in joining together in World Day of Prayer services. In 1998 they wrote the program for women throughout the world. These services play an important role in bringing our churches closer together.

The Middle East Council of Churches (MECC). Another instrument toward Christian unity is the Middle East Council of Churches (MECC) founded in 1974. It continues to be the only platform for full ecumenical cooperation in the region with representatives from all four Christian families: the Oriental Orthodox, the Eastern Orthodox (Chalcedonian), the Catholic, and the Evangelical churches.[127]

The MECC grew out of various interchurch developments in the Middle East dating back to a 1902 encyclical, issued by the ecumenical patriarch in Constantinople, raising the issue of Christian unity and Orthodox relations with Roman Catholics and Protestants.

From the mid-1920s until the early 1960s the mantle of ecumenism was carried by missionaries living and working in the Jerusalem area who cooperated to form the Near East Christian Council in 1956.

By the early 1960s the mission agencies ceded their involvement in favor of churches acting as agents of mission; in 1962 a fellowship called the Near East Council of Churches was formed.

These intensified contacts and dialogues between Protestant churches and Eastern and Oriental Orthodox churches in the region brought about significant processes of reconciliation and healing among the churches, and in May 1974 the Middle East Council of Churches came into being. The process of reconciliation continued to grow. In 1990 the seven Catholic churches of the Middle East joined the MECC as its fourth family. Finally, the Middle East Council of Churches was a fully inclusive council.

The MECC has continued to bring our churches together in a significant way, and it has opened many doors of communication among members. Currently the MECC is in crisis for various reasons, including reasons relating to finance and structure, but strong attempts are being made by the local churches to revive it on the basis of its uniqueness and significance. The MECC is the main framework of ecumenism for the mainline churches in the Middle East, and this crisis has motivated all member churches to work together in claiming local ownership and stake in the MECC. It is my vision that the newly emerging structure of the MECC will concentrate on the Christian presence and witness in the Middle East, promoting ecumenical spirituality and *diakonia* with a basis in the self-understanding of the local churches, while providing common ground for Christian–Muslim interfaith dialogue.

Fellowship of Middle East Evangelical Churches. The Fellowship of Middle East Evangelical Churches (FMEEC) is an association of Reformed, Anglican, and Lutheran churches in the Middle East who confess one God—Father, Son, and Holy Spirit—and one Lord and Savior, Jesus Christ. They hold the Holy Bible to be the sole foundation for Christian doctrine. They confess justification by the grace of God through faith in Jesus Christ, and good works as the fruit of faith. The objectives of the fellowship are to strengthen the mission and ministry of the Protestant churches, to promote leadership training and formation of the laity of both men and women, and to bring the member churches to a closer unity through working and learning together.

There has been a long tradition of motivation for unity among the Evangelical churches in the Middle East. The Evangelical churches were active in the developments throughout the twentieth century among the missionary organizations, which eventually led to the establishment of the MECC. But the member churches of the MECC are not in full communion. Therefore, the quest for unity remains a priority for FMEEC. In 2005 a proposal, actively promoted by the ELCJHL, was launched which aimed at a formal agreement between the churches of the Reformed and Lutheran traditions in FMEEC. In January 2006 The Amman Declaration of Lutheran and Reformed Churches in the Middle East and North Africa, a full-communion agreement between these churches, was signed. This agreement establishes the mutual recognition of Baptism, eucharist, ministry, and ordination, and provides a formal link to the Community of Protestant Churches in Europe (formerly the "Leuenberg Fellowship"). The signatory church bodies commit themselves to close cooperation and common witness.

Relations between the ELCJHL and the Anglican church. The Anglican Diocese of Jerusalem belongs to the Province of the Episcopal Church in Jerusalem and the Middle East. The relations between the Lutheran church and the Anglican church have been close since the middle of the nineteenth century. In 1841, a joint British Anglican and Prussian Evangelical bishopric was established in Jerusalem, in which the office of bishop alternated between the two churches until 1886. However, one must recognize a difference in focus between the two churches during this early period. Much of the Anglican work was derived from The London Society for Promoting Christianity among the Jews, established in 1808. Among the German Lutherans was a strong diaconal focus in education for Arab boys and girls. When the two churches agreed to go their separate ways, Anglicans established congregations in Jerusalem and to the north while the Lutherans worked in Jerusalem and in areas to the south. Differences between German Lutherans and Anglicans on European soil likely created barriers preventing cooperation in the Middle East. However, by the mid-1970s both the Anglican church in Jerusalem and the ELCJHL elected Palestinian bishops, leading to greater cooperation.

However, the Anglican Diocese of Jerusalem was not a signatory of the 2006 Amman Declaration of Lutheran and Reformed Churches in the Middle East and North Africa, although the Anglicans are an integral member of FMEEC and known as "evangelicals" in the region. This was, however, in keeping with Anglican ecumenical practice globally, whereby Anglican churches only enter into full communion with churches that have an episcopal ministry in apostolic succession. This means that, at the present time, the Anglican and the Lutheran churches do not have formal relations of full communion.

This is a paradox in light of the history of the two churches. I believe the way forward is to explore how the two churches can enter into a bilateral relationship of full communion in line with the Porvoo Common Statement, Called to Common Mission, or the Waterloo Agreement. The ELCJHL would then be in similar dual relationships with the local Anglican and Reformed churches as the Lutheran churches in Denmark, Norway, Estonia, Latvia, and the ELCA. In practice they would act as mediating churches in the relationship between Anglican churches on the one hand and Reformed churches on the other hand.

The importance of international dialogues for our mission. For the churches in the Middle East the development of international relations between the different Christian world communions to which we belong is very important. We all see ourselves as members of larger church families in which ecumenical developments among them can be a great stimulus for us locally. It is important that global ecumenical agreements are well received and supported locally. But for this to succeed, such international dialogues should not only concentrate on theological issues, but should also provide proposals and encouragement for local cooperation in mission and *diakonia*. We must also make sure that we do not continue to export our tensions to new places. One example is China. We are happy that the Word of God is being proclaimed and that the churches there are growing rapidly. Denominational differences should not lead to competition there. Rather, we would like to see cooperation, encouragement, and mutual support. Ecumenism has always arisen out of concern for the churches' mission. So also should it continue today.

Current Continuing Points for Ecumenical Dialogue

And yet, even with these important ecumenical partners and amidst a Christian population that is as small as ours in the Middle East, there are still many points of ecumenical dialogue, just as there continue to be important points of ecumenical dialogue in the larger ecumenical sphere.

And, as I choose to view them as points of dialogue rather than points of contention, I do not wish to provide answers at this time, but rather I wish to put forward continuing points, both local and international, that I believe deserve active and passionate ecumenical dialogue for the sake of our common mission:

How can we put aside our fears of conversion and cross-ecumenical proselytism so that the bridges of ecumenical dialogue can be built strong?

How do we approach diversity, both within our own churches and within our ecumenical partnerships? In what ways can our diversity lend strength to our dialogue? For example, can the clear policy of the LWF for the ordination of women become an integral point of ecumenical diversity and pluralism within our church—a point that encourages strengthened ecumenical dialogue?

How do our language choices continue to impede dialogue? And how can we work to encourage continued dialogue surrounding language choices? For example, when mainline evangelical church bodies are rather referred to as ecclesiastical communities by the Vatican, what are the implications? How does this affect our ongoing dialogues on the theology of justification, sacramental theology, ministry, and the apostolic succession?

How can we better develop a deeper theology of accompaniment with our ecumenical partners in the Middle East and throughout the world who witness in a Muslim world?

Amidst the growing evangelistic movements in the world, how do we continue to open the doors of ecumenical dialogue?

How do we, in the midst of ecumenical dialogue, take into consideration our call to interfaith dialogue with our brothers and sisters of diverse faiths?

And, how do we actively continue to live out our call to mission, even as we work for freedom of religion in our pluralistic world?

How can we better address the growing fundamentalism within Christian churches?

How can intentional ecumenical and interfaith dialogue provide an alternate way forward to the imposed secularism that threatens to strip our world of public religion?

And, finally, amidst these questions of internal ecumenical dialogue, how can we come together—the LWF, the WCC, the Vatican, the Ecumenical Patriarch, etc.—to form a common and overarching strategy of *diakonia* and cooperation in our work toward the eradication of poverty, an end to armament, and the care of creation, as we address issues of justice and gender balance, and lend our hands in moments of great and immediate need?

The Role of Religion in the Middle East

In any religious practice, there is always present a dialectic between scripture and tradition, the practical implication and implementation. As theology impacts life, so life impacts theology. As our world becomes increasingly global and pluralistic, the influences of practical life are expanding the religious dialectic in many parts of the world. But this pluralism has been a part of the religious dialectic of the Middle East for as long as humanity has existed, and, in this unfolding religious history, issues of conflict and reconciliation have always been present.

In the Middle East we do not need dialogues in order to establish interfaith relationships. We are a region of interfaith relationships. But that is also the reason we should have more interfaith dialogue! It is a paradox that, even if extremist forms of religion have increasingly played a greater role in the Israeli–Palestinian conflict, established religious perspectives have rarely been taken into account in peace negotiations. In the quest for a just and enduring peace, our genuine religious beliefs and our high level of mutual understanding has much to contribute.

Rabbi David Rosen and others have noted that the failure of the Oslo Peace Accords probably has much to do with the absence of religious perspectives. If peace negotiations are to succeed in the Middle East, religion must be brought to the table. If religion is left out of the picture, the whole religious field is easily left in the hands of extremists. And that is how religion becomes more a part of the problem. I believe that religion can contribute significantly. I believe that religion can be part of the solution.

So how should we proceed in the interreligious sphere? I agree with Imam Yahya Hendi who says that we must in all sincerity ask ourselves the difficult question of whether our politics are consistent with the main tenets and directions of our faiths. We must be willing to be self-critical and to challenge our fellow Christians when they have adopted destructive, extremist ideas.

We still have a long way to go. We need to recognize, among other things, how religious differences actually play into our ethnic interrelations. We spoke for example earlier of the role of forgiveness. This is a concept that is central and well known to us as Christians. It also exists in both Judaism and Islam, but with different meanings and implications. In the two other faiths, there are certainly strong beliefs in God's graciousness and mercy. But in Judaism[128] and Islam[129] these beliefs do not take shape in individual or collective forgiveness as we know it in Christianity.

As religious leaders we face a major challenge. We face the reality that the general reputation of religion has been seriously damaged as a result of extremist abuses of faith language and faith practices. In my view, the way forward is for the three religions to discuss the common values shared between them. A natural consequence of this would be that the three faiths open themselves up for critical self-assessment in light of the faith issues in question.

Middle East Interfaith Initiatives for Reconciliation

It is important for me to draw your attention to three interfaith initiatives that have special importance not only for the Middle East, but also for the complex interreligious situation of the world at large.

"A Common Word Between Us and You." The first initiative I wish to highlight is the Muslim document, "A Common Word Between Us and You," first published in September 2007. This is a theologically substantial and moving document in which 138 Muslim scholars from all Islamic countries and regions in the world express what they see as fundamental Muslim teaching and also the primary common ground between Christianity and Islam. According to the statement, the most fundamental common values between Islam and Christianity, and the basis with the highest potential for future dialogue and understanding, are shared emphases on the love of God and the love of neighbor. "A Common Word" documents these shared emphases by referencing significant passages in the *Qur'an* and the Bible. Rather than engage in polemics, the signatories have adopted what they see as the traditional and mainstream Islamic position of respecting the Christian scripture and calling Christians to be more, not less, faithful to it.

As of October 2010, seventy-one Christian responses to "A Common Word" had been published. These responses from official church representatives and scholars together represent a very significant documentation of how Christians can speak from different vantage points to many of the same fundamental issues of faith—in Christianity and jointly with teachings of Islam—in spite of the fact that Christian traditions are at least as diverse within the Christian family as are Muslim traditions. This process is a good example of how interfaith exchanges—a kind of dialogue—help to bring about a renewed consciousness on fundamental tenets of faith both *within* and *between* religious families.

The World Interfaith Harmony Week. The second initiative is the World Interfaith Harmony Week, proposed by King Abdullah II of Jordan and adopted by the United Nations General Assembly in October 2010 to be recognized the first week in February each year. When Prince Ghazi of Jordan, Special Adviser on Religious Affairs to King Abdullah, presented the initiative before the UN General Assembly, he stated: "The misuse or abuse of religions can . . . be a cause of world strife, whereas religions should be a great foundation for facilitating world peace. The remedy for this problem can only come from the world's religions themselves."

I call on all the churches in the world to recognize and assign the first week of February to be the World Interfaith Harmony Week, in order that we may together combat all kinds of anti-Semitism, Islamophobia, Christianophobia, or xenophobia, in order that religion will be the true source of forgiveness and reconciliation in every civilization and culture.

Council of Religious Institutions in the Holy Land. The third initiative I wish to highlight is the Council of Religious Institutions in the Holy Land (CRIHL, http://www.crihl.org), established in 2005. For several decades there have been a number of attempts to bring together a three-way discussion of Jews, Muslims, and Christians. We are now seeing some success. The council gathers together distinguished leaders of all three religions into one forum. These include the Chief Rabbinate of Israel (including both Ashkenazi and Sephardic chief rabbis), the heads of the local churches of the Holy Land (including also the Lutheran church), the Ministry of Islamic *Waqf* at the Palestinian Authority, and the Islamic *Sharii'a* Courts of the Palestinian Authority. We are thankful to the Church of Norway for sending the Rev. Dr. Canon Trond Bakkevig to assist as facilitator and convener. Taking into consideration the volatile political situation, I consider this council to be a modern miracle of our Lord.

This council's mission statement shows its foundation in the core values of love of God and love of neighbor. It says:

> As religious leaders of different faiths, who share the conviction in the one Creator, Lord of the Universe; we believe that the essence of religion is to worship G-d and respect the life and dignity of all human beings, regardless of religion, nationality and gender.

The mission statement also shows that the commitment of these leaders goes beyond the mere theoretical and moves into the realm of action:

> We accordingly commit ourselves to use our positions and good offices, to advance these sacred values, to prevent religion from being used as a source of conflict, and to promote mutual respect, a just and comprehensive peace and reconciliation between people of all faiths in the Holy Land and worldwide.

In particular the council has undertaken three initiatives. The first initiative is media monitoring. Whenever derogatory and inciting statements by religious leaders are identified in the mainstream media, they are brought to the council for evaluation and, when necessary, response. Sometimes concerns are handled in a discreet, private way, and at other times public responses are made. Members of the council have expressed appreciation for this means to put a check on verbal abuses and thus provide for relationship building.

A second initiative is the Israeli–Palestinian schoolbook project. A United States Department of State grant helped launch this program in August 2009 under the leadership of Dr. Bruce Wexler of Yale University. A joint research team including one Israeli professor, one Palestinian professor, and seven research assistants, all fluent in both Hebrew and Arabic, have been studying 700 Palestinian and Israeli textbooks in order to analyze how "the other" is portrayed in each group's educational materials. The goal was to complete the study by the end of 2010 and to present the findings to the council in 2011. The study has taken more time than originally anticipated, but the council looks forward to the opportunity to analyze the findings. When this has been done, their findings will be forwarded to the educational ministries of the Palestinian Authority and Israel. Depending on the findings, the council will decide what actions may be necessary to correct negative portrayals and to promote accuracy in depicting the other. This is an essential step in laying the foundation of reconciliation at the very the grassroots of our societies—in and for our children.

A third initiative is our ongoing discussion concerning the significance of Jerusalem in all three religions. In only a short time, the CRIHL has made impressive progress in building relationships and understanding among the religious leaders of Jerusalem and also programs that greatly impact the general public. After building a relationship of trust, we are now approaching a discussion concerning the significance of Jerusalem in all three religions. We are asking: Why is Jerusalem dear to the three religions? On what do we agree? On what do we disagree? How do we reach agreement on the main religious issues regarding the Holy City?

Perhaps now you can understand why I refer to this as the miracle of Jerusalem.

Conclusion

Let us not underestimate the importance and potential of these developments in interfaith relations. Let us at the same time realize that these developments are merely the beginning. As our history of ecumenical dialogue and relationship shows us, the journey is long, but the way toward reconciliation is possible. In order to have the desired effect for reconciliation and peace in today's world, we must be willing to walk the way of confession and repentance, reconciliation and forgiveness together in openness.

May we be truly open to meaningful dialogue—a dialogue that holds the power to reshape and reform us all—rooted in the faith and *diakonia* Jesus calls us to live out as one in God by the power of the Holy Spirit.

This is Christ's prayer for us:

> That they may all be one. As you, Father, are in me and I am in you, may they also be in us. . . . That they may become completely one, so that the world may know that you have sent me and have loved them even as you have loved me (John 17:21, 23).

Jerusalem Today and Tomorrow

Four Visions

Chicago, Illinois • May 2011

Dear sisters and brothers in Christ:

I am an Arab Palestinian Christian Evangelical Lutheran. I was born in Jerusalem and grew up in the shadows of shrines of each of the Abrahamic faiths. I lived three minutes from the Holy Sepulchre, four minutes from the Jews' Western Wall, and five minutes from the Muslims' Dome of the Rock. This impressed upon me the need to be inclusive, never exclusive, in my approach. It taught me that there are other legitimate points of views and perspectives. But at the same time, I never lost my identity or beliefs because of that. On the contrary, I believe it strengthened my identity and my faith in my risen Lord.

And it allowed me the opportunity to see that it is not just Christians who are passionate about Jerusalem, the place of our Lord's death and resurrection.

Jerusalem is important to Jews for many reasons. Jerusalem is, in Jewish thought, the place where the name of God dwells. As the location of ancient Israel's First and Second Temples, it was the center of Jewish religious life. Jews consider the Western Wall the last remnant of the temple complex and so is today Judaism's holiest site. According to the Torah, Jews are to visit Jerusalem each year for Feast of Tabernacles, Passover, and Shavuot.

But even though I knew all these facts, it wasn't until the Six-Day War in 1967 that I understood what Jerusalem meant to them. After Israel captured Jerusalem's Old City, I saw crowds of Jews pour into the city, crying and singing as they made their way to the Western Wall.

Similarly, Jerusalem is important to Muslims for many reasons. Jerusalem was Muhammad's destination on his "Night Journey." The al-Aqsa ("Farthest") Mosque, located in Jerusalem's Old City, is Islam's third holiest site for this reason. The area around the mosque, according to the Qur'an, is to be referred to as "The Blessed Land." Jerusalem was also the first *qiblah*, or direction that Muslims should face when praying. Some Muslims say that worshipping in Mecca is worth 1,500 times elsewhere; in Medina worth 1,000, and in Jerusalem worth 500.

But Jerusalem's importance to Muslims became clear to me one day after I met a woman, a shopkeeper, in Lebanon. When she heard I was from Jerusalem, she came around the counter and began to hug me. "Woman, what are you doing? Get away!" I said, feeling a little embarrassed and trying to pull away from her. She said, "You are from Jerusalem. I want to touch you. I will never get to Jerusalem in all my life, but when I touch you, I have touched the Holy City, and thus I am blessed."

It is clear to me that Jerusalem is beloved in all three religions. And so it seems obvious to me that peace will not reign in the City of Peace unless a way is made for three faiths and two peoples to share the city.

Over the years, many people have offered their visions for the city, which generally represent four distinct theological conceptions of Jerusalem.

Jerusalem–City of the Past

The first vision of Jerusalem emphasizes the New Testament understanding and de-emphasizes Jerusalem as the central place within the Old Testament purposes of God. Does Jerusalem continue to have any special, enduring place within God's purposes in the time after the coming of Christ? Adherents to this view base their argument on the words of Jesus as well as the New Testament as a whole. This interpretation speaks of God's decisive and completed judgment upon the city and is concerned now for the universal spread of the Gospel beyond its previously narrow confines in the land of Palestine. This position focuses on texts such as:

• Jesus' several warnings of judgment upon the city (not least in the apocalyptic discourse).

• "You will worship the Father neither on this mountain nor in Jerusalem . . . the true worshipers will worship the Father in spirit and truth" (John 4:21, 23).

• Epistles focusing on the new or heavenly Jerusalem (Galatians 4:26; Hebrews 2:12; Revelation 3:12; 21:2).

• The missionary mandate to the disciples in Acts 1:6-8 not to be concerned with the restoration of Israel but to be Jesus' witnesses to the ends of the earth, guided by the Holy Spirit.

- The whole message of the Epistle to the Hebrews that the Christ figure is the one who the temple and Jerusalem had represented.

- The general lack of concern with the physical Jerusalem in theological terms throughout the New Testament.

This was exactly the view of Eusebius, the greatest scholar of his day. He said, "No, the city of Jerusalem might be of great interest from a historical point of view but theologically its significance in the present and for the future is nil." For this group, Jerusalem is not qualitatively different. Although Western theologies, including the Protestant movement, see the historical importance of Jerusalem and its place in salvation history, they believe its importance lay only in its past, not its present. They believe the promise that "wherever two or three are gathered in the name of Christ, there is Holy Ground," whether it is in Jerusalem, Oslo, Washington, Stockholm, or Helsinki.

St. Jerome wrote once to his followers, "The gate of heaven is open everywhere, as it is open in Jerusalem, so it is open in Italy, Britain and everywhere." St. Athanasius (296-373) also said, "Where the Holy Communion is celebrated, there is Jerusalem." Thus for some church fathers, Jerusalem is a blessing for the whole world because of the salvific act and the resurrection, but our faith is not in any one city, but in the living Christ, present everywhere, where he is worshipped in spirit and truth.

Jerusalem—City of the Incarnation

The second theological vision can be called the incarnational approach. Proponents of this view would base their understanding of Jerusalem's uniqueness, not on its role in the Old Testament period, but on the fact that the city "played host" to great events of the New Testament, most notably the crucifixion, death, resurrection, and ascension of our Lord and Savior Jesus Christ.

Cyril of Jerusalem, in his cathechetical lectures delivered in 348 CE, expressed this vision: Had Jerusalem's treatment of Jesus resulted in the crucifixion? Had that affected Jerusalem's status in God's sight? Cyril would have turned this argument on its head by developing the Johannine teaching concerning the cross as truly the revelation of Christ's glory: The Cross was a "crown not a dishonor and glory of glories for the worldwide church." The fact that the salvific event, combined with other events of the Testaments, had occurred in Jerusalem and nowhere else could only mean one thing: Jerusalem had been and still was a city of special significance in God's sight. Hence, Cyril pointedly refers to his contemporary Jerusalem as a "Holy City," referring to the strange event in the passion narrative (unique to Matthew 27:53) when the saints who had fallen asleep were raised and . . . "went into the holy city." Jerusalem was truly a Holy City in a theological sense, special to God and not simply to the faithful through its many historical associations.

One can see that this attitude is adapted by Orthodox and Catholic theologians. Father Rafiq Khoury, of the Latin Patriarchate in Jerusalem, writes that just as there is the history of salvation, there is also the geography of salvation. Even we Palestinian Christians who live in Jerusalem emphasize the Holy City as a city of resurrection and a city of crucifixion. It still has a deep meaning in our understanding. I wonder if that is because it reminds us of the historical events of the mystery of salvation, because certainly it has no eschatological connotations for us.

This vision makes these points:

1. The cross reminds us of redemption. Thus, Jerusalem calls people penitently to meet the crucified Redeemer. Christians need to be incarnationally present, yet they need to be prophetically outspoken. This presents the church with a challenge which needs to be heard in Jerusalem as much as anywhere else.

2. Some think that there is a special sense of spiritual warfare in Jerusalem. While the power and goodness of Christ may be celebrated in Jerusalem, it is not impossible that Jerusalem could also be a place where evil holds sway, where the battle between good and evil is particularly heightened, even if the ultimate victory of Christ is assured through the historical resurrection (Ephesians 6:12; 1 Corinthians 2:8; Colossians 2:15).

However, this vision is significant because it emphasizes that every stone and holy place inspires us to revive our faith in the Lord. This is the reason that pilgrims come for spiritual edification.

Jerusalem—A City Restored

A third theological vision of Jerusalem, the restorationist approach, sees Jerusalem's significance in the imminent future. This restorationist approach is directed to those living in or closely associated with West Jerusalem. This is very much the modern, new city, the part of the city inhabited by the Jewish people and built with all their attendant excitement in being restored as their "capital," Jerusalem, after 2,000 years of relative absence. Some Jewish Zionists with religious convictions interpret this event with eschatological hopes of the return of the Jewish messiah. Others contend that, in the restoration of the Jewish people to this city, God has, as it were, returned to God's permanent address.

Just as this was the center of the Jewish nation from the time of David through 70 CE, so now it is appropriately the center of a revived Jewish nation in the Holy Land today. If this was the place God had chosen as a special dwelling place for God's name and God's people in special ways in the Old Testament, so today it is a place of special significance in God's purposes and a place of potential special spiritual blessing. This is indeed the "Zion" so beloved by the psalmist: "For the Lord will rebuild Zion and appear in his glory" (Psalm 102:16).

Jewish eschatological thinking and Christian restorationists agree on such a thing with one distinction, that the Messiah to be expected is Jesus returning. Their prayer is that God will reveal himself in Jesus to Zion and thereby to the world at large. In this way Jerusalem will once again prove to be the epicenter of God's purposes.

The Messianic Jewish movement and some who work in mission to the Jews would see the return of the Jewish people to the land as but a stage within God's continuing dealings with the Jewish people, a prelude to the time when hearts will be turned to faith in Jesus, their Messiah. This return to the land and Jerusalem is but a pre-evangelistic period to enable the Jews to be prepared to believe in the Yeshua, the Messiah.

This idea contrasts with the Christian Zionists, who rely on a particular brand of eschatology claiming it is acceptable in the return for Christians to identify supportively with Israel, leaving "their conversion" as such in the hands of God. But the Christian Zionists also promote the rebuilding of the Third Temple in the place of the Dome of the Rock to hasten the second coming of Jesus and to ignite Armageddon, where those who do not believe in the Messiah will be killed by the sword of Christ. I am scared of this Christian right. They seek Christ the military general, not the Christ of the cross.

The Catholic bishops in Illinois declared this theology "false teaching." I call it heresy. My Christ is always the Christ of the cross who comes to save the world freely with his precious blood and not to coerce people into faith. Such ideology is so dangerous because it leaves Jerusalem in constant tension, especially twice a year, when so-called "defenders" of the temple advocate and try to lay the foundation stone of the Third Temple and cause more fighting in Jerusalem. This misguided ideology creates perpetual tension, not only for the Muslim community, but also for the Palestinian Christian church and the Jewish community.

Vision of a New Jerusalem—A City of Unity and Reconciliation

The three previous visions of Jerusalem are all considered "Christian" and "biblical." Yet they stand in almost total contradiction to one another. As adherents of these visions compete to shape Jerusalem's future, the city they love has become a place of brokenness, fear, and pain.

It is like the Tower of Babel that we read about in Genesis, where everyone is struggling to be the highest, to be in control of everything and everyone. Even the religious and political groups here are splintered, competing for resources, power, and agendas. It does not help that people from afar feel the right to create visions and push their agendas for Jerusalem.

But for me, visualizing my hopes and dreams for Jerusalem is more than a theological exercise. It is my home. It is the place of my family, my church, pastors, friends, and schools. And I believe there is another vision for the City of Peace—a vision that integrates most fully God's promise of peace and reconciliation known to us in Jesus Christ. It is the vision as articulated in Ephesians:

> But now in Christ Jesus you who once were far off have been brought near by the blood of Christ. For he is our peace; in his flesh he has made both groups into one and has broken down the dividing wall, that is, the hostility between us. He has abolished the law with its commandments and ordinances, that he might create in himself one new humanity in place of the two, thus making peace, and might reconcile both groups to God in one body, through the cross, thus putting to death that hostility through it. So he came and proclaimed peace to you who were far off and peace to those who were near; for through him both of us have access in one Spirit to the Father. So then you are no longer strangers and aliens, but you are citizens with the saints and also members of the household of God, built upon the foundation of the apostles and prophets, with Christ Jesus himself as the cornerstone. In him the whole structure is joined together and grows into a holy temple in the Lord; in whom you also are built together spiritually into a dwelling place for God. . . . And the Gentiles have become fellow heirs, members of the same body, and sharers in the promise in Christ Jesus through the gospel (Ephesians 2:13-21; 3:6).

In this spirit, I visualize Jerusalem as a city of Pentecost as described in Acts, where:

- Confused languages become a single language of love and hope.
- Understanding replaces confusion and anger.
- Repentance, forgiveness, healing, and reconciliation replace war, spiraling violence, and hatred.

The new Jerusalem is a city of unity and reconciliation, where there is no domination, no occupation, no wall, no terror, no suicide bombing, no home demolitions, no bloodshed.

In the new Jerusalem, there is unity and sharing. Ears and eyes are open to hear and see the reconciling work of God for all of God's children. Human dignity will be upheld for all. No one group will rule over the other. Jews, Muslims, and Christians will live together peacefully, praying at their holy sites with the assurance that justice and equality and security are guaranteed for all.

For decades, the world's peace community has tried to help this vision become reality. In its 1947 partition plan for Palestine, the UN proposed that Jerusalem be a *corpus separatum*–a city belonging to no one group but to the world and administered by the United Nations. The November 1947 UN General Assembly Resolution 181 states:

> The City of Jerusalem shall be established as a *corpus separatum* under a special international regime and shall be administered by the United Nations. The Trusteeship Council shall be designated to discharge the responsibilities of the Administering Authority on behalf of the United Nations.

The December 1948 UN General Assembly Resolution 194 proposed that the city's holy places be protected and made available to worshippers:

> Resolves that, in view of its association with three world religions, the Jerusalem area, including the present municipality of Jerusalem plus the surrounding villages and towns, the most eastern of which shall be Abu Dis; the most southern, Bethlehem; the most western, Ein Karim (including also the built-up area of Motsa); and the most northern, Shu'fat, should be accorded special and separate treatment from the rest of Palestine and should be placed under effective United Nations control.

Dozens of UN resolutions have been proposed since then in an effort to achieve this earthly New Jerusalem. These include:

- UN Security Council Resolution 242, November 1967 (after the war: withdrawal from occupied territories; designating Ambassador Gunnar Jarring as UNSG special representative).

- UN Security Council Resolution 252, May 1968; UN Security Council Resolution 267, July 1969; UN Security Council Resolution 298, 1971 (stop expropriation and settlement in Jerusalem); UN Security Council Resolution 271, September 1969 (protest against arson of the al-Aqsa Mosque).
- UN Security Council Resolution 338, October 1973 (after the war, recalling Resolution 242).
- [17 September 1978: signing of the Camp David accords; Jerusalem omitted from the text, although the U.S.A. had already declared Israel's annexation from East Jerusalem as illegal]
- Israel withdraws from Sinai, April 1982 (i.e., "91 percent of the occupied territories")
- UN Security Council Resolutions 476 and 478, June-August 1980 (deploring the Jerusalem Basic Law adopted by the Knesset).
- [UN Security Council Resolution 605, December 1978 (beginning of first Intifada; deploring situation in OPT, including Jerusalem)].
- October-November 1991, Madrid; 13 September 1993, Oslo agreement signed in Washington, D.C.
- UN Security Council Resolution 1073, September 1996 (grave concern about situation in Jerusalem and other OPT).
- UN Security Council Resolution 1397, March 2002, and UN Security Council Resolution 1435, September 2002 (support for the Quartet and the Arab Peace Plan).
- UN Security Council Resolution 1435, November 2003 (support for the Road Map).

In December 2009, the European Union's Foreign Affairs Council declared that Jerusalem must be shared: "If there is to be a genuine peace, a way must be found through negotiations to resolve the status of Jerusalem as the future capital of two states" (Council conclusions on the Middle East Peace Process, Foreign Affairs Council, 8 December 2009). But we are a long way from realizing this vision. In fact, every day the "facts on the ground" create more and more barriers to peace. Jerusalem does not need more walls or weapons. We need God's vision of reconciliation, justice, healing, and hope, not only in Jerusalem, but to the ends of the earth. We need the Messiah that saves Palestinians and Israelis from fear and all predicaments.

We, as the church, must speak the prophetic truth that the road to peace is not through weapons and war but through active nonviolence, reconciliation, and re-humanization. We are sent to carry this cross of peace and justice in the face of dehumanizing occupation and into every isolated corner where violence and hate live.

In 1994, leaders of Jerusalem's thirteen local Christian churches met to discuss the status of Jerusalem and the situation for Christians there. Their statements are still pertinent today:

> Jerusalem is a city holy for the people of the three monotheistic religions: Judaism, Christianity and Islam. Its unique nature of sanctity endows it with a special vocation: calling for reconciliation and harmony among people, whether citizens, pilgrims or visitors. And because of its symbolic and emotive value, Jerusalem has been a rallying cry for different revived nationalistic and fundamentalist stirrings in the region and elsewhere. And, unfortunately, the city has become a source of conflict and disharmony. It is at the heart of the Israeli-Palestinian and Israeli-Arab disputes. While the mystical call of the city attracts believers, its present unenviable situation scandalizes many. . . .
>
> When the different sides involved now speak of Jerusalem, they often assume exclusivist positions. Their claims are very divergent, indeed conflicting. The Israeli position is that Jerusalem should remain the unified and eternal capital of the state of Israel, under the absolute sovereignty of Israel alone. The Palestinians, on the other hand, insist that Jerusalem should become the capital of a future state of Palestine, although they do not lay claim to the entire modern city, but envisage only the eastern, Arab part.

Perhaps you can see from these statements that there are really five elements that must be considered in Jerusalem for any just peace solution: Jews, Christians, Muslims, Israelis, and Palestinians.

The Christian leaders also said:

> [T]hrough a prayerful reading of the Bible, Christians recognize in faith that the long history of the people of God, with Jerusalem as its center, is the history of salvation which fulfills God's design in and through Jesus of Nazareth, the Christ. . . . In the vision of their faith, Christians believe the Jerusalem of the Prophets to be the foreseen place of the salvation in and through Jesus Christ. . . . In the Acts of the Apostles, Jerusalem is the place of the gift of the Spirit, of the birth of the Church, the community of the disciples of Jesus who are to be His witnesses not only in Jerusalem but

even to the ends of the earth. In Jerusalem, the first Christian community incarnated the ecclesiastical ideal, and thus it remains a continuing reference point.

Furthermore, I will point out that the Book of Revelation proclaims the anticipation of the new, heavenly Jerusalem. The Holy City of Jerusalem is considered to be the image of the new creation and the aspirations of all peoples, where God will wipe away all tears, where there will be no more death or mourning, or crying or pain, because the former world has passed away (Revelation 21:4). For Christians, then, it is no wonder that Jerusalem is so important. I ask: Lord, do you mean that this will be the heavenly Jerusalem now or sometime in eternity? Do you intend it to be a foretaste of that heavenly Jerusalem by making it inclusive for all people at all times?

The Christian leaders noted that Jerusalem is significant for Christians for two essential, inseparable reasons:

> 1. A Holy City with holy places most precious to Christians because of their link with the history of salvation fulfilled in and through Jesus Christ;
>
> 2. A city with a community of Christians which has been living continually there since its origins.

Unfortunately, this community is dwindling due to emigration, the growth of extremism, lack of vision for a just peace, and imposed restrictions such as reunification permits. We are saying, "What is Jerusalem without Palestinian Christians?"

They went on:

> In so far as Jerusalem is the quintessential Holy City, it above all ought to enjoy full freedom of access to its holy places, and freedom of worship. . . . Local Christian communities should have the right to worship and to carry out their religious, educational, medical and other duties of charity, as well as having their own institutions . . . and the right to have their personnel run these institutions.
>
> In claiming these rights for themselves, Christians recognize and respect similar and parallel rights of Jewish and Muslim believers and their communities. Christians declare themselves disposed to search with Jews and Muslims for a mutually respectful application of these rights and for a harmonious coexistence, in the perspective of the universal spiritual vocation of Jerusalem.

All three religions should be able to feel "at home" and at peace with one another in a shared Jerusalem. Experience shows that a guarantee is necessary for this to happen because Jerusalem is too precious to be dependent solely on municipal or national political authorities, whoever they may be. As the Christian leaders said:

> Jerusalem [must] not be victimized by laws imposed as a result of hostilities of wars but to be an open city which transcends local, regional or world political troubles. This statute, established in common by local political and religious authorities, should also be guaranteed by the international community.

Finally, the Christian leaders concluded:

> Jerusalem is a symbol and a promise of the presence of God, of fraternity and peace for humankind, in particular the children of Abraham: Jews, Christians and Muslims. We call upon all parties concerned to comprehend and accept the nature and deep significance of Jerusalem, City of God. None can appropriate it in exclusivist ways. We invite each party to go beyond all exclusivist visions or actions, and without discrimination, to consider the religious and national aspirations of others, in order to give back to Jerusalem its true universal character and to make the city a holy place of reconciliation for humankind.

There will be no solution for our current problems in Jerusalem until all the parties concerned think not only of themselves, but also of the other parties. Jerusalem is dear to all three Abrahamic religions. That is why the patriarchs and heads of local Christian churches in Jerusalem developed a statement on the status of Jerusalem in 2006.

> We believe that a stable, open Jerusalem depends on the following:
>
> • The human right of freedom of worship and of conscience for all, both as individuals and as religious communities.
>
> • Equality of all inhabitants before the law, in coordination with international resolutions.
>
> • Free access for all—citizens, residents or pilgrims—at all times, whether in peace or in war. Jerusalem should be an open city.
>
> • The rights of property ownership, custody, and worship, which the different churches have acquired throughout history, should continue to be retained by these same communities. These rights, which are already protected in the *Status Quo* of the Holy Places

according to the historical *firmans* and other documents, should continue to be recognized and respected.

• The various Christian holy places in the city, wherever they are, must remain united in geography, whatever the solution envisaged.

In Revelation, the New Jerusalem is described as a place where God will wipe away every tear from our eyes. I long to see the day when there is no weeping, no suffering in my city. I believe that when God chose Jerusalem to be the dwelling place, it was meant to be a place of unity and connection between God and all the people, not a place of division and hatred.

Let us pray to Christ and join hands as the worldwide church for the peace, justice, and reconciliation that passes all human understanding. Let us pray that this city, which was the place of the dwelling of God's name and where God and humanity were reconciled through Jesus Christ, will be the place of reconciliation between Palestinians and Israelis, East and West, North and South. Let us pray that everyone who comes to Jerusalem will be blessed and experience the presence of Immanuel, God with us, and be reconciled with Jesus Christ, our reconciler.

Listen again to the promise of Ephesians:

> For he is our peace; in his flesh he has made both groups into one and has broken down the dividing wall, that is, the hostility between us... So he came and proclaimed peace to you who are far off and peace to you who are near. For through him both of us have access in one Spirit to the Father. In him, the whole structure is joined together and grows into a holy temple in the Lord, in whom you also are built together spiritually into a dwelling place for God (Ephesians 2:14, 17, 18, 21, 22).

What Does the Lord Require of Us?
A Vision of Peace through Justice

The Ecumenical Review • June 2011

"What does the Lord require of you but to do justice, and to love kindness, and to walk humbly with your God?" (Micah 6:8).

When I think of the concept of a *just peace,* my thoughts always turn to these beautiful words from the prophet Micah. They are so short and concise, but they say so much to our current situation in Israel–Palestine, just as they did some 2,600 years ago when the prophet walked these same hills, when he longed in his heart for a true and enduring peace, and when he courageously stood up among the people and spoke out a word from the Lord which would reach the hearts of the people, and especially those rulers who often acted from self-interest rather than what was good for all, let alone what the Lord required.

Micah, of course, was a contemporary of the great prophet Isaiah, whose words are quoted in the New Testament almost more than any other Old Testament writer. The context was the occupation of the Assyrian army, having already destroyed the Northern Kingdom and exiling all its surviving inhabitants. The words of Micah are set in the form of a courtyard drama where God calls witnesses to testify the case for Israel. The people are advised that showy acts of religiosity are not the answer; not sacrifices or burning incense or loud recitations of prayer. There are simply three things that they must do:

- Do justice.
- Love kindness.
- Walk humbly with your God.

Surprisingly, the one term that is missing from Micah's list is that of peace.

The New Testament, however, is filled with images of peace:

- Jesus, the Prince of Peace.
- Peace on earth among those whom God favors.
- Blessed are the peacemakers.
- Peace I leave with you; my peace I give you. I do not give to you as the world gives.

Yet when it comes to the Old Testament, the number of verses speaking about war far outnumber the references to peace. (According to one concordance, the term "war" occurs 227 times, while the term "peace" occurs 192. There are many other verses describing acts of war.)

Interestingly, the prophet Micah himself appears wary of talk of peace. Those prophets who cry "Peace" will be left in the dark, completely without vision. The assumption is that these all too ready declarations of peace occur because it puts bread on their tables (Micah 3:5-6). How similar this is to the warnings of Jeremiah and Ezekiel about those who go around proclaiming "Peace, peace" when there is no peace (Ezekiel 13:10; Jeremiah 6:14). The implication is clear: efforts for peace for the sake of peace are doomed to failure. But when the people do what the Lord requires—namely to do justice, love kindness, and walk humbly with your God—then a real and lasting peace can occur. This is how we understand a just peace.

It has been estimated that in the twentieth century no less than fifty different peace proposals were offered to settle the Israeli–Palestinian conflict. They all failed. There has been no easy peace. The reason? They all failed to begin with the principle of justice. A case in point is found in the Oslo Peace Accords of the 1990s. This approach began with confidence-building measures, opportunities for the two parties to meet together around less controversial issues and development relationships. The difficult issues were put off for a later date. These final issues were what we might call justice issues, and while relationship building was taking place, injustices continued day after day and undercut any benefits from these relationship building meetings and the small steps that seemed to be taking place. The Oslo agreements did provide a start—and we are thankful for that—but now it is time to begin with the approach of Micah—to begin by doing justice.

There is another important implication in Micah's approach. Peace is not merely a matter of words or concepts. Think tanks have arisen in all the major cities of the world to discuss how to solve all the problems of the world. Politicians debate the issues, and scholars write dissertations. Yet, as a skeptical public often says, talk without action is nothing. Perhaps that is why Jesus said, "Blessed are the peacemakers," not "Blessed are the peace talkers." The opposite is also true as "activists" mobilize people for demonstrations and protests, sometimes harming the greater movement toward peace. The wisdom of the prophet is that the concept and the action are combined. The concepts are laid out: justice, kindness, and humility, while coupled with a call for action: *do* justice, *love* kindness, *walk* humbly.

Do Justice

Micah begins with the Hebrew word *mishphat,* a term used in the legal system—appropriate for his image of the ancient courtroom setting. It focuses on what is legally expected, what rights individuals have as humans created in the image of God. This concept of *mishphat*/justice is often intertwined with *tzedek,* the idea of righteous acts. So it is not surprising that Joachim Jeremias, who spent his formative years in Jerusalem where his father was *Propst* for the Lutheran Church of the Redeemer, referred to justice as the central concept of the Bible.[130]

The principle of justice begins with the assumption that all people are created equal and that both parties in negotiations must treat each other equally. The difficulty is that this has not been the case. It does not bode well for peace when the two sides do not approach the negotiation table as equals.

Karl Barth notes, "God always takes his stand unconditionally and passionately on this side and this side alone: against the lofty and on behalf of the lowly; against those who already enjoy right and privilege and on behalf of those who are denied it and deprived of it."[131] This is the message of God to Moses at the burning bush, having heard the cry of those oppressed. This is the message of the prophets, always taking the side of the widow, the orphaned, the poor, and even the alien in the land. Justice begins with the assumption of equality and expects that there be mutual respect, that each side views the other as a gift from God. For Palestinians and Israelis this equity is based on a number of factors: First, both sides can affirm a belief that the same God has created Jews, Muslims, and Christians, Palestinians and Israelis, that all are endowed with the image of God, and that love for God is transferred into love for neighbor as oneself. Second, this same creator God has provided the land with all its resources as a gift for the benefit of all these people. It is not to be squandered, nor is it to be used as a source of domination of one group over the other. Third, both peoples have a long and rich heritage with roots in the land. To argue over who was in the land first or who had the longest claim or whose claim is more legitimate by differing theological standards is to deny the importance of the first principle and it is counterproductive. Fourth, both Israelis and Palestinians have the right of self-determination because of who they are, not because of events occurring in Europe or any other part of the world, and not because any third party has granted it. It is a basic human right. Fifth, Palestinian and Israeli census figures put the two groups roughly on an equal footing. With nearly five million Israelis and five million Palestinians, the two sides have equal needs in being able to fulfill a reasonable livelihood.

The starting point must begin with such a declaration of equality and mutual recognition of the rights of the other. Palestinians must view Israelis as equals. Israelis must view Palestinians as equals. Nothing short of this is acceptable.

On the basis of this principle of equity, the already articulated declarations of international law, including the Geneva Conventions and the resolutions of the United Nations, serve as the obvious foundation for just solutions. Some may ask: Is there absolute justice? I would answer: No, but there is rational justice in this world that aims at creating security, justice, freedom, coexistence, and acceptance of the other.

For me, this means consistent support for the following:

1. A two-state solution. From the Palestinian point of view, full recognition of Israel has been assumed with the signing of the Oslo Peace Accords and affirmed by the full assembly of the Palestinian National Authority in 1998. From the Israeli point of view, opinion polls have demonstrated that the majority of Israelis now accept the reality of a Palestinian state. A division of land for the existence of the two states is an absolute necessity. United Nations Resolutions 242 and 338 should be the basis for this part of the solution. By signing the Oslo Peace Accords in 1993, the Palestinians already relinquished to Israel land designated in the 1949 armistice—seventy-eight percent of historic Palestine—with twenty-two percent of historic Palestine designated as a new Palestinian state along the borders of 1967. Palestinians should be allowed full use of resources such as water and mineral resources.

2. An end to Israeli settlements. All settlements should be discontinued. Israel should be encouraged to resettle these residents within Israeli borders and to provide compensation for them. Settlers who might remain by mutual consent should be dealt with under Palestinian law with full rights and responsibilities.

3. A political solution for refugees. Consistent with United Nations statements in 1948 and 1949 and with Resolution 242 made by the United Nations Security Council on November 22, 1967, there must be "a just settlement of the refugee problem." The 1947-49 combat created refugees numbering 750,000, many of whom continue to live with their descendants in refugee camps. Additional refugees were created by the 1967 war, some of them second-time refugees. What does such a settlement entail? I would suggest that the issue be divided into two important components. First, there must be recognition of the injustice created in 1948. Second, a just and reasonable political settlement must follow.

4. A shared Jerusalem. The heads of churches in Jerusalem, in their 2006 statement, speak to the concept and necessity of a shared Jerusalem for all—Christians, Muslims, Jews, Israelis, and Palestinians as two peoples and three religions. Because of the complexities of this arrangement, Jerusalem should be given a special status that is guaranteed by the international community.

5. Regional cooperation. The new Palestinian state will not be large enough to compete on a global basis, and should take a cue from our European brothers and sisters who have come together in the European Union. The establishment of a Middle Eastern Union with neighboring Arab states could help all parties involved.

The security of Israel is dependent on freedom and justice for Palestine. And freedom and justice for Palestine is dependent on the security of Israel. This is a symbiotic relationship and a key formula for justice in the Middle East.

I also believe that the Palestinians must see God in the Israelis, and the Israelis must see God in the Palestinians. Thus, we recognize the humanity of the other, and thus we will mutually recognize in each other the human, religious, civil, political, and national rights. Only then, will Palestine and Israel become a promised land of milk and honey for both Israelis and Palestinians alike.

Love Kindness

While doing justice is tied closely to human rights, the concept often translated as "love kindness" can perhaps best be tied closely to the concept of compassion. This term is chosen deliberately. The root of the verb '*achabat* is "to burn, kindle, set on fire"—so one has a passion for acts of kindness done to the other. While justice is something humans are obligated to do, Micah calls us to have a passion to go beyond what is expected.

English translations here commonly translate *chesed* as "kindness." Luther chose the word *Gnade*, the same term he used in the New Testament for c*haris*, grace. In other contexts, "mercy" seems the appropriate term. Kindness seems to imply politeness or civility. More is expected by Micah. This phrase denotes acts of compassion which are undeserved and beyond the expectation of right. The ancient rabbis enumerated certain deeds which are performed wholly out of goodness, unselfishly, and without ulterior motives such as burying the dead, comforting mourners, visiting the sick, restoring peace between disputing parties.

Yes, Jesus said, "Blessed are the peacemakers." The overriding ethic of the Sermon on the Mount fits with this: Love your enemies. Turn the other cheek. When compelled to walk one mile, go two. When required to give up your robe, give also your tunic.

In the Middle East, it seems that religion has often been the problem. At least it is a powerful undercurrent that affects the political issues that have been problematical. I would propose that religion can just as easily be the solution. We can begin very simply with two principles: love of God and love of neighbor.

Jesus referred to these as the two greatest commandments (Matthew 22:37-40). Rabbi Hillel taught the same; it comes directly out of the Torah. Islam teaches the same.

On 13 October 2007, 138 Muslim clerics and scholars issued a document called "A Common Word Between Us and You" as a foundation point in dialogue between Muslims and Christians. This document emphasizes that the need for common ground is not merely academic:

> Finding common ground between Muslims and Christians is not simply a matter for polite ecumenical dialogue between selected religious leaders. Christianity and Islam are the largest and second largest religions in the world and in history. Christians and Muslims reportedly make up over a third and over a fifth of humanity respectively. Together they make up more than 55% of the world's population, making the relationship between these two communities the most important factor in contributing to meaningful peace around the world. With the terrible weaponry of the modern world; with Muslims and Christians intertwined everywhere as never before, no side can unilaterally win a conflict between more than half of the world's inhabitants. Thus our common future is at stake. The very survival of the world itself is perhaps at stake.

"A Common Word" thus speaks directly about the two core principles mentioned above:

- The commandment to love God fully is (thus) the first and greatest Commandment of the Bible.

- There are numerous injunctions in Islam about the necessity and paramount importance of love for—and mercy towards—the neighbor. Love of the neighbor is an essential and integral part of faith in God and love of God because in Islam without love of the neighbor there is no true faith in God and no righteousness.

"A Common Word" recognizes that differences still emerge, yet the time has come to focus on the commonalities:

> Whilst Islam and Christianity are obviously different religions—and whilst there is no minimizing some of their formal differences—it is clear that the Two Greatest Commandments are an area of common ground and a link between the *Qu'ran*, the Torah and the New Testament.

Thus the document ends with a very basic appeal: "Let us respect each other, be fair, just and kind to one another and live in sincere peace, harmony and mutual good will."

Some have criticized "A Common Word" for its lack of depth. Yet it is a start, an important place to begin the dialogue. With such core values as love of God and love of neighbor, there is a clear basis to evaluate those who claim to love God and claim to speak for God, and who yet take extremist measures through violence and hatred. In his book, *When Religion Becomes Evil*, Charles Kimball writes:

> Whatever religious people may say about their love of God or the mandates of their religion, when their behavior toward others is violent and destructive, when it causes suffering among their neighbors, you can be sure the religion has been corrupted and reform is desperately needed. . . . Conversely, when religion remains true to its authentic sources, it is actively dismantling these corruptions.[132]

So the first letter of John offers a clear caution: "Those who say, 'I love God,' and hate their brothers or sisters, are liars; for those who do not love a brother or sister whom they have seen, cannot love God whom they have not seen" (1 John 4:20). Similarly Muhammad said, "None of you has faith until you love for your neighbor what you love for yourself."

When mainline Christians, Muslims, and Jews—and especially their leaders—remain silent and timid about these core values, they allow themselves to be held hostage by the extremists, and they, in a sense, contribute to the problem. Thus, it is critical that mainline Christians speak out forcefully when extremist Christians threaten to burn copies of the Qur'an, engage in hate speech against Islam and Muslims, promote Islamophobia, misrepresent its teachings, or defame its prophet. It is equally critical that Christians speak out against all forms of hate speech toward Judaism or the Jewish people and the practice of any form of anti-Semitism. Likewise, we expect Jews and Muslims to speak out forcefully when extremists offer defamations against the other—be they Muslim, Jew, or Christian.

The same imperative is there for Muslims to speak out against extremism in Islam. Perhaps this has best been expressed in the Amman Message, a statement issued on 9 November 2004, calling for tolerance and unity in the Muslim world. This message was delivered in Amman as a sermon by Sheikh Iz-al-Din-Tamimi to an audience of King Abdullah II of Jordan and a group of Muslim scholars. It calls for all Muslims to emphasize these core values of compassion, mutual respect, tolerance, and freedom of religion. The following year 200 Muslim scholars from fifty countries came together to elaborate further on three points: First, they clarified in a sense what constituted "mainline" Islam by what historic schools of Islamic jurisprudence were considered acceptable. Second, they summarized the basic beliefs within Islam that are shared by all of these eight schools of jurisprudence. Third, they clarified the acceptable procedures for issuing *fatwas* (rulings). In this way, these Muslim leaders set a framework that makes it easier to identify extremism and to reject such ideas.

What I have been discussing in the last few paragraphs pertains to Muslims and Christians, while the Israeli–Palestinian conflict involves Muslims, Christians, and Jews. However, two important points can be made. First, worldwide it is imperative that Muslims and Christians, as the largest religious groups, begin seeking common ground. The failure to achieve such an understanding in other parts of the world affects us here in Jerusalem. Second, the role of Christianity in Jerusalem, even as a small minority, has also been likened to the salt of the earth. The already existing positive relationship with Muslims means that the Jerusalem church can provide an example for Christians in other parts of the world; it also means that Christianity can serve as a bridge to seeking ground between Muslims, Jews, and Christians.

As far as the first point, King Abdullah II of Jordan this past September proposed the idea of holding a week of interfaith harmony each February. In

October, the UN General Assembly passed this proposal (Resolution 65/L 5) with the backing of twenty-nine cosponsoring countries—mostly with high Muslim populations. World Interfaith Harmony Week encourages all states to "spread the message of interfaith harmony and goodwill in the world's churches, mosques, synagogues, temples and other places of worship . . . to each according to their own religious traditions or convictions." The resolution itself cites seven previous UN resolutions over the previous eleven years that call for the promotion of a culture of peace, of mutual tolerance, and for interfaith dialogue. It also specifically mentions the initiative of "A Common Word" as important grounding especially in terms of the two core principles of love of God (or alternatively, love of the good) and love of neighbor.

The United Nations Assembly minutes show that this proposal was adopted without a vote, and the only concern raised was from the Vatican who preferred the term interfaith dialogue rather than interfaith harmony. However, speaking for King Abdullah II, his special envoy Prince Ghazi bin Mohammad of Jordan demonstrated that such an effort must go beyond the three great monotheistic religions; he thus cited Confucius as the source for the term harmony with the connotation of "beautiful and dynamic interaction between different elements within a whole." Similarly, the resolution, while showing dependence on "A Common Word" and speaking of "love of God and love of neighbor," includes the alternative concept of "love of the good" in deference to Eastern religions.

So it is clear that "A Common Word" is moving beyond being simply a Christian–Muslim dialogue. It is also important that Christians and Jews, as all peoples of the world, recognize that this is a Muslim initiative and the role that King Abdullah has played.

In 1991, I was a founding member of a group that would come to be known as the Jonah Group, a group of local Christian and Jewish leaders, offering a forum for dialogue on issues of key importance in the local arena. Together, we are seeking the path of justice. We read the biblical texts and reflect together what acceptance of the other, justice, self-defense, coexistence, and exodus mean to Palestinians and Israelis today. It is essential to nurture a theological understanding in dialogue that finds the core values that will make Palestine and Israel a blessing to all nations.

This is one of the places in which Christians have a role to play in the Middle East. We are called to work with Jews and Muslims to find the core values of love of God and love of neighbor. And when we begin with the core values of love of God and love of neighbor, it puts us on an equal footing, where mutual respect and appreciation make serious and honest dialogue possible. This is how we can understand the concept in Micah of loving kindness or having a passion for kindness, real and sincere openness to the other.

For several decades there have been a number of attempts to bring such a three-way discussion together. We have had some success. Since 2005 the Council of Religious Institutions in the Holy Land (CRIHL) has brought together the leadership of all three religions in one forum. These include the Chief Rabbinate of Israel (including both Ashkenazi and Sephardic chief rabbis), the heads of the local churches of the Holy Land (including also the Lutheran church), the Ministry of Islamic *Waqf* at the Palestinian Authority, and the Islamic *Shari'a* Courts of the Palestinian Authority. I consider this council to be the modern miracle of our Lord, taking into consideration the volatile political situation.

This council's mission statement shows its foundation in the core values of love of God and love of neighbor. It says:

> As religious leaders of different faiths, who share the conviction in the one Creator, Lord of the Universe; we believe that the essence of religion is to worship G-d and respect the life and dignity of all human beings, regardless of religion, nationality and gender.

The mission statement also shows that the commitment of these leaders goes beyond the mere theoretical and moves into the realm of action:

> We accordingly commit ourselves to use our positions and good offices, to advance these sacred values, to prevent religion from being used as a source of conflict, and to promote mutual respect, a just and comprehensive peace and reconciliation between people of all faiths in the Holy Land and worldwide.

In particular the council has undertaken three initiatives.

The first initiative is in media monitoring. Whenever derogatory and inciting statements by religious leaders are identified in the mainstream media, they are brought to the council for evaluation and, when necessary, for a response. Sometimes concerns are handled in a discreet, private way, and at other times public responses are made, depending upon the case. Members of the council have expressed appreciation for this means to put a check on verbal abuses and thus provide for relationship building.

A second initiative is the Israeli–Palestinian Schoolbook Project. A United States Department of State grant helped launch their program in August

2009 under the leadership of Dr. Bruce Wexler of Yale University. A joint research team of one Israeli professor, one Palestinian professor, and seven research assistants, all fluent in both Hebrew and Arabic, have been studying 700 Palestinian and Israeli textbooks in order to analyze how "the other" is portrayed in each group's educational materials. The goal is to complete the study by the end of 2010 and to present the findings to the council in 2011, and through the council to the educational ministries of the Palestinian Authority and Israel. Depending on the findings, the council will decide what actions may be necessary to correct negative portrayals and to promote accuracy in depicting the other.

A third initiative is the Emerging Religious Leaders program which seeks to build popular support among Israelis and Palestinians towards a peaceful resolution of the conflict, by shifting the way young religious leaders perceive each other, view the conflict, and by creating ways to resolve it. This program is still in the initial stages, seeking funding which would make possible common study of sacred study, overseas and local travel, and a five-day wilderness expedition to build relationships.

In a short time, the CRIHL has made impressive progress in building relationships and understanding among the religious leaders of Jerusalem and also through programs that greatly impact the general public. This seems to be a perfect example of Micah's idea of loving kindness.

To live with other religions, cultures, races, languages. and traditions is an art. But it is an art we must learn, practice, and perfect if we want our children to be able to live together in peace–with human rights, dignity, religious freedom, cultural liberty, and justice for all.

Walk Humbly with Your God

We have seen how Micah's call to do justice and to love kindness must be at the center of all peacemaking. Yet all this may be incomplete without Micah's call to walk humbly with your God. The Hebrew term for walking is *ŷlecet,* a term related to the Jewish concept of *halakah*, a term that summarizes all ethical action. A person's daily walk—all walking—carries an ethical dimension. The future depends on an avoidance of reckless and self-centered action that diminishes the other.

The Hebrew term *hatznēa'* has usually been translated as "humbly," ever since Luther's translation of the German Bible. However, Delbert Hillers notes that the term can also refer to "employment of discretion, prudence, and wisdom."[133] The New English Bible thus translated this as walking wisely with your God. Perhaps the best approach is to include both ideas in the concept of peacemaking.

How does one walk humbly with God? The first point is that one must be ready to confess wrongs that have been done, to seek forgiveness and reconciliation. The late Pope John Paul II held that there is "no peace without justice, no justice without forgiveness." These were not just empty words. He humbled himself in asking for forgiveness for past actions against the Jewish people carried out by members in the Roman Catholic Church. This is the kind of example that must be set to show that forgiveness is not a sign of weakness, but one of strength. The difficulty is that politicians by nature try to avoid any admission of wrong or words of regret as if they would weaken them from future actions.

Perhaps the most instructive example from the Bible is that of David when Nathan reproached him for the sin against Bathsheba and Uriah, and David confessed, "I have sinned" (2 Samuel 12:13). The beautiful Psalm 51 shows the depth of confession and also the prayer to create a clean heart and a new and right spirit for the future.

Here religious leaders must take the first step, then national days of prayer and repentance must follow. In this way, statesmen may also learn that through confession of sin of the past new doors are opened for living life abundantly in peace. Repentance and forgiveness are at the core of one walking humbly.
This is not the end but only the beginning. As individuals we must employ discretion, prudence, and wisdom in one's daily walk, not recklessly to offend and create new areas of friction. Walking humbly means walking wisely.

As nations, we must employ discretion, prudence, and wisdom by setting policies that work proactively for peace. To begin, nations must bring an end to the major arms industry and arms trade that has blanketed the earth with military weapons. When governments provide more weaponry and dozens of fighter planes as an incentive to come to the peace table, it is counterproductive. It only sets up talks for failure and provides even greater arsenals to renew fighting and hostility. The Middle East does not need more weapons with which to destroy itself. It needs an honest political will to bring justice and reconciliation to the people. If that does not happen, then the voice of moderation will no longer prevail, and extremism will hold us hostage.

To walk wisely means bringing an end to weapons of mass destruction. If the industrial nations of the West are addicted to such a so-called strategy of security, that is their problem. But for us in the Middle East: Please let us be a nuclear free zone, a chemical weapons free zone, a biological weapons free zone.

Finally, to walk wisely means rechanneling government spending on programs that create life, not death. If the money spent on weapons were now spent on HIV/AIDS programs, people would have a chance to grow old along with their vine and fig tree. If the money spent on weapons were now spent to fight the enemy of hunger, desperate starving people would not have a reason to turn to violence. If the money spent on weapons were used to build schools with peace education programs, young people could grow up learning to live together in their own independent states, to dream together of their futures, and to have a shared vision to create a better Middle East for their children and grandchildren.

This is not an easy task. But it is what the Lord requires of us: to do justice, to love kindness, and to walk humbly with our God.

The Church's Commitment to Non-Violence

Third International Conference
"Violence, Nonviolence, and Religion"

Bethlehem University • 9 February 2011

There is no country where religion is used and misused as much as here in Israel/Palestine. People use their holy writings to justify occupation, to justify home demolitions, to justify detentions of honest, hardworking people—in short, the writings are used to justify violence. Even God's name is invoked to justify violence.

Martin Luther once said that the Bible is like a forest, where one can find all kinds of interesting things if one wanders aimlessly without a compass. But with a good compass, which you find in Christ, you will find peace, justice, and reconciliation. In particular, if we follow Christ's Sermon on the Mount, we will find our way through the forest. With a compass of loving your enemies, turning the other cheek, and seeing in the other the image of God, one can find the peace for which we all hope.

When Alexander the Great was on his quest to conquer the world—with his army and all the might and power of Greece—he was traveling through the forest in ancient India when he came upon a Jain monk, sitting and meditating peacefully, unperturbed by this mighty army. Why didn't this monk move out of the way? Did he not know who Alexander was? Did he not see the mighty army coming? Alexander was so impressed with such a man of nonviolence, that he got down off his horse, observed the monk for a long time, and then ordered his army to turn around and begin its journey back to Greece. No army could stand in the way of Alexander, but this man of peace was able to turn him back.

This ancient Jain philosophy guided Mahatma Gandhi in his quest for freedom and independence against the mighty British Empire—and through Gandhi, Martin Luther King Jr. learned nonviolence against segregated American society and Desmond Tutu against apartheid in South Africa.

The Jains of India have a beautiful concept called *ahimsa*, that is usually translated as nonviolence. Yet "nonviolence" may not be the best translation for *ahimsa*. Jains themselves suggest that more accurately we might use the term "non-harming."

• "Violence" suggests the idea of intentionality, while Jains believe that much harm is done to other humans and to our planet even unknowingly.

• "Violence" may suggest primarily physical harming; the Dijambra monks remind us by their white masks that many of us harm others through our words and attitudes without ever touching the other.

• "Violence" suggests a direct connection with persons, while Jains would suggest that harm is caused to many victims without ever seeing them. Take for example the whole issue of global warming, where our dependence on fossil fuels and my own driving habits lead to a major change in weather patterns. There are thousands of victims of hurricanes, cyclones, and flooding whom we will never see or meet face to face.

The same can be said for taking political sides. When we chose too quickly or without delving deeply into the issues, it can harm many people.

As the Gospel of John reminds us, God created the world so that all people could have life and have it abundantly. Every action of ours that prevents that from happening is harming them and in a sense could be called violence. Every failure of action could likewise be described as acts of violence. All humans share the same Creator, so all must equally be given those basic rights of food, shelter, health care, education, and general well being.

According to the unanimous resolution of the United Nations General Assembly, we are to recognize the first week of February as a Week of Interfaith Harmony—an initiative by His Majesty King Abdullah II of Jordan. This week of harmony is based on the simple premise that all religions share the basic core values, namely love of God and love of neighbor as self. How can anyone in the name of religion—any one who claims to love God—turn to violence against their neighbor, against any human created in the image of God? The First Epistle of John says, "Those who say, 'I love God,' and hate their brothers or sisters, are liars; for those who do not love a brother or sister whom they have seen, cannot love God whom they have not seen" (I John 4:20).

In his book, *When Religion Becomes Evil,* Professor Charles Kimball writes: "Whatever religious people may say about their love of God or the mandates of their religion, when their behavior toward others is violent and destructive, when it causes suffering among their neighbors, you can be sure the religion has been corrupted and reform is desperately needed."[134]

We are called to dismantle these corruptions, these misuses of religious texts that use violence to achieve selfish ends. Misusing a religious text is itself a form of violence.

All religions agree that killing is evil; we learn it in the Ten Commandments. Yet Jesus announces in the Sermon on the Mount that "thou shall not kill" goes much further than simply murder. What about injuring someone else? What about beating with a stick? What about torture? What about holding up a hospital patient at the check point? Jesus goes much further. Anyone who is angry against brother or sister is guilty of murder. It is not simply an act of physical harm. Its goes back all the way to our attitudes. Similarly, Jesus goes on to say that anyone who insults another is guilty of murder. Anyone who humiliates another, who despises another, who mistreats another—this is violence. Perhaps the violence of the tongue is the worst violence of all, as the letter of James declares.

Religion must always take a stand with nonviolence. There is no returning evil for evil (Romans 12). Dr. Martin Luther King Jr. reminded us how violence can be a downward spiral: "Returning hate for hate multiplies hate, adding deeper darkness to a night devoid of stars. Darkness cannot drive out darkness; only light can do that. Hate cannot drive out hate; only love can do that. Hate multiplies hate, violence multiplies violence, and toughness multiplies toughness in a descending spiral of destruction."[135]

Yet we must not confuse pacifism (nonviolent response) with passivism (mere compliance). If we allow the latter to be the case, then evil triumphs, hate triumphs, darkness triumphs. We are called to resist evil, but resist evil with good, resist violence with nonviolence. This is the message of the "Kairos Palestine Document."

For sixty-two years Palestinians have been struggling to live in their own land. At times Palestinians have turned to violence. The church is called to support the struggle for this abundant life. The way is always and only nonviolence.

Who remembers the names of the armed policemen confronting civil rights marchers in Selma, Alabama? But we remember Martin Luther King marching, arms joined with his brothers. Who remembers the driver of the tank in Tianamen Square in Beijing in 1989? The young man who stood there defiantly will be remembered forever. Who remembers the generals of war? People remember those politicians who dared to make peace.

For me, nonviolent struggle is an integral part of spirituality that teaches us to see the image of God in the other. This nonviolent way is the only way for justice, peace, reconciliation, forgiveness, and acceptance of the other.

May God guide us to continue in our nonviolent struggle for the sake of humanity.

Bring Religion Back to the Front Lines of Peace

Washington Post Guest Voices • September 30, 2010

"Can Religion Solve Conflicts in the Middle East?"

For Common Ground News Service • 17 September 2010

Is religion the problem in the Middle East conflict? Or can religion be the solution?

Many people, especially those in the secular world, have opted for the former, observing the negative side of religion so often covered in the news. Those who attract the cameras are people we call hardliners, those who appear inflexible, and leave no room for compromise. They are the ones fanning the flames of the conflict and creating the image that religion is at the heart of the ongoing struggle. .

Is the problem religion or extremism in religion? The answer can be found in an early Christian text: "Those who say, 'I love God,' and hate their brothers or sisters, are liars; for those who do not love a brother or sister whom they have seen, cannot love God whom they have not seen" (1 John 4:20). At the heart of Christianity are two principles: love of God and love of neighbor, as Jesus himself taught (Matthew 22:37-40). Yet this was not original to Jesus. It came from the Jewish Torah. Islam teaches the same principle.

The problem is not Islam, or Judaism, or Christianity. The problem is when certain individuals, claiming to be speaking for God or defending God act counter to this core teaching that love for God shows itself in respect for the other. We call such individuals extremists.

In his book, *When Religion Becomes Evil,* Wake Forest University Professor Charles Kimball writes: "Whatever religious people may say about their love of God or the mandates of their religion, when their behavior toward others is violent and destructive, when it causes suffering among their neighbors, you can be sure the religion has been corrupted and reform is desperately needed. . . . Conversely, when religion remains true to its authentic sources, it is actively dismantling these corruptions."

I see a second problem, hinted at by Kimball. When mainline Christians, Muslims, and Jews—especially their leaders—remain silent and timid about these core values, they allow themselves to be held hostage by the extremists, and they contribute to the problem.

So the solution is not to remove religion from the political discussion, but to ensure that religion plays a role as the guardian of the politicians. We as religious leaders need to become more engaged and speak out more forcefully to "dismantle the corruptions" and give a vision of life together in all its diversity in the Middle East.

I would like to suggest three steps that we religious leaders can take to bring religion back into the public sphere in a positive way. Religion must be prophetic, it must serve as a catalyst for reconciliation, and it must offer peace education for future generations.

There are plenty of examples throughout history when religion has turned political rather than prophetic, when it legitimized the political power of the day rather than offering a self-critical prophetic word, when it remained silent and complicit rather than risk losing privileges and status. The Hebrew prophets are our example in addressing truth and justice. The situation in Palestine–Israel today needs prophetic voices that call for security for Israel and justice for Palestinians in order to achieve historic reconciliation.

The late Pope John Paul II held that there is "no peace without justice, no justice without forgiveness." He humbled himself in asking for forgiveness for past actions of members of the Roman Catholic Church against the Jewish people. We need statesmen and religious leaders to learn from him, acknowledge the wrongs we have done to each other, and enable new beginnings.

Reconciliation is not simply the absence of hatred. Our people need to learn how to create a shared vision of common values and a shared hope for the future. This is why peace education is crucial. We can start by teaching about other religions without prejudice and misrepresentation—just as the Council of Religious Institutions in the Holy Land has begun a project monitoring Israeli and Palestinian textbooks. Religion can have a positive role in the current peace talks when it emphasizes love of God showing itself in love of neighbor.

To live with other religions, cultures, races, languages, and traditions is an art. But it is an art we must learn, practice, and perfect if we want our children to live together in peace, with human rights, dignity, religious freedom, cultural liberty, and justice for all. To this end we religious leaders must play an active role.

The Role of Religion in the Middle East

Chicago Council of Religious Leaders

18 May 2011

I greet you from the city of Jerusalem, a city holy to three faiths. I am an Arab Palestinian Christian Evangelical Lutheran. Many people no longer think of Christians residing in Jerusalem. They assume that Israelis are Jews and all Palestinians are Muslims. Yet Christians today comprise two percent of the population, far smaller than a century ago, but still a presence. I was born and raised in a Palestinian family, refugees from the 1948 war in the Old City of Jerusalem. My house was just a stone's throw from the Church of the Holy Sepulchre, just three minutes walk from the Haram al-Sharif, just five minutes from the Western Wall. Just around the corner was the Lutheran Church of the Redeemer where I was attracted as a youth to its evangelical theology.

My family roots go back to the early church of the Book of Acts. This also means that we Jerusalem Christians have lived side by side with Muslims for nearly 1,400 years. As Arab Christians we have been praying to Allah for 2,000 years. As Arab Christians, we share the same country, the same culture, the same Arabic language, the same plight, the same struggles, the same destiny, and the same emerging Palestinian state. So our histories and future are shared and linked.

Our family lived side by side with many Muslim families in the Old City. We didn't really think that much about it. We were neighbors. We shared each others' joys. We shared each others' sorrow. I have fond childhood memories of a close family friend, Abu Mahmud. Our families would visit each other in our homes. It didn't seem that different. During Ramadan, they always brought us *Qatayef*—the delicious pancakes filled with walnuts and cinnamon and dripping with honey. At Christmas we always brought them our favorite Christmas cakes. One year their children noticed, "Why do the Younans have a Christmas tree and we don't?" So we went over to their house and decorated a tree for them.

The Role of Religion in the Middle East

In the Middle East we do not need dialogues in order to establish interfaith relationships. We are a region of interfaith relationships. But that is also the reason why we should have more interfaith dialogue! It is a paradox that even if extremist forms of religion have increasingly played a greater role in the Israeli–Palestinian conflict, established religious perspectives have rarely been taken into account in peace negotiations. In the quest for a just and enduring peace, our genuine religious beliefs and our high level of mutual understanding has much to contribute.

Rabbi David Rosen and others have noted that the failure of the Oslo Peace Accords probably has much to do with the absence of religious perspectives. If peace negotiations are to succeed in the Middle East, religion must be brought to the table. If religion is left out of the picture, the whole religious field is easily left in the hands of extremists. And that is how religion becomes a part of the problem. I believe that religion can contribute significantly. I believe that religion can be part of the solution.

So how should we proceed in the interreligious sphere? I agree with Imam Yahya Hendi who says that we must in all sincerity ask ourselves the difficult question of whether our politics are consistent with the main tenets and directions of our faiths. We must be willing to be self-critical and to challenge our fellow Christians when they have adopted destructive extremist ideas.

As religious leaders we face a major challenge. We face the reality that the general reputation of religion has been seriously damaged as a result of extremist abuses of faith language and faith practices. In my view, the way forward is for the three religions to discuss the common values shared between them. And a natural consequence of this would be that the three faiths open themselves up for critical self-assessment in light of the faith issues in question.

Middle East Interfaith Initiatives for Reconciliation

It is important for me to draw your attention to three interfaith initiatives that have special importance not only for the Middle East, but also for the complex interreligious situation of the world at large.

"A Common Word Between Us and You." The first initiative I wish to highlight is the Muslim document "A Common Word Between Us and You," first published in September 2007. This is a theologically substantial and moving document in which 138 Muslim scholars from all Islamic countries and regions in the world express what they see as fundamental Muslim teaching and also the main common ground between Christianity and Islam. According to the statement, the most fundamental common values between Islam and Christianity, and the basis with the highest potential for future dialogue and understanding, are shared emphases on the love of God and the love of neighbor. "A Common Word" documents these shared emphases by referencing significant passages in the *Qur'an* and the Bible. Rather than engage in polemics, the signatories have adopted what they see as the traditional and mainstream Islamic position of respecting the Christian scripture and calling Christians to be more, not less, faithful to it.

As of October 2010, seventy-one Christian responses to "A Common Word" had been published. These responses from official church representatives and scholars together represent a very significant documentation of how Christians can speak from different vantage points to many of the same fundamental issues of faith—in Christianity, and jointly with teachings of Islam —in spite of the fact that Christian traditions are at least as diverse within the Christian family as are Muslim traditions. This process is a good example of how interfaith exchanges—a kind of dialogue—help to bring about a renewed consciousness on fundamental tenets of faith both *within* and *between* religious families.

The World Interfaith Harmony Week. The second initiative is the World Interfaith Harmony Week, proposed by King Abdullah II of Jordan and adopted by the United Nations General Assembly in October 2010 to be recognized each year in the first week in February. When Prince Ghazi of Jordan, Special Adviser on Religious Affairs to King Abdullah, presented the initiative before the UN General Assembly, he stated: "The misuse or abuse of religions can . . . be a cause of world strife, whereas religions should be a great foundation for facilitating world peace. The remedy for this problem can only come from the world's religions themselves."

I will repeat here for you what I said in an interview in February in my role as president of The Lutheran World Federation: "The World Interfaith Harmony Week is significant for the Lutheran World Federation and all of its member churches because there is no place in the world in which Lutheran churches live on their own. Lutheran churches, rather, live with other religions—sometimes in a minority position, sometimes in a majority position, but never alone."

I call on all the churches in the world to recognize and assign the first week of February to be World Interfaith Harmony Week, in order that we may together combat anti-Semitism, Islamophobia, Christianophobia, or xenophobia, in order that religion will be the true source of forgiveness and reconciliation in every civilization and culture.

Council of Religious Institutions in the Holy Land. The third initiative I wish to highlight is the Council of Religious Institutions in the Holy Land (CRIHL), established in 2005. For several decades there have been a number of attempts to bring together a three-way discussion of Jews, Muslims, and Christians. We are now seeing some success. The council gathers together distinguished leaders of all three religions into one forum. These include the Chief Rabbinate of Israel (including both Ashkenazi and Sephardic chief rabbis), the heads of the local churches of the Holy Land (including the Lutheran church), the Ministry of Islamic *Waqf* at the Palestinian Authority, and the Islamic *Shari'a* Courts of the Palestinian Authority. And, to assist as facilitator and convener, we are thankful to the Church of Norway for sending the Rev. Dr. Canon Trond Bakkevig. Taking into consideration the volatile political situation, I consider this council to be a modern miracle of our Lord.

This council's mission statement shows its foundation in the core values of love of God and love of neighbor. It reads:

> As religious leaders of different faiths, who share the conviction in the one Creator, Lord of the Universe; we believe that the essence of religion is to worship G-d and respect the life and dignity of all human beings, regardless of religion, nationality and gender.

The mission statement also shows that the commitment of these leaders goes beyond the mere theoretical and moves into the realm of action:

> We accordingly commit ourselves to use our positions and good offices, to advance these sacred values, to prevent religion from being used as a source of conflict, and to promote mutual respect, a just and comprehensive peace and reconciliation between people of all faiths in the Holy Land and worldwide.

In particular the council has undertaken three initiatives. The first initiative is in media monitoring. Whenever derogatory and inciting statements by religious leaders are identified in the mainstream media, they are brought to the council for evaluation and, when necessary, for response. Sometimes concerns are handled in a discreet, private way; at other times public responses are made, depending upon the case. Members of the council have expressed appreciation for this means to put a check on verbal abuses and thus provide for relationship building.

A second initiative is the Israeli–Palestinian Schoolbook Project. A United States Department of State grant helped launch their program in August 2009 under the leadership of Dr. Bruce Wexler of Yale University. A joint research team of one Israeli professor, one Palestinian professor, and seven research assistants, all fluent in both Hebrew and Arabic, have been studying 700 Palestinian and Israeli textbooks in order to analyze how "the other" is portrayed in each group's educational materials. The goal was to complete the study by the end of 2010 and to present the findings to the council in 2011. The study has taken more time than originally anticipated, but the council looks forward the opportunity to analyze the findings. When this has been done, their findings will be forwarded to the educational ministries of the Palestinian Authority and Israel. Depending on the findings, the council will decide what actions may be necessary to correct negative portrayals and to promote accuracy in depicting the other. This is an essential step in laying the foundation of reconciliation at the very the grassroots of our societies—in and for our children.

A third initiative is our ongoing discussion concerning the significance of Jerusalem in all three religions. In only a short time, the CRIHL has made impressive progress in building relationships and understanding among the religious leaders of Jerusalem and also programs that greatly impact the general public. After building a relationship of trust, we are now approaching a discussion concerning the significance of Jerusalem in all three religions. We are asking: Why is Jerusalem dear to the three religions? On what do we agree? On what do we disagree? How do we reach agreement on the main religious issues regarding the Holy City? Perhaps now you can understand why I refer to this as the miracle of Jerusalem.

Conclusion

Catholic theologian Hans Küng said, "No peace among nations without peace among religions. And no peace among religions without dialogue." We need only look at news headlines to see the truth in his statement.

I do not need to tell you about the enormity of the challenge we face. You know from your own contexts that the stakes are high. I hope that my words today encourage you to continue fostering respect and esteem for people of diverse faiths so that faith takes its rightful place as something that unites and empowers us for the common good of humanity.

To live with other religions, cultures, races, languages, and traditions is an art. But it is an art we must learn, practice, and perfect if we want our children to be able to live together in peace, with cultural liberty and justice for all.

Brothers and sisters:

It is time to liberate our world from the extremism and hate that seeks to dominate and distract us from promoting common values of love, justice, peace, and human dignity.

It is time that religious leaders from every faith and ethnicity have the courage to stand up and denounce any violence or hate done in the name of religion, and name it as blasphemy.

How many more deaths, shattered cities, walls of concrete will it take before we refuse to further destroy one another?

If ever there was a time to transform our swords into plowshares, our hatred into love, our oppression into freedom, occupation into liberation, it is now!

May God continue to use us all as peacemakers, instruments of this healing, ministers of reconciliation, and brokers of justice. Thank you.

Why Lutherans Should Recognize Interfaith Harmony Week

Lutheran World Federation Interview

www.lutheranworld.org • February 2011

Interviewer: This first week of February marks the launch of the first "World Interfaith Harmony Week" as proclaimed by the Secretary General of the United Nations. I had the opportunity this week to sit down with the Right Reverend Munib A. Younan, bishop of the Evangelical Lutheran Church In Jordan and the Holy Land (ELCJHL) and president of The Lutheran World Federation (LWF) and ask him a few questions about the significance of this week. Here's what Bishop Younan had to say.

Interviewer: Interfaith dialogue has been a growing focus around the world in recent years. It might surprise some readers to know that this proposal for the World Interfaith Harmony Week came out of Jordan. What is the significance of Jordan as the country of this initiative's birth?

> Younan: It is very fitting that the proposal for World Interfaith Harmony Week came out of Jordan, as Jordan is a country in which Muslims and Christians have been living in harmony for 1,400 years. Jordan is already a paradigm of Christian–Muslim coexistence, and it is the political will of King Abdullah II of Jordan that this paradigm should continue to be developed not only in Jordan and in the Middle East, but also throughout the world. It is my wish that we Arab Christians can be of help to those countries in which Islamophobia is growing by sharing how we here in the Middle East live with other religions, combating not only Islamophobia, but also anti-Semitism and anti-Christian sentiments and actions, whoever the perpetrator.

The Jordan Times called this week an "occasion for people to express their own religious teachings about tolerance, respect for others and peace, in hopes of bringing people together across the globe." How does our Lutheran theology speak to this?

> In a time of extremism, the core religious values of love of God and love of neighbor should be promoted. I find that our Lutheran theology of creation and our theology of redemption both speak to this. We are created equally. And we are redeemed equally. Together, these theologies provide a strong basis from which to dialogue with our sisters and brothers in humanity from all religions, while we also have a strong basis from which to combat any kind of exclusivity, extremism, or superiority complex.

Bishop Younan, your church is situated in the midst of one of the most diverse interfaith centers of the world. What particular significance is the World Interfaith Harmony Week to the Middle East region?

> Our church has a prophetic role in the Middle East. Its prophetic role is to serve our Lord and our neighbor. Our strength is not in our numbers, but in our witness for love, for justice, for hope, for forgiveness, and for reconciliation. This we do through our educational ministries and through interfaith dialogue with Muslims and with Jews, and through the Council of Religious Institutions in the Holy Land (CRIHL), which is comprised of the two chief rabbis, the Islamic court, the minister of religious affairs in Palestine, and the heads of churches. And for me, as long as the church is an integral part of the fabric of its society, it carries in itself a living witness.

What is the significance of the World Interfaith Harmony Week for The Lutheran World Federation and its member churches?

> The World Interfaith Harmony Week is significant for The Lutheran World Federation and all of its member churches because there is no place in the world in which Lutheran churches live on their own. Lutheran churches, rather, live with other religions—sometimes in a minority position, sometimes in a majority position, but never alone.

> I call on all our member churches in The Lutheran World Federation to designate the first week of February as World Interfaith Harmony Week—a time in which to enter into dialogue with the

religions that are living in their context, and to find the common values that promote justice, coexistence, peace, toleration, and life together, and to work together for the eradication of poverty, the promotion of the role of women, and the reconciliation of our world. Our aim is that religion will not be a source of conflict and problems, nor a reference for any kind of violence, but that religion would become the source of the solution in our broken world.

Finally, what is your appeal to the global human community this week?

My appeal is this: that religion be the source of harmony, justice, and reconciliation in this world. Find from the holy writings what builds this world in the love of God and love of neighbor, not what divides it. Find from the holy writings the common values of our shared humanity. Thus, we can live in harmony.

Suggestions for Christian–Muslim Dialogue

Kuala Lumpur • March 2011

I greet you from the city of Jerusalem, a city holy to three faiths. I am an Arab Palestinian Christian Evangelical Lutheran. Many people no longer think of Christians residing in Jerusalem. They assume that Israelis are Jews and all Palestinians are Muslims. Yet Christians today comprise two percent of the population, far smaller than a century ago, but still a presence. I was born and raised in a Palestinian refugee family from the 1948 war in the Old City of Jerusalem. My house was just a stone's throw from the Church of the Holy Sepulchre, just three minutes walk from the Haram al-Sharif, just five minutes from the Western Wall. Just around the corner was the Lutheran Church of the Redeemer where I was attracted as a youth to its evangelical theology.

My family roots go back to the early church of the Book of Acts. This also means that we Jerusalem Christians have lived side by side with Muslims for nearly 1,400 years. As Arab Christians we have been praying to Allah for 2,000 years. As Arab Christians, we share the same country, the same culture, the same Arabic language, the same plight, the same struggles, the same destiny, and the same emerging Palestinian state. So our histories and future are shared and linked.

Our family lived side by side with many Muslim families in the Old City. We didn't really think that much about it. We were neighbors. We shared each others' joys. We shared each others' sorrow. I have fond childhood memories of a close family friend, Abu Mahmud. Our families would visit each other in our homes. It didn't seem that different. During Ramadan, they always brought us *Qatayef*—the delicious pancakes filled with walnuts and cinnamon and dripping with honey. At Christmas we always brought them our favorite Christmas cakes. One year their children noticed, "Why do the

Younans have a Christmas tree and we don't?" So we went over to their house and decorated a tree for them.

Because of our shared backgrounds and years living together, we rarely differentiate nationally between Christians and Muslims. All of us belong to the same land, and the land belongs to us. I prefer not using the term minority, speaking of our status defined by our numbers, with all the implications that the term minority implies. Likewise, the concept of *dhimmi*—once used in the Ottoman Empire, and still used in Islamic countries where *shariah* law is practiced, and where Christians receive special privileges in return for taxation—this concept of *dhimmi* is not applicable. We Christians are part and parcel of Palestinian society. With that understanding we come together as equals for Muslim–Christian dialogue.

Diapraxis

A Danish Lutheran theologian, Lise Rasmussen, called the union of interfaith dialogue and advocacy "diapraxis." "I see dialogue as a living process, a way of living in coexistence and pro-existence," Rasmussen wrote. "By diapraxis I do not mean the actual application of dialogue but rather dialogue as action. We need a more anthropological contextual approach to dialogue where we see diapraxis as a meeting between people who try to reveal and transform the reality they share," she said.

By adopting this kind of prophetic dialogue for life, we engage our faith in ways that:

- Address people's suffering
- Challenge structures of injustice
- Build modern civil society

All too often religion has been part of the problem, dividing rather than uniting humanity. Our dialogue must work to bring us together to deal with the problems. Religion must be the solution, not the problem.

Today Christians and Muslims number over one-half of the world population, perhaps as much as two-thirds. According to a Gallop poll in 2008, fifty-three percent of Westerners have a negative view of Muslims. At the same time thirty percent of Muslims feel negatively about Christians. This is a tragic development in a global society where people can be easily be brought together by technological advances in communications and transportation. A productive Christian–Muslim dialogue is critical not only for the future of the Middle East, but also for the survival of our planet. Let me share with you a number of principles that will help us to respect and value people of diverse faiths.

Religious leaders are to model respect for other religions

As religious leaders, we carry a heavy responsibility. As religious leaders, we set the example for our followers in their words and deeds. Here are a few ways religious leaders can model respect for other religions:

1. Intentional engagement with the other. As in all relationships, intentional engagement involves dialogue. When you meet someone, you learn their likes and dislikes, their background and their hopes and dreams through conversation. If you hope to befriend this person, you listen without judgment. You respond to their questions in the hope of increasing their understanding of you.

The same is true in interfaith dialogue. We dialogue, above all, to erase our ignorance of one another. We dialogue in order to learn how the other seeks to be understood. For instance, I want Muslims to know that Christianity has many faces and that Christians who call for antagonism toward other religions do not speak for me or for Christianity.

In order to understand what dialogue is, it is important to say what it is not: Dialogue is not an occasion for converting, challenging, or analyzing another's beliefs. It is not intended to be a course in comparative religion. Its aim is not judging the other religion from the standpoint of our own doctrines.

In dialogue, we are set free from a system of exclusive doctrinal claims in order to listen to each other, seek mutual understanding, and, on this foundation, pursue our shared values. In this way, religion becomes a positive force in a broken world, seeking peace, justice, *diakonia*, acceptance, coexistence, freedom, and human rights for all.

If we want our children to behave appropriately, we must behave in like manner. As faith leaders, we must engage with each other in healthy, respectful, and public ways so that those we lead will see people of other faiths as neighbors and allies for life, not enemies.

2. Honest representation of the other. Self-defense is instinctive. If someone lies about you, you defend yourself. Perhaps we can apply this instinct to the defense of the other.

As religious leaders, we have a responsibility, first, to understand the other as they want to be understood and, next, to share that understanding with our people. It is our duty to ensure that our people get an accurate picture of the other, not just the prejudices they hear in the streets. Our preachers must be responsible. We must oppose those who selectively read sacred writings of other faith traditions in an effort to tarnish their reputations. We must not allow extremists to kidnap our holy writings for their own purposes. We must not tolerate the language of mutual denunciation, dehumanization, and demonization. In particular, Muslims and Christians must agree to speak out against blasphemy in Pakistan. And so we must teach our people a new language—the language of love and respect.

This is one of the main efforts of the Council of Religious Institutions in the Holy Land, the first Jewish, Muslim and Christian council in the Middle East. Because this change must begin with faith leaders themselves, we established a hotline for monitoring derogatory remarks by clergy, imams, and rabbis about other faiths. We jointly call on all religions to teach the right thing about the other and use the same language at home, at work, in the synagogue, at church, in the mosque, and at temple.

This applies to our schools as well. We must ask ourselves if our school curricula– especially history and religion classes—teach the right thing about the other. How can we expect future generations to build civil society with the other if they do not see them as equal partners? For this reason, the Council of Religious Institutions in the Holy Land is working with both ministries of education in Israel and in Palestine to develop a curriculum of tolerance for use in Israeli and Palestinian textbooks.

It is essential that each religion must be understood not as we other religions interpret it, but in the way that religion wants to be understood. One example is His Majesty King Abdullah II of Jordan's Amman Message, a 2004 statement calling for tolerance and unity in the Muslim world. The Amman Message condemns Islamic extremism and emphasizes Islam's core values of compassion, mutual respect, tolerance, acceptance, and religious freedom. Following is an excerpt:

> On religious grounds, on moral grounds, we denounce the contemporary concept of terrorism which is associated with wrongful practices wherever they come from—including assaults on peaceful civilians, killing prisoners and the wounded, unethical practices such as the destruction of buildings, and ransacking cities. These despotic attacks on human life transgress the law of God, and we denounce them.
>
> As the *Qur'an* says, "Take not life which God hath made sacred, except by way of justice and law" (Al Anaam, 51). . . . No human whose heart is filled with light could be an extremist. We decry the campaign that portrays Islam as a religion that encourages violence and institutionalizes terrorism.

Another example is "A Common Word Between Us and You," the 2007 open letter signed by 138 Muslim scholars from different schools of Islam all over the world calling for peace between Muslims and Christians. The document calls people to work for common ground and understanding between the faiths based on the common commandments to love God and humanity.

I believe the approach taken in this document is a healthy trend in interfaith dialogue and interfaith relations. Instead of focusing on differences in doctrine and "comparative religion," leaders are lifting up and building on common positive values, such as peace, justice, forgiveness, and reconciliation. Comparative religion can result in arrogance and foster superiority that one religion is better than the other, and thus create division and intolerance. In dialogue for life, we are focusing on common values that help us live together and grow from our common search for God. It is important that each religion speak to its own adherents and seek to define itself, rather than being labeled by the other. This also promotes important dialogue within each faith as well, since there are many faces of each religion, which is important to recognize in a time when extremist voices are getting stronger and trying to claim they are the only "true voices" of their religions.

Dr. Miroslav Volf, professor of theology at Yale Divinity School, addresses this subject in his paper on "A Common Word":

> Lest someone think that this is too quick and somewhat cheap triumph of religion over conflict, let me make plain what I am not saying about the significance of finding commonality between Christianity and Islam in the dual command of love. First, to have the dual commandment of love in common, does not mean to be amalgamated into the same religion. Even if there is significant agreement on the love of God and neighbor, many other differences remain—differences that are not accidental to each faith but which define them. For instance, Christians continue to believe that the One and Unique God who is utterly exalted above all created beings, is the holy Trinity and that God has shown unconditional love for humanity in that Jesus Christ as God's Lamb bore the sins of the world; Muslims do not share these beliefs. Similarly, Muslims revere the Prophet Muhammad as the "seal of the prophets" and the Holy Qur'an as sacred Scripture, whereas Christians do not. An agreement on the love of God and neighbor does not erase differences. It enables people to accept others in their differences,

leads them to get to know each other in their differences, and helps them live together harmoniously notwithstanding their differences.

You know you understand the other faith when you can tell their story to their satisfaction. That is why I say that it is the responsibility of Arab Christians to be the voice of Islam in the West. Likewise, Arab Muslims have the responsibility of being the voice of Arab Christians to the Arab and Muslims worlds. This will promote an honest representation of the other.

3. Ethical conduct toward the other. In early 2005, an American magazine reported that guards at a U.S. prison camp had deliberately damaged a copy of the *Qur'an*. That September, a Danish newspaper published a dozen cartoons depicting the prophet Muhammad. I, as a religious leader, responded to these events by calling for a code of conduct to be signed by Arab Muslim and Christian leaders.

The Jordanian Interfaith Coexistence Research Center in Amman, Jordan, the church of Norway, and the ELCJHL convened forty-eight Muslim and Christian leaders in January 2008 to develop and sign this code of conduct. The resulting Amman Declaration calls for mutual respect of all religions' holy places and symbols and makes an appeal for worldwide religious toleration.

It says in part that

> We, as people who believe in the One God, and as people who own the legacy of coexistence in this region, Muslim and Christian, seek in this difficult era to build together our present and future society, in a spirit of mutual responsibility so that comprehensive peace and real justice prevail in our region and in the world as a whole. To achieve this, we undertake the commitment and pledge to call for the following to be implemented, not in our region only, but in the world as a whole:
>
> • Respect of religious freedom and belief.
>
> • Respect of all messengers, prophets, holy books, and religious texts and prohibition of their desecration.
>
> • All holy places should be respected and made freely accessible to believers.
>
> • All religious symbols must be respected and any desecration should be prohibited and prevented.

- Respect for responsible freedom of expression which does not harm the belief and feelings of others.
- To continue dialogue and human cooperation so that justice, peace, development and decent living, called for by the human and religious teachings of the heavenly religions, can be achieved.

Is this not the least that we expect for ourselves? Therefore, I hope that a code of conduct like this will be observed not only by Muslims and Christians but also by other religions as well.

Last September, when a man claiming to be a Christian pastor in the United States threatened to burn copies of the Qur'an at his church on September 11, I issued a public statement condemning him. I said, "If we are silent, we are complicit . . . [in this action] and we will bear the responsibility for a spiral of violence." I followed this with an op-ed piece for *The Washington Post* online edition. I assure you, as a Christian bishop, I will not remain silent when Islam is defamed. And I appeal to you as Muslim leaders that you do the same when you hear that Christianity is being defamed.

Religious leaders are to model respect for people who practice other religions.

Just as we respect other faith traditions, we should respect each faith's practitioners. We should seek full human rights for people of all faiths, not only our own. I am not talking about narrow self-interest here, but about the "fullness of life," as it is stated in my tradition, for all.

According to Article 18 of the Universal Declaration of Human Rights, "Everyone has the right to freedom of thought, conscience and religion; this right includes freedom to change his/her religion or belief, and freedom, either alone or in community with others and in public or private, to manifest his/her religion or belief in teaching, practice, worship and observance."

This touches on a very sensitive issue—that of mission, as it's known in Christianity, or *ad-dawah*, as it's called in the Muslim world.

Christianity and Islam are known to be missionary religions. It is in fact central to my call as a Christian, for my Lord and Savior calls me to go, preach the gospel, and make disciples (Matthew 28:19-20). Islam also calls its believers to call others to submit to God and Islamic teachings.

I think it is necessary to respect the missionary endeavors of every religion; however, I agree with Khalif Omar al-Khattab, who says: "Your freedom ends where the other's freedom starts." We religious leaders should not allow our countries to become missionary battlefields. What kind of world would that be?

But as long as they do not use coercion or financial incentives, I think everyone should be allowed to answer that call and tell others about their religion. And, if one is truly convinced, he or she should be free to follow their conscience. Religious leaders should not call for that person's elimination but respect their decision if they have freely chosen to change their religion. In a pluralistic world, it is unavoidable that people will choose to adopt new religions. As religious leaders, we should establish practices that support this basic human right. One such model is presented by the Islamic Council of Norway and the Church of Norway Council on Ecumenical and International Relations, which presented a joint declaration on the freedom of religion and the right to conversion in 2007.

Allow me to present an example from my own church, as well. We in the ELCJHL believe that education—of Christians, Muslims, and Jews—is a key to building tolerance and coexistence. In our educational programs, approximately forty-five percent of our students are Muslim. We do not seek to convert the children but to educate them to live together with other religions in peace and mutual respect, so that they may come to understand the other as the other wants to be understood. We are preparing future leaders—both Muslim and Christian—to work together to build a modern, democratic, civil society with freedom of religion, expression, and living together as equal citizens with equal rights and equal responsibilities.

As a helpful step to promote this respect and good will, I would appeal to all of you to mark your calendars to observe the Week of Interfaith Harmony, the first week of February each year. This was an initiative of King Abdullah II of Jordan that was adopted unanimously by the UN General Assembly last October. The resolution encourages all countries of the world to "spread the message of interfaith harmony and goodwill in the world's churches, mosques, synagogues, temples and other places of worship . . . to each according to their own religious traditions or convictions." It specifically mentions the initiative of the "Common Word" document as important grounding especially in terms of the two core principles of love of God (or alternatively, love of the good) and love of neighbor.

I will repeat here what I said in an interview last month for the LWF website: "The World Interfaith Harmony Week is significant for The Lutheran World Federation and all of its member churches because there is no place in the world in which Lutheran churches live on their own. Lutheran churches, rather, live with other religions—sometimes in a minority position, sometimes in a majority position, but never alone."

This Week of Interfaith Harmony is an opportunity for all of us to grow in our respect of other religions.

Religious leaders are to oppose extremism.

One of the great challenges of the twenty-first century will be to reclaim faith as a force for justice, peace, and love, rather than being part of the problem. Ever since the September 11 tragedy in the United States, to a large extent, the world has focused on the growing threat of Muslim extremism. But no religion has a monopoly on hate or extremism. All of us are equally responsible and equally called to work together to seek the common, positive values of love, compassion, justice, and peace, and together to uphold the sacred value of all, regardless of color, race, creed, or religion.

Dr. Charles Kimball, professor of comparative religion at Wake Forest University and writer on Middle East religions and relations, writes in his book, *When Religion Becomes Evil*, that the five markers of this phenomenon are:

- Absolute truth claims
- Blind obedience
- Establishing the "ideal" time
- When all ends justify the means
- The declaration of holy war

He writes,

> Whatever religions people may say about their love of God or the mandates of their religion, when their behavior toward others is violent and destructive, when it causes suffering among their neighbors, you can be sure the religion has been corrupted and reform is desperately needed. When religion becomes evil, these five corruptions are always present. Conversely, when religion remains true to its authentic sources, it is actively dismantling these corruptions.

It is so interesting to me that often the people who call themselves fundamentalists—in any religion—have often abandoned the most basic fundamental of all: "Love God and your neighbor as yourself."

Why is this? What can we do about it? The world is crying out for better vision and leadership in today's increasingly violent, extremist, and militarized world.

Lutheran historian Martin Marty says that extremism grows where injustice, oppression, and poverty flourish. I believe this is true in the Middle East. The heart of the problem in the Middle East is the unresolved and continuing oppression, injustice, and ongoing occupation of Palestine. People here see the West standing for justice and freedom for its friends while it is building walls, physically and symbolically, around Muslims and the Arab world. Here, the test of the West for justice is whether they can help bring a just end to the Israeli–Palestinian conflict. Until there is some justice achieved here, rather than the acceleration toward greater discrimination, Western claims of bringing democracy and freedom to the Middle East will seem like a cruel joke. Clever extremists will use democratic systems to come to power. Extremism will grow.

It is high time we moderate people of faith stand up and take back our religions! We who are grounded in the real fundamentals of love, compassion, justice, and peace must affirm together that God has created every human life—indeed all of creation—to be cherished, protected, and nurtured. We must stop demonizing one another in the name of God and instead try to see God in the other. We will then learn and grow from one another about what will give life, love, *salaam*/peace to this earth.

But lest it sound like I am focusing on the extremism of the "other," I remind myself and other Christians to clean our own kitchens before we criticize someone else's. We have our own extremists, such as Christian Zionists and others.

Religious leaders must create a united front to oppose extremism, for extremism tries to transform political injustice into religious wars and conflicts, in which the only winner is extremism itself. Former U.S. Secretary of State Condoleezza Rice agreed with me when I told her, "Extremism cannot be combated by shelling or bombarding but by education and interfaith dialogue."

I believe the "neighbor" spoken about in the holy writings is every person, regardless of faith, doctrine, culture, ethnicity, or gender. It is the role of religious leaders to make all efforts to educate our followers to apply this teaching universally.

Religious leaders are to provide leadership for *diakonia* and confronting social problems.

Religious leaders in their dialogue are to move beyond intellectual dialogue to dialogue for life. Religions must not see themselves as rivals, but rather as potential partners for the service of people of all religions, ethnicity, gender, or political affiliation. God did not call us to serve our own followers or people only but to be servants of God to help humanity have life and life abundantly. Common service illustrates that religions are not in competition but complement each other's service and *diakonia* for the sake of humanity itself.

Last summer when the country of Pakistan was hit by devastating floods, I wrote in my first public statement as the president of the LWF: "The flood does not differentiate along ethnic, political, or religious lines; neither should we. This is the time to unite behind our common humanity."

Religious leaders must tackle the social-ethical issues in our own societies before they become a source of dissension. We must discuss such social-ethical issues based on the theology of creation that God created us equally in order that we know each other and solve together the sensitive questions—questions such as mixed marriages, the role of women, state religion, citizenship, and other issues that require frank and transparent deliberations and dialogue by religious leaders.

Religious leaders must cooperate together on global issues. God calls us to work together on issues of eradicating poverty, HIV/AIDs, gender equality, global warming, and climate change. Can we also work together to stop the proliferation of both conventional and nuclear armaments? Can we call on politicians to stop building nuclear weapons and instead use the money for education, eradicating poverty, and helping fund research to find treatment for contagious and serious diseases such as malaria, HIV/AIDs, and cancer? Can we convince political leaders to sign an international agreement to fight climate change, which devastates especially poor nations in the South? We have many challenges before us as religious leaders. I ask you, can we have more joint projects together?

Religious leaders are to be prophetic.

Throughout history, religion has often been used to legitimize the political power of the day. Sometimes religious leaders opted to be quiet and be complicit rather than to confront injustice, for fear of losing their rights.

Instead, religious leaders must use the power of religion to speak truth to power and to promote justice in their societies and the world. Prophetic leaders do not seek to please the powerful or maintain the *status quo*. In the Old Testament we find many examples of the prophets challenging injustices and abuses of power. Driven by a commitment to live out the commands to love God and the neighbor, prophetic leaders use their power to call for justice and secure human rights for all people, especially those dispossessed and marginalized by society.

Certainly Amos made no points with rulers when he said, "Take away from me the noise of your songs; I will not listen to the melody of your harps. But let justice roll down like waters, and righteousness like an ever-flowing stream" (Amos 5:23-24).

The prophet Jeremiah suffered as he uttered powerful and painful oracles against his own people. Jesus Christ suffered crucifixion for challenging the religious and political institutions of his time.

I believe religious leaders have not spoken enough about justice. Perhaps they represented their government's policies and ignored justice; maybe they were concerned only with their own internal problems and interests, and ignored the burning issues of the world. For example, how many Asian countries suffer now under oppression, lack of human rights, social injustice, occupation, colonialism, and the like? Religious leadership has not spoken enough about this. If religious leaders only raise their voices in a concerted way, they will become a beautiful, effective symphony of justice that will disrupt injustice and end violations of human rights. People today speak about freedom and democracy, but only from their own narrow national interests. We say that justice is the first priority for many countries in Asia and the developing world in order that freedom and democracy may be realized. It is our call as religious leaders to work for justice and only justice.

I agree with His Royal Highness Prince Ghazi of Jordan who says that the issues of the Palestinian occupation and the sharing of Jerusalem are two major issues for dialogue between Muslims and Christians. Both Muslim and Christian leaders are raising their voices for a just end to the illegal Israeli occupation, which would include two nations living side by side on 1967 borders, a shared Jerusalem, a stop to all settlement activity, a solution to the refugee issue, and the sharing of resources. Such a solution may bring about further regional cooperation.

We believe in justice and security for both Palestinians and Israelis. The litmus test for the West—that is, the European Union and the United States—is whether they can bring about justice with a single, uniform standard throughout the entire Holy Land.

Religious leaders are to be catalysts for reconciliation.

According to Encyclopedia Britannica, nearly eighty-five percent of people throughout the world profess belief in God. Together we can have a huge impact on fostering reconciliation throughout the world.

Followers of Abrahamic faiths find the rationale for reconciliation in the creation story. Genesis 1:27 says that we all—whether male, female, Jew, Muslim, Christian, Buddhist, Hindu, deist, agnostic, or atheist—are created in God's image. This means we all share equal humanity and are all equally worthy of love and respect.

Simply put, reconciliation is the restoration of friendship or harmony. I believe people of faith are reconciled when they acknowledge God in the other. Our Hindu friends call this *namaste,* roughly translated "the divine in me sees the divine in you." When you consider another person an equal, it is only logical to recognize their religious and other human rights. God calls us to seek together the values our faith traditions hold in common, such as justice, peace, forgiveness, respect, toleration, and love.

We Palestinian Christians believe this work of reconciliation is the very heart of our faith tradition. It was the work of Jesus during his public ministry in ancient Israel, and it was the mission he passed on to us when he returned to God. Indeed, reconciliation is a priority for all religious leaders in the Middle East. Reconciliation is not simply the absence of hatred. Our people need to learn how to create a shared vision of common values and a shared hope for the future.

But before reconciliation can take place, each tradition must take responsibility for its actions. The late Pope John Paul II provided an example when he confessed the sin of some members of the church who persecuted the Jews throughout history. In doing so, he set an example for forgiving the past, shaping the present, and providing a common vision for the future.

Muslims and Christians have not been innocent toward each other throughout history. We have abandoned our core faiths when we have dehumanized each other. One example is the crusades, which harmed Muslim, Jewish, and Christian communities. Another is the xenophobia, Islamophobia, Christianophobia, and anti-Semitism that pervades our world. Another example is when Muslims accuse Christians of being *kuffar* (apostates) or *mushrikiin* (pantheists). It is time we evaluate our history and take stock of the present in order to shape the future. Repentance and forgiveness provides the environment in which reconciliation can take place.

In the year 2000, a Church of Norway study called *Vulnerability and Security* states the potential well: "The great world religions have both similarities and fundamental differences. And one of the most important similarities is actually a conviction that it is part of the innermost essence of religion to be a source of peace and reconciliation."

Catholic theologian Hans Küng said, "No peace among nations without peace among religions. And no peace among religions without dialogue." I hope that my words today encourage you to continue fostering respect and esteem for people of diverse faiths so that faith takes its rightful place as something that unites and empowers us for the common good of humanity.

To live with other religions, cultures, races, languages, and traditions is an art. But it is an art we must learn, practice, and perfect if we want our children to be able to live together in peace, with cultural liberty and justice for all.

Sermons about Love for Neighbor and Reconciliation

Fear Not!

Christmas Message

Bethlehem • 24 December 2010

Luke 2:10

When we think of the Christmas story, the most common words that come to mind are peace, joy, hope, faith, and love. Christmas is a pleasant time when families come together, when choirs sing, and when children are filled with fantasies. Yet the first two words of Christmas are "Fear not!"

> In that region there were shepherds living in the fields, keeping watch over their flock by night. Then an angel of the Lord stood before them, and the glory of the Lord shone around them, and they were terrified. But the angel said to them, "Fear not! For see—I am bringing you good news of great joy for all the people: To you is born this day in the city of David a Savior, who is the Messiah, the Lord (Luke 2:8-11).

It was the same when the angel appeared to the aged priest Zechariah at the temple: "Fear not!"

And when Gabriel appeared to the young girl Mary in Nazareth: "Fear not!"

And when Joseph learned that Mary was pregnant and an angel appeared to him in a dream: "Fear not!"

In first century Palestine, there were so many reasons for them to be afraid:

• For Zechariah, the impotency of old age and the potential loss of mental and physical abilities.

• For Mary, a young vulnerable girl, pregnant outside of marriage in a patriarchal society.

- For Joseph, the pressures of leading an upstanding and righteous life with religious zealots judging him on the basis of Mary's pregnancy.

- For the shepherds, the threat of the natural world with wild animals about to attack their flocks during the darkness of night and the lawlessness of thieves and bandits who would not be afraid of using violence for material gain.

- For all of them, questions about God's presence in their lives when God seemed so very far away.

And yet "Fear not!" was the message of the angel to all of them. And it was not the terrifying, life-destroying, bad news they might have expected. It was good news of great joy for each one of them and for all people. "Fear not! For I bring you good news of great joy!"

> For God so loved the world that he gave his only Son, so that everyone who believes in him may not perish but may have eternal life (John 3:16).

For Zechariah, for Mary, for Joseph, for the shepherds, the message was very simple: "God has not forgotten you. God is not far away or removed from your lives. God hears your cries of loneliness, inadequacy, uncertainty, doubt, and fear about who you are, what is your purpose in life, how you fit in with your relationships to others, your relationship to this vast universe, and most of all your relationship to God—to God who comes in the form of a child born in a humble manger, among common people like you, on a still, silent night, in a small village like Bethlehem. This is good news of great joy. God loves you. Fear not!"

In the first epistle of John, we are told: "There is no fear in love, but perfect love casts out fear" (1 John 4:18). And so the first word of Christmas must be that spoken by the angels, "Fear not!" It is the first, the middle, and the last word of Christmas. "Fear not!" Here in Bethlehem and Jerusalem, and into the whole world, "Fear not!" Then, 2,000 years ago, and today at Christmas 2010, "Fear not!"

There are many issues today that cause us to fear: health problems like cancer and diseases like HIV/AIDS, economic issues like job loss and decreasing funds for retirement, family issues like divorce or the death of a spouse, environmental issues like global warming and disappearing natural resources, international tensions and the development of more destructive weaponry, extremism in politics and religion. Once again we need a Christmas angel proclaiming, "Fear not!"

Yes, here at Christmas time 2010 in the Middle East, we once again long for a heavenly angel to comfort us with these words, "Fear not!" Our people are in danger of drowning in fear. Christians in many parts of the Middle East are increasingly cowering in fear and becoming timid in their witness. Just a little over a month ago in Baghdad at Our Lady of Salvation Church terrorists gunned down two priests and fifty-one defenseless worshippers. Since then, another three were killed in Mosul, and an elderly Christian couple were murdered in their own home in Baghdad. So how do Christians respond? In an Associated Press story, one woman, afraid to give her name, said she lives in a constant state of fear, keeping her children indoors and out of school. In less than fifteen years, the number of Christians in Iraq has declined from 1.25 million to only 400,000. For centuries Christians and Muslims have lived side by side, yet today religious extremists are holding hostage the moderate majority, Christian and Muslim alike. Iraqi Christians are once again in need of a Christmas angel proclaiming, "Fear not!"

A similar picture is developing in Egypt where Coptic Christians have fresh in their memories the drive-by shooting that left six Christians dead in Nag Hammadi as they were leaving church after last year's Christmas Eve mass. As we welcome another Christmas season, there are heightened tensions in Egypt. We ask both sides—Christians and Muslims alike—to dialogue concerning their differences for the sake of their long-standing relationship. We announce to them from Jerusalem, "We are praying for you." And we say, "Fear not!"

These and other situations have resulted in the U.S. State Department "International Religious Freedom Report" for 2010 reminding us that: "The right to believe or not to believe, without fear of government interference or restriction, is a basic human right." To believe without fear, to worship without fear, is a fundamental human right. Yet, because of extremism, people are afraid.

These and other situations were the reason that the Vatican recently held its synod on the Middle East to: "Confirm and strengthen Christians in their identity through the Word of God and the Sacraments. . . . And to give new life . . . so that they might provide an authentic witness of joyful and attractive Christian life."[136]

I hope that the World Council of Churches will hold a similar conference so that we Christians of the Middle East will have a coordinated strategy and be strengthened in the process.

Here in Jerusalem and the Holy Land, including Jordan, we are not facing the same problems of persecution as our sisters and brothers in many countries of the Middle East. There may be social and political problems, but we thank God for the religious freedom we enjoy. Here Christians today number only 1.7 percent of the population, with many Arab Christians emigrating because of the political situation and the lack of willingness and resolve to bring about a just peace, because of lack of jobs, because of lack of housing, because of the difficulty of travel, and because of the rise of extremism on both sides.

Palestinians and Israelis today face a common enemy: fear. In the absence of justice and peace, the common denominator is fear—fear of the other, fear for the future, fear that freedom is not coming, fear that children will grow in hatred, fear of insecurity, fear of the occupation. Fear is our common prison that keeps us locked up in cycles of mistrust and shattered dreams. It is a fear that builds nonproductive "facts on the ground." It is a fear that will only vanish when there is peace based on justice and reconciliation built on forgiveness. We proclaim that such a just peace is possible today. We pray that all political leaders will seize the opportunity before it is too late. The same message of the first Christmas rings true today: "Fear not!" There is a child who was born into a world of fear in order to take away that fear and to bring peace to earth and good will to humankind.

The Christmas message must speak loud and clear once again, "Fear not!" We are in need of a heavenly angel, a messenger of God, who says, "Do not be afraid." Fear not, Zechariah. Fear not, Joseph. Fear not, Mary. Fear not, shepherds. Fear not, Palestinian Christians. Fear not, Arab Christians. God hears you. God loves you. God empowers you. God calls you to be a vibrant and living witness in this place at this critical time in history.

When the angels appeared to the Beit Sahour shepherds, the promise of good news overshadowed all their fears. The announcement of God's love for them and the world cast out all the fear that might have prevented them from traveling to Bethlehem amid the crowds and the Roman soldiers on that first Christmas night.

The announcement of God's love for them brought them to the manger where they bowed in humble worship to the long-promised Christ child, where they prayed, where they uttered songs of thanksgiving, where they were fed spiritually and strengthened in order to return to their normal, mundane, and sometimes exhausting tasks of daily life. Luke describes this return in such encouraging words: "The shepherds returned, glorifying and praising God for all they had heard and seen, as it had been told them."

For the shepherds, the dangers were still there. The threats of violence were still very real and no different than before. The demands of making a living, of supporting their families, and of sharing with their neighbors and communities—none of that was different from the day before. In many ways, their lives had not changed, but their spirits had. They went about their daily tasks glorifying and praising God for all they had heard and seen. From the beginning of those two small words—"Fear not!"—the shepherds were called to witness; they were sent out, unafraid, to share the good news with those around them.

Likely their home communities, their friends, and even their families met them with some reluctance, perhaps with skepticism and doubt. Those around them were still living in fear. I wonder how the shepherds began their stories about that first Christmas night? Most likely it was with those same two words, "Fear not!" And their witness would have provided a contagion that changed families, transformed communities, and encouraged others no longer to live in fear, but to share in that vibrant witness of the hope that came to Bethlehem in the child born in a manger.

Our task as a church is to be the salt of society, the leaven of the dough. Our task today is to provide education. It is also our task to provide our society with educated individuals who promote the values of human rights, freedom of religion, and democracy. Our task is to train leaders who will become teachers, lawyers, and professionals who will contribute to the well being of society. Our task is to provide a witness of nonviolent struggle against injustice, to promote religious toleration, to provide a model of peoples of different religious and ethnic backgrounds learning to see God in the other, and to love our neighbor as ourselves. We can no longer be timid or afraid about our witness to the world. At this time of hopelessness, it is essential that we Christians develop a theology of witness and coexistence focusing on the reasons that the babe of the manger calls us—like the shepherds of old—to witness here in the Holy Land.

Today Christians in the Middle East are just a small minority, living in a world filled with danger and filled with what must seem to be insurmountable challenges. And so it was with those first shepherds of Beit Sahour, only three or four of them, perhaps one or two still children, all uneducated and untrained in speech. I could understand if they had been timid in telling the story. But Luke tells us they went home glorifying and praising God. And I could understand if today's Christian community remained timid about its witness. But then I hear again those first two little words of the Christmas message: "Fear not!"

The angels call to us from the first Christmas.

"Fear not!"

They speak to us when we hear the Christmas story once again.

"Fear not!"

And from the manger in Bethlehem we continue to hear.

"Fear not!"

Living Stones

Fifth Sunday of Easter

Grace Lutheran Church, La Grange, Illinois

22 May 2011

"Like living stones, let yourselves be built into a spiritual house" (1 Peter 2:5).

Grace, mercy, and peace from our Lord Jesus Christ.

Jerusalem is well known for its beautiful stone buildings. You have all seen the magnificent photographs of Jerusalem, with all the white limestone houses. Prominent in every photograph of the Old City is my own church, the Evangelical Lutheran Church of the Redeemer, right in the center of the Old City with its tall white limestone tower, a prominent landmark.

In 1918, at the beginning of the British Mandate, Governor Sir Ronald Storrs began enforcing a law that only white limestone, quarried from the hills surrounding Jerusalem, could be used in construction. No painted wood houses. No red-brick houses. Everything in white limestone. Today, there is even a *Wikipedia* entry for "Jerusalem Stone," it is so typical for Jerusalem.

Even in Jesus' day visitors often remarked about the amazing quality of Jerusalem stone. In fact shortly before Jesus' death, after visiting the Jerusalem temple, the disciples used to the fishing villages of Galilee remarked to Jesus, "See what beautiful stones and what beautiful buildings!" So I wonder if St. Peter, living far off in Rome, was just a little homesick for his beloved Jerusalem when he wrote to the Christians in Turkey with these words: "Like living stones, let yourselves be built into a spiritual house."

One of my fondest memories growing up in the Old City of Jerusalem was the sound of stonecutters preparing the stone for a new building. We could hear the sound of the chisel on stone from long distances away, and we would run to watch. It was fascinating how skilled the stone cutters were. These craftsmen could tell just by the sound as they hewed the rough stone, whether the stone was a dead stone or a living stone. That is exactly what they called them. The dead stones were tossed away in a pile, but the living stones were the ones that would fit perfectly in place and add beauty to the building.

The stone cutting trade has been active in Jerusalem for over 2,000 years, and today there are over 650 Palestinian stone-cutting enterprises. The most skilled are amazing artists. A look at the Redeemer stone altar and pulpit helps one to understand how stones can be described as living, how they can be cultivated and hewn to serve God in providing beauty to this land called holy. Our pulpit in Beit Jala includes the carved words: "Open my lips, and my mouth shall declare your praise" (Psalm 51:15). Simon Peter was very observant seeing how something material could serve such a spiritual purpose.

In my early years as a pastor, after I began working with people, I asked a skilled stonecutter, "What do you think is easier to hew, to shape, to mold? A stone or a human?" He laughed at me and answered, "I enjoy working with stones. They can be molded and worked. Humans can be less workable, more stubborn."

> Like living stones, let yourselves be built into a spiritual house,
> to be a holy priesthood, to offer spiritual sacrifices acceptable to
> God through Jesus Christ.

I take the stone cutter to be Jesus. Jesus with his chisel continues to hew and mold us. Through Baptism he washes us to become living stones and through Holy Communion he nourishes us to be ready to be hewn, cut, molded, and shaped, that our lives may be offered up for the purposes of God. Christians are not in this world for themselves, but they are placed here to serve others. The sole controlling principal in this service is love. And Jesus, always with his chisel, takes away the unnecessary pieces of hatred, anger, sinful thinking, and jealousy, and molds us in love. As the song says, "His banner over me is love," and he thus calls us to be agents of love.

Sometimes people think that vocation and call is only for the clergy or the church professional. When Peter talks about being a holy priesthood, we remember Martin Luther's focus on the priesthood of all believers. The woman cleaning in her kitchen, the man building a house, the secretary in the office, the teacher, the truck driver—all have callings that contribute to the work of Christ's kingdom. God does not work through us at the same time, in the same place, in the same work. God moves at different times and in different places, in different works, in different people, but always guided by the same spirit and the same faith. Every stone of the building plays an important role. Every stone helps it achieve its function. Every stone adds to its beauty. It is our evangelical understanding, that Christ hews us to be servants of love in order that we may serve human beings regardless of their gender, political or religious affiliation. And love keeps no record of its works, for it thinks only about the other; when it accomplishes good, its deed appears as a gift and not a duty. To be preserved, such love must constantly be given new life by faith, faith in Jesus Christ as Savior and Lord.

In particular we can think of Simon himself—the one named by Christ as Peter, the Rock—the disciple who wrote these very words. Think of all those episodes where he seemed so hardheaded and rough-edged that he needed to be shaped and hewn by Jesus himself. Think of how it must have been as Jesus first called him, a common fisherman, to become a fisher of human beings. Think of how it must have been for this man full of doubts as he saw first hand how Jesus healed the sick. Think of how it must have been as Peter watched the faces of people listening to Jesus' preaching of the kingdom of God having come into their midst. Think of how it must have been as Peter heard Jesus' voice calling him to come to him on the water. Think of how it must have been as Peter ran to the tomb on Easter morning to see if it was really true that Jesus had risen from the dead, to bring to people like Peter the hope of the abundant life.

Yes, Peter was a rough stone, but Jesus hewed him, molding him and shaping him to become a living stone, fit together with all those ancient stones of the disciples and early Christians to be built into a spiritual house.

The same is true of Mary Magdalene, a woman possessed by seven spirits. She followed Jesus and loved him, allowing herself to be molded by him. Who would have thought that she would have been chosen to be the first to proclaim the resurrection.

> Once you were not a people,
> but now you are God's people;
> once you had not received mercy,
> but now you have received mercy (1 Peter 2:10).

That was Peter's own story and also the story of Mary Magdalene. That is our story today.

> But you are a chosen race, a royal priesthood, a holy nation, God's
> own people, in order that you may proclaim the mighty acts of

him who called you out of darkness into his marvelous light (1 Peter 2:9).

We are called, hewn, shaped, and molded to be witnesses of God's mighty acts from Jerusalem into all the world.

Simon Peter understood well the practice of building houses in Jerusalem—not only the way the stones were hewn, but also the practice of building a sturdy house that was passed on for generations. Here in Chicago, a common practice is that a young married couple first may rent a small apartment; then, after a few years, buy a small house; then after their family grows, buy a larger house with more bedrooms; and then when reaching retirement, might sell that house to buy a smaller house or perhaps a condo. In Jerusalem, the family house is precious and continues in the family for generations. When children are born, the sturdy stone house is expanded with additional rooms; with marriages and grandchildren, the house continues to grow, a living structure. The dwelling place of younger generations depends on the well-placed stones of earlier generations.

So it is very common today for tourists and pilgrims—millions each year—who come to Jerusalem to see the ancient stones of the Bible. Everyone wants to visit where Christ walked, where he slept, where he taught, where he died. Everyone wants to see the churches built by Christians over the centuries at these historical places. Everyone wants to see the stones—to touch them, to photograph them, to see for themselves the beautiful stones and all that they stand for. Long ago this land became know as the Holy Land—holy not because the stones are holy, but because the Holy One of God made himself manifest in this land. In truth, however, those many visitors soon become bored when they look only at the stones in the ground. The stones are good, they are beautiful, but we must be careful not to turn them into relics, as if they were holy themselves. They are holy only insofar as they are witnesses to the mighty acts of a holy God.

I always say that there is a difference between a tourist and a pilgrim to the Holy Land. Tourists come to see the dead stones, the history of the land, and the archaeology. Pilgrims come to revive their faith while encountering the living stones, so when they leave their own faith is revived, as is also the faith of the living stones, the Christians of the Holy Land. Both will be called a holy race, servants of love, accompaniers of each other wherever they are called.

Eusebius, bishop of Caesarea, once said, "Every place where you worship the Lord in Spirit and in truth is holy land." Likewise, "Every place where the Holy Communion is celebrated is Jerusalem."

What Eusebius is telling us that what really matters are the living stones, the people who worship the Lord in spirit and truth, the people who celebrate Holy Communion, the people who give a vibrant witness to the mighty acts of God. For 2,000 years, the Christians of Palestine have been those living stones, who in their day-to-day lives, in good times and bad, in their struggles and in their suffering, have provided that witness. These living stones of Jerusalem are like the stones in that first room of this generations-old house that has grown just as the family of God has grown throughout the world.

We look at those earlier generations of living stones with appreciation, knowing how many of them left their own homes, their comfortable lives, and their security to allow themselves to be placed into this spiritual structure, all the while giving new meaning to these holy places. We look with heartache when later generations of living stones have been forced from the homes as refugees. We look with sorrow when we see their houses demolished today to make room for others to take their place. We look with sadness when today's young people are emigrating because of the difficulties of the political situation, because of growing extremism, and because of lack of jobs and housing.

This is the reason that we call upon the living stones not to emigrate, telling them that the Lord calls them to stay in our country for a holy service. We are living in the land of Calvary. We are to carry the cross whatever the price. For we know that after Golgotha there is resurrection. As long as we serve in love in Jerusalem and in the Holy Land, we are reflecting the resurrection in our lives and reflecting Christ's love. Christianity in Jerusalem has survived 2,000 years. We did not survive because of wealth, bank accounts, property, or investments. We survived because of the living witness of love and forgiveness that we have carried. The church is always to be prophetic. That means we must always proclaim the Gospel and administer the Sacraments. We are to care for the living stones.

Continued emigration has reduced Christianity in Israel and Palestine to only 1.7 percent. We are anxious and afraid about the vulnerability that comes with such small numbers. Yet we do not sit by idly, doing nothing. We continue our vibrant witness and continue an active role in society, serving as the balance between Jews and Muslims. We continue to focus on education that teaches our children to live together with the other in religious freedom and with respect to build a civil society. We have established in particular a leadership training program with thirty young people who are being hewn through

Bible study, theology, and leadership theory as living stones to play a dynamic role in the future of our church.

> Like living stones, let yourselves be built into a spiritual house, to be a holy priesthood, to offer spiritual sacrifices acceptable to God through Jesus Christ.

Like living stones, let yourselves be built into a spiritual house and do not forget those other stones in the same structure.

We are all living stones, witnessing to the mighty acts of God. We are all living stones, living out our callings by God, the master builder. We are all living stones, fit together with each other in a communion which brings us into greater appreciation of each other and the gifts that are offered. Like living stones, let yourselves be built into a spiritual house.

As a holy priesthood we are all called to a formidable task. When thinking of the challenges before us I am reminded of a story about the gatekeeper of heaven who one day encountered one of heaven's residents crying about being so bored, "All we do is sing and worship all day. What else can I do?"

So the gatekeeper gave that individual a small shovel and the task of leveling Mount Everest in the Himalayas. After 7,000 years that individual returned, having completed the task. But after two weeks in heaven, the resident soon grew bored again. The gatekeeper of heaven gave him a teaspoon and said, "Go an empty the Pacific Ocean." 20,000 years later the task was finished, and he returned to heaven.

Again boredom set in, and that individual followed with a request: "Give me work that will take longer."

So the gatekeeper responded, "Go, teach the people the love of Christ." For people to learn the love of God and love of neighbor, it will take an eternity, and it is a task that never ends until Jesus comes again. It is easy to love God whom we have not seen, but difficult to love one's neighbor whom one sees every day.

This is the reason that we are called to serve our fellow human beings. As Arab Christians, we feel that we have a vocation. We are called by Christ to be proclaimers of forgiveness in a region full of hatred and anxiety. We are called to be instruments of peace in a land of walls, separation, and strife. We are called be brokers of justice in a region that is full of oppression and blatant injustice. We are called to be promoters of human rights including women's rights in a region that violates their rights. We are called to be initiators of dialogue in a region where religions is misused to be a source of conflict. We are called to be ministers of reconciliation and apostles of love. We ask you, being an integral part of the family of living stones: Pray for us. Do not leave us alone. Accompany us so that we, together as a holy nation, may proclaim Christ and advance Christ's kingdom.

May God bless you as you carry out a living witness in our world today.

Reformed for Costly Discipleship and Creative *Diakonia*

Reformation Day

The Lutheran Church of the Redeemer, Jerusalem

31 October 2009

Matthew 5:1-12

The grace of our Lord Jesus Christ, the love of God the Father, and the communion of the Holy Spirit be with you all ever more. Amen.

Dear sisters and brothers in Christ,

It is a great privilege to celebrate Reformation Day year after year in this church in Jerusalem. For us, the day of Reformation is not only a celebration of events that took place around 500 years ago, but in fact, it is an ecumenical celebration in which we join with other churches to celebrate that the church of God continues to preach the Gospel in its truth and purity and to rightly administer the sacraments. In this sense, it is an ecumenical thanksgiving service, and Christ empowers us to declare the Good News in Jerusalem.

On this day, we celebrate the fresh proclamation of the Gospel by Martin Luther. You might say that we in the Middle East had a Reformation of our own 170 years ago, when German missionaries brought a fresh proclamation of the Gospel to Jerusalem, where it originated two millennia ago. This means that when people need a fresh proclamation of the Gospel, God sends disciples to renew the Good News of salvation and liberation. This is the heart of the Reformation: that the church should always to be ready to be reformed to live out the Good News of salvation in terms of justification by grace alone, through faith alone, in Christ alone.

The evangelical movement in the Middle East lived out that Good News through *diakonia* in education, social work, health work, and ecumenism. Its missionaries did not intend to establish a new church in the Holy Land, but our Palestinian ancestors insisted on it, in response to the message and service of the loyal missionaries.

This year, the ELCJHL celebrated the fiftieth anniversary of the royal recognition of our church. We also celebrated the thirtieth anniversary of the Arab Lutheran bishopric. In our Reformation Day service three decades ago, the first Arab Lutheran bishop, Daoud Haddad, was consecrated. For this festive occasion, Bishop Haddad chose to preach on the Beatitudes, as found in Matthew 5:1-12. That is why I have chosen this text for today.

This familiar and beloved text is found in both St. Matthew's and St. Luke's gospels, but in different settings. St. Matthew sets the Beatitudes as the preamble of the Sermon on the Mount. St. Luke places the Beatitudes immediately after the call of the disciples. This is why one scholar calls them "the ordination address of the Twelve." Some consider the Beatitudes to be "the compendium of Christ's doctrine." Others see them as the "Magna Carta of the Kingdom." Others speak of a "manifesto of the King." Many Christians and non-Christians are inspired by the depth of wisdom they contain. It is said that even Mahatma Gandhi found guidance for his life in them.

The "blessed are . . . " language of the Beatitudes goes back to Old Testament worship language. Psalm 2:12 says, "Blessed are all who take refuge in him." Psalm 84:5 says, "Blessed are those whose strength is in you." King Solomon in his proverbs says, "Blessed is the man who finds wisdom, the man who gains understanding" (Proverbs 3:13). The books of Daniel and Revelation also use language of blessing those who persevere in the face of affliction and persecution.

Although we often read the Beatitudes as individual verses, some theologians say that they are meant to be read together as a unit. The Beatitudes are a complete whole and cannot be divided. Each phrase implies the next. It is said that when lived out, a person manifests all the attributes described here simultaneously. For example, the one justified by faith cannot be poor in the spirit without mourning. That one cannot mourn without hungering and thirsting for righteousness or without being meek and being involved in peacemaking. It is impossible to manifest one of these attributes—and receive the blessing pronounced upon it—without manifesting the others also. They may appear in varying degrees in different people, but all are present, as they are meant to be.

What do the beatitudes mean for us today? The beatitudes are not another set of commandments or a code of conduct for Christians. Instead, the Beatitudes are Christ's clear call to a costly discipleship and a creative *diakonia* for the healing of this globalized, materialistic, unjust world.

1. The Beatitudes call us to a costly discipleship.

In his inaugural sermon, Bishop Haddad, our first Arab bishop, asked, "What kind of people does our world need today? Does our world need politicians, economists, administrators, diplomats, teachers, or reformers?"

I would answer him today that the world needs people in all these important professions. But in the Beatitudes Jesus is saying that our world needs more than professional expertise. Our world needs people who are ready for a costly discipleship. It needs true disciples who are justified by faith and are ready to deny themselves, take up their crosses, and follow Jesus in order to change the world. It needs every baptized believer to live out the Beatitudes in their daily lives. Our world needs true disciples who do not pursue their own interests or seek to acquire power and influence. Instead, Christ needs disciples today who, like the first disciples, respond to the power of his call. Indeed, it is their response to his call that made them poor and mournful and hungry.

This is how Dietrich Bonhoeffer explained it:

> He calls them blessed, not because of their privation, or their renunciation they have made, for these are not blessed in themselves. Only the call and the promise, for the sake of which they are ready to suffer poverty and renunciation, can justify the beatitudes. . . . External privation and personal renunciation both have the same ground—the call and the promise of Jesus. Neither possesses any intrinsic claim to recognition.

One of our youth recently asked me about this text. "Here in the Middle East, we live in a multicultural, multireligious society," he said. "We are few in number. What do the Beatitudes mean for us?"

The Beatitudes were preached to the disciples, who were also few in number, I reminded him. Then as now, Jesus' call is not dependent on numbers or context or the prevailing political situation; it comes to all believers at all times. Jesus calls his hearers blessed not because of what they have but because they recognize what they lack.

In this year of anniversary celebrations, the Arab Evangelical Lutheran church has commemorated God's faithfulness in allowing us to become an established church. Like all churches here in the Holy Land and throughout the Middle East, our numbers are comparatively small. But our strength is not in numbers or buildings or bank accounts or political power. The strength of Christ's church in the land of resurrection is always in its vital proclamation of the Gospel of salvation and its positive commitment to society. Its strength is the Holy Spirit working in and guiding us, empowering us to reflect God's love through prophetic, costly discipleship. Its power in us, the local expression of worldwide Lutheranism, is revealed when we fulfill the call for living witness and creative *diakonia*. Are we ready for it?

2. The Beatitudes call us to creative *diakonia* for the healing of the world.

There is old Arab story of a king who gave each of his three sons a precious gift. He gave the first prince a special telescope to reveal the invisible. He gave the second prince a flying carpet to transport him anywhere he wished to go. He gave the youngest prince a miraculous apple to heal any disease.

Thanking their father, the three princes took their gifts and went out into the world. One day, by coincidence, the brothers found themselves together in one town. The first prince used his telescope and saw that their youngest sister was sick. So the second prince used his flying carpet to transport them back to the palace. The third prince used the miraculous apple to heal their beloved sister.

When the king learned of what they had done, he said, "Well done, my sons. When you use whatever gift you have with the gifts of others, you can change the world."

I believe the King of kings has gifted the church abundantly and calls us to cooperate like the three princes for the healing of the world. We can use our special telescope to reveal hidden injustice, like human trafficking and systemic poverty. We can use our flying carpet to accompany those who struggle alone against hegemony and extremism. We can use the miraculous apple to cure those who suffer from ailments of body, mind, and spirit. We can use all our gifts to promote abundant life, as the Gospel of John calls it, or as the late Palestinian poet Mahmoud Darwish put it, "On this earth there is that which deserves life and is worth living for."

Closer to home, we can see that our sister, our country of Palestine–Israel, is also in dire need of this healing. She is sick with injustice, hatred, bloodshed, extremism, division, occupation, and oppression. Palestinians and Israelis are dying for justice and peace. Jerusalem, the place where God and humanity were reconciled, needs reconciliation among the three faiths and two nations that seek to share it.

I know it is possible, for God has used the church to bring healing to another lingering, festering wound. Today in Augsburg, Germany, events are planned to celebrate the tenth anniversary of the Joint Declaration on the Doctrine of Justification between The Lutheran World Federation and the Roman Catholic Church. In this declaration, the church bodies agreed on the basic truths of justification by faith and ended centuries of condemnation against each other.

Dear sisters and brothers, the tasks are momentous: comforting those who mourn, satisfying those who hunger and thirst for righteousness, standing with the meek, the merciful, and the persecuted. The call is clear: "You are the salt of the earth. . . . You are the light of the world."

On this Reformation Day, may we all be open to the work of the Holy Spirit to reform us as individuals, as churches, as the people of God, to be renewed daily in our costly discipleship for the healing of the world.

Let us close with St. Augustine's reflection on the beatitudes:

> What does it mean to follow if not to imitate? The proof of this is that Christ suffered for us, leaving us an example that we should follow in his footsteps (1 Peter 2:21).
>
> Blessed are the poor in spirit. So imitate him who for your sake became poor although he was rich (2 Corinthians 8:9).
>
> Blessed are the meek. Imitate him who said: "Learn from me, for I am meek and humble of heart" (Matthew 11:29).
>
> Blessed are they who mourn. Imitate him who will weep over Jerusalem (Luke 19:41).
>
> Blessed are they who hunger and thirst after righteousness. Imitate him who said: "My food is to do the will of the one who sent me" (John 4:34).
>
> Blessed are the merciful. Imitate him who came to the help of the man who had been wounded by robbers and lay half-dead and despairing on the ground (Luke 10:33).
>
> Blessed are the clean in heart. Imitate him who committed no sin and no deceit was found in his mouth (1 Peter 2:22).
>
> Blessed are the peacemakers. Imitate him who prayed on behalf of his persecutors: Father, forgive them, they know not what they do (Luke 23:34).

Blessed are they who are persecuted for the sake of righteousness. Imitate him who suffered for you, leaving you an example that you might follow in his footsteps (1 Peter 2:21).

Oh good Jesus, I see you with the eyes of faith you have opened within me. I see you calling out and saying, as though berating humankind: "Come to me and place yourselves in my school.

May the peace that surpasses our understanding keep your hearts and minds in Christ Jesus. Amen.

With Eyes and Ears on Jesus

Transfiguration Sunday

Kuala Lumpur • 6 March 2011

Matthew 17:1-9

I greet you from the city of Jerusalem where, as we begin this season of Lent, forty days of fasting and preparation, Jesus served and died, but where he rose again.

I come from Jerusalem, a city set on a small mountain. The biblical writers always talked of going up to Jerusalem, the Psalmists wrote the Songs of Ascent for pilgrims who made their approach. Our Psalm today (Psalm 99) calls it Zion, God's holy mountain, where we are to praise his holy name, worship, and extol him as the Lord our God.

Today the city is embroiled in conflict and suffering. Yet pilgrims come by the thousands and the tens of thousands. They pass daily by my office window saying, "It's good to be here. Wouldn't it be nice to stay awhile?" And sometimes they do. Sometimes they overstay their welcome. Sometimes they lose their own identity, what psychologists refer to as the Elijah syndrome. I can tell you in particular about a middle-aged man named Adam, a Lutheran pastor from the U.S.A., who arrived in Jerusalem thirteen years ago and stayed. He stayed because he loved our mountain. He stayed because he said it made him feel closer to God. He stayed, letting his visa and passport expire, becoming virtually a homeless beggar dressed in clothes left behind at a five-dollar-a-night youth hostel. Just last week, after taking up a collection, we put him on a plane and said, "John, it's time to leave the mountain. It's time to go home."

Kuala Lumpur is a wonderful city to visit, set in this huge valley called the Klang Valley resting between the Titiwangsa Mountains to the east and several minor mountain ranges in the north and south. It is good to be here. It is good to take a break from our daily routines and gather with LUCAS and all the Asian Lutheran Leaders, and meet in such a beautiful city—a beautiful city with modern architecture and a skyline of high-rise buildings including the two largest twin buildings, the Petronas Twin Towers—450 meters high, eighty-eight floors, built at a cost of more than $1.6 billion.

I can imagine what it must be like to take the elevator to the highest floor, to look out at the spectacular view—no poverty, no unemployment, no war, no religious strife, no staff arguments, no worries about how to meet our budgets, no confrontations with a staff member in need of discipline, no secretary coming for counseling because of a death in the family, no domestic dispute, no diagnosis of cancer, no eviction order from one's home announced just one week ago by local soldiers. I can imagine sitting at the top of such a skyscraper looking out endlessly at the beauty of God's creation wanting to linger, wanting to delay getting back on the elevator and return to the bottom floor, to the waiting taxi, to our homes, to all the responsibilities awaiting us.

For those of us gathered together, it is not just the location that attracts. And it is not the solitude. We thrive on each others' company, the time we spend together, our mutual sharing, the encouragement we offer one another, and the challenging and honest words we speak to one another. This is the accompaniment that we share with each other.

Matthew tells us that, as Jesus is transfigured, speaking with Moses and Elijah, Peter suggests that they stay there. "I will make three dwellings here." Peter could have many motives, but maybe one is the natural desire to make the experience of transformation into something more manageable, more predictable, more permanent.

How much easier to build the tent, enclosing and containing the experience in some way, rather than to be that tent ourselves—living witnesses, temples of the Holy Spirit.

As Peter is speaking, God interrupts him. God tells the disciples and tells us, that we must listen to Jesus; we must keep on listening to him. It is a continual process, not something that can be enshrined and then mechanically repeated.

Why is it that Peter offers to build three tents? Obviously, he and the disciples are standing in the presence of three great figures: Moses, Elijah, and a transfigured Jesus. If you remember the story of Moses, you will remember that he did not die (Deuteronomy 34:6). He simply went to the top of Mount Nebo, where he gave himself into the hands of God. Likewise the great prophet Elijah did not die; rather God took him up into heaven in a fiery chariot. And with Jesus transformed and clothed in white, Peter, James, and John are allowed a glimpse into the resurrection.

The three tents are symbolic. The tent of Moses is the legislation—a tent for the law and the commandments. The tent of Elijah is the tent of prophesy, for though there is no prophetic book written under his name in the Old Testament, he is the greatest of the prophets. So the Law and the Prophets met there on the mountain with the Lord.

How is this to be interpreted?

1. The kingdom of the Lord is a kingdom of meekness and fervency. Moses was known for his humble and meek character. Elijah was known for his zeal. They both waited for the Lord.

2. The goal and fulfillment of the Law and Prophets is Jesus. Origen said: "Thou who are the glory of Moses is the law. The wisdom of the prophets. They are Moses and Elijah with him."

3. Law and Prophesy bowed to Jesus. They are subservient to him.

What does this mean for us today? We feel comfortable and secure in our churches, in our traditions, in our cultures. We want to stay there where it is comfortable. However, the tent is not long lasting or enduring. The tent will fade away and decay. Sometimes we look at our global tent, filled with racism and prejudice, filled with war and the spread of armaments, filled with multinational corporations that are stronger than many nations and that exploit the poor—we look at this global tent and are satisfied, thinking we are enjoying its pleasures as a band-aid covering over all its difficulties. This global tent too will fade away. Its comfort and security will come to an end. We are to get out from under the protection of this tent and ask: What is reliable, what endures, what is long lasting?

When we read the Bible, sometimes the interpretation may leave a tent of law or sometimes a tent of false prophesy, but the tent that endures is the tent of the gospel. The Bible is not an easy book. It contains so much; the language is different; the culture and the customs are different. Yet Jesus is our guide. Jesus is the compass. Martin Luther often said, "*Was treibt Christum.*" Whatever points to Christ, that is what is important for us. That is what endures and remains. This is the reason that it said, "Peter, James, and John only saw Jesus on the mountain."

And so Jesus stands alongside Moses and Elijah, on top of the mountain. Yet the voice speaks clearly to Peter, James, and John, "This is my son, my beloved! Listen to him!"

There are so many voices speaking in the world today. There are so many so-called prophets seeking to give us answers and solutions. There are so many so-called Christians, saying "Listen to me!" "My way is the right way."

There are many voices of extremism that we hear today. Voices that deny the other their humanity because of their different culture or tradition or race or even gender; voices that deny the other the freedom of religion as they claim their religion is the only right way; voices that even deny the other religion to use the terminology they believe in; voices that call for revenge, killing, or accusing other human beings as being infidels; voices that want no peace, no justice, and no freedom.

But the voice from heaven speaks clearly, "This is my son, the beloved. Listen to him."

And we understand him the clearest through the cross. Jesus does not stay on the mountain to build a kingdom, to erect a cathedral, to establish an empire. He leads Peter, James, and John down the mountain to the plain, to the valley below where people are suffering, where people are struggling, where people are praying and asking for help. He leads them down the mountain and to Jerusalem, where he gives up the brilliant white robe and takes upon himself a crown of thorns. For it is only through dying that he is resurrected; it is only through the cross that we have life; it is only through Golgotha that we find a dwelling place that lasts forever.

This is the reason I call upon you as you struggle in your everyday life not to look to yourself, but to Jesus Christ your Savior.

"This is my son, the beloved," the voice calls from heaven. "Listen to him."

May the peace that surpasses all human understanding keep your hearts and minds in Christ Jesus. Amen.

Jesus' Strategy Session for the Early Church

Opening Worship
Lutheran World Federation Council Meeting

Geneva, Switzerland • 8 June 2011

John 14:1-14

Sisters and brothers in Christ, grace and salaam.

John 14 is part of a section from the Fourth Gospel known as Jesus' farewell discourse. Chapters 13 through 17 take place in the Upper Room at that final meal together on that Thursday evening before Jesus is arrested, tried before the high priest and Pilate, and crucified. While the Synoptics focus on Jesus' eucharistic meal, John focuses on Jesus' teaching, thus the common title for this section: Jesus' farewell discourse.

I wonder, however, if in a sense, this section is misnamed. Farewell implies that these are Jesus' last words, the end, a moment that is final. Unlike the final lectures of other great teachers, this is not the end. This is just the beginning. Yes, this is the end of Jesus' earthly ministry (looking at things from Jesus' perspective). But if we approach this from the disciples' perspective, this session marks new beginnings, a transition from following Jesus as disciples to charting their future as the church with Jesus' continued guidance through the Spirit whom the Father will send in Jesus' name. From the disciples' perspective this is not the end, but a new beginning. It is not farewell, but in a sense their orientation session to a new and exciting life under the guidance of the Spirit. For them, it is a planning session, a strategy session to chart out the way ahead. Here in John 14, Jesus addresses the disciples to help them discern the journey before them.

And how does he help them discern in Journey?

- "I do not want you to be troubled," Jesus begins in John 14:1. Yes, there are difficult times ahead. And they must be realistic about the way ahead of them.
- "Peace I leave with you; my peace I give you."
- "I will not leave you orphans," he says in the verses just following this section.
- "I will send to you the Paraclete, the Spirit, who will lead you in all truth."
- "A new commandment I give you, that you love one another," that you continue to engage the world, with all of its challenges, difficulties, setbacks, roadblocks, detours, and—yes—even persecutions.
- Pray! "If for anything you ask in my name, I will do it."

So here in the Upper Room Jesus has this dialogue with the disciples to help them discern the journey. And it is a dialogue, not just a sermon and a lecture. The disciples have lots of questions and queries about how to discern the way:

- Philip asks, "Lord, aren't you going to show us the Father?"
- Thomas asks, "Lord, we do not know where you are going. How can we know the way?"

Many people see such questions as a sign of weakness, as simply the foolishness of disciples who continually fail to understand, as disciples who have been so preoccupied with themselves that they haven't paid attention. But I see their questioning as their strength. They are engaged. This is the time for discernment, and they understand the consequences for the journey before them.

And Jesus' response? He provides words of comfort and assurance, but words that are also challenging and encouraging them to take up the journey he offers. These are words familiar to all of us, "I am the way, the truth, and the life."

What comfort these words must have had for the disciples! You have nothing to worry about. All been prepared for you. Life is a gift from God. It is yours. Trust God. Trust me.

Yet there's more to it. In John, words often have a double meaning. Life often has the connotation of eternal life; life together as Jesus and the Father are one, and we and God are one forever. Yet in John, that word, life, also speaks to the here and now: "I have come that you might have life, and have it abundantly." Life is not just something for the future. It begins now in the present.

And Jesus is the way: "I am the way, the truth, and the life." Yes, Jesus offers the way to the Father. Jesus is both the mediator of salvation and also a norm of life. Life is ours because Jesus has established that relationship that brings us into unity with God. In that way, we can add nothing to it; it is God's gift. And that gift frees us up to discern the journey before us in the present, to empower us to be agents of God's love to the world around us. Because Jesus is the way to the Father, we can now focus on the present challenges. What is the way? What is the way for us to engage the world?

Again Jesus says it very simply, "I am the way, the truth, and the life." What is the way that Jesus has shown? It is the way evident throughout the Fourth Gospel:

• The way engages the other, whether it is the Jewish scholar Nicodemus (chapter 3) or the Samaritan woman at the well (chapter 4). This is the way of worshipping in spirit and in truth.

• The way gives sight to the blind (chapter 9), feeds the hungry (chapter 6), helps the lame to walk (chapter 5). This is the way of healing.

• The way accepts the sinful adulteress and offers forgiveness (chapter 8), while challenging those who hide behind double standards. This is the way of love and forgiveness.

• The way places a child into the midst and declares, "Of such is the kingdom of God." This is the way of inclusion.

• The way provides a model for *diakonia*, a model of service, washing the feet of the disciples (chapter 13). This is the way of mission and *diakonia*.

How do we discern the journey? Look no further than the way of Jesus. "I am the way, the truth, and the life."

It is no accident that the early Christians in the Book of Acts—similar to the Essenes in the Qumran community—were known as Followers of the Way.

• Followers of the Way—not a straight, smooth, paved way, but one with curves, potholes, bumps, and detours.

• Followers of the Way—not one with the answers all spelled out in advance, but one that constantly raised questions for continued discernment.

• Followers of the Way—with dangers, threats, financial difficulties, challenges, and set backs.

• Followers of the Way—with the Spirit guiding you into all truth.

We have come to Geneva to meet together, to reflect together, to pray together, and to deliberate together under the theme, "Discerning the Journey." If the council would have sat at the feet of Jesus in his farewell discourse, then would we be like Philip, insecure about our future and longing for answers that span the next seven years? If the council were to have the impetus like Peter, then would we declare, "We will follow your way, whatever the cost?" If the council would be like Thomas, would we ask to just put our finger in Jesus' hands and side, showing our doubts and reservations? Would we be like those relying on reason and logic, when the way of Christ is seldom logical and rarely reasonable?

This is why Christ calls us to discern the way. How do we discern the way:

• First, by praying in his name that he may guide us. As we pray are we not in a sense continuing in the dialogue of discernment that the disciples shared with our Lord in the Upper Room? Are we not seeking guidance and direction, no different than the disciples in those early days in Jerusalem? As we begin our strategic planning, faced with difficult circumstances, bold challenges, and tough choices, we have Christ's invitation before us: "If in my name you ask me for anything, I will do it?" May we pray with the psalmist:

> Make me to know your ways, O Lord;
> Teach me your paths.
> Lead me in your truth, and teach me,
> For you are the God of my salvation;
> For you I wait all day long (Psalm 25:4-5).

• Second, by remembering those who have traveled the way of Jesus before us. Today, especially we remember Columba, Aidan, and Bede, Renewers of the Church in the British Isles. Certainly, their way was filled with obstacles and challenges, but, like the disciples, they were able to discern the way to change the course of history for this small section of the world.

• Third, by accompanying each other, asking questions, but trusting that the Lord will accompany us as we accompany each other. There is a story of a king who gave each of his children a straw. When they took the straw in their hands, he instructed them to break it. Every one broke it easily. Then he handed them another straw and instructed them to gather all the straws together in a bundle. They gathered them together, and he instructed them to use their muscles and all their strength to break this bundle of straw. Nobody could break it. So he told them, if you each work separately, you will be easily broken. But if you work in accompaniment to serve the world, then no one can break you, just like the straw.

It is the same as we discern the way. If each of us remains insecure, individualistic, each one working separately, we will discover many different ways, but not the way of Christ, the way of accompaniment, the way of communion, as difficult as it is. In our queries and in our questions we come to the table together, confused, seeking clarification, and asking questions. As he breaks the bread, he will send his Paraclete, the Holy Spirit to lead us as a communion of Christ in his holy name.

What we accomplish this week has important implications for the way in which the churches of our communion will work with each other in engaging the world.

We discern the journey with challenges no smaller than those faced by the disciples.

We discern the journey with gifts no less than those provided by Jesus who is the way, the truth, and the life.

And so Jesus invites us to pray: Lord, be with us in our discernment of the journey before us. Fill us with questions that help us delve more deeply into the challenges before us. Fill us with your Spirit to lead us into the truth. Fill us with your love for the sake of the world. With confidence we come before you asking in your name. Amen.

I Am the Resurrection and the Life

Easter Message

The Lutheran Church of the Resurrection
Jerusalem • 24 April 2011
"I am the resurrection and the life" (John 11:25).

Christ is risen. He is risen indeed.

In a world of suffering and death, these words of resurrection and life transcend us. Jesus first addressed these words to Martha of Bethany when Jesus stood at the tomb of his good friend Lazarus (John 11:25). This occasion is one that has profound meaning because Jesus shows clearly his emotions in the face of death, weeping openly over the death of his friend.

Martha understood fully that God always stands on the side of life. "Lord, if you had been here our brother would not have died," she said, pleading to Jesus. The whole Bible reveals this theology of life, as God meant it to be. God chooses wholeness for us. God chooses dignity of life. God chooses the abundant life. So Jesus proclaimed in the previous chapter of John, "I have come that you may have life, and have it abundantly" (John 10:10).

That is the whole reason for Jesus' life and ministry. That is the whole reason that John has recorded these stories, including Lazarus being brought forth from the tomb. "These signs have been written," says John in his summary conclusion, "that you might believe that Jesus is the Christ, the Son of God, and that believing you might have life" (John 20:31). That is why every child in Sunday school is taught, "For God so loved the world that he gave his only begotten son, that whoever believes in him will not die, but have eternal life" (John 3:16).

Over the last few weeks as we have been viewing images of destruction and despair from Japan, I have thought often about Jesus' sorrow over the death of Lazarus and also the tears that must be flowing over the sight of dead bodies, damaged homes that appear as if they were a mere Lego toy village, and the catastrophic possibilities emerging from the ruined nuclear reactors.

On Ash Wednesday, we marked a cross of Christ on our foreheads. Just two days later, the earthquake and tsunami marked a cross of death on this island nation. Our Lenten journey is one that cannot be made without weeping at the death and destruction throughout the entire global community.

We look at this destruction and ask, "What is life?"

As a country, Japan seemed to have achieved so much. We looked up to Japan as a model of a country successfully recovering after the Second World War. It was so developed, economically secure, without the problems afflicting so much of the world. And yet so quickly, that is gone, crushed, washed away.

How is it that people one day can be busy going about their daily lives, and then the next day it is over so suddenly? How is it that people one day are so wrapped up in their families, their homes, their cars, and material possessions, and the next day they are sitting there like Job with nothing left behind? How is it the young people one day so full of life and energy, of joy and laughter, can so suddenly find themselves lying on the seashore, lifeless corpses. How can it end so quickly? Maybe this is the way Jesus felt during Holy Week, that life was so fleeting, so fragile, so cheap. What is the meaning of life?

As I sit before my television weeks after the earthquake and tsunami in Japan and see the continuing discovery of bodies, I am drawn to reflect on my own mortality. Does not this tragic event hit us all? Is not this a wake-up call to shake us up, causing us to wonder when our time will come? This was Luther's understanding of the first use of the law, always accusing, always pointing out where we in our humanity come up short. Is this in a sense a sign from God that human beings have forgotten the real meaning of life and resurrection? Do we as humans spend our efforts focusing on narrow problems and ourselves? Is this a reminder of our addiction to the material side of life and neglect of the spiritual?

Do we need a deeper spirituality to put us in touch with the abundant life described in John's Gospel? With all the fighting, with all the killing, with all the actions hindering people from achieving their own basic rights, how can we be sure that life is worth it? I believe the resurrection is the feast of life. It is the feast that reminds us that Jesus has overcome death by his own death and resurrection and has granted life—and life abundant—for every human being.

What is going on in the Arab world? Why is it happening now? We watch the television coverage; we see people taking great risks; we hear interviews of those empowered to challenge the system. They are telling us that they are ready to lose everything, all of their material goods, to gain freedom.

As Christians we understand that Christ did not mean for us to live just any life. So we look positively to political and economic reforms in the Arab world. Maybe the Arab world is experiencing a new spring, a spring where the blossoms of life are becoming more tangible, where people are aching for life, for equal opportunities, for economic growth, for a modern civil society, for freedom of expression.

But, it seems that the seed of freedom that has been implanted in every living conscience will never die. Even if this seed of freedom has been quiet or dormant, or if it has been silenced by oppression or fear, when it does wake up it seeks life with dignity, whatever the cost. Such a suppression of this precious human inclination for freedom resembles in a way the oppression of Christ on the cross and his death. When he arose, he trampled all that humiliates and oppresses, and he set before us a wide table of this feast of abundant life for the present and the future.

United States Treasury Secretary Timothy Geithner said last Saturday—a day we refer to as the Saturday of Lazarus—to the International Monetary Fund (IMF) that the world economy will grow at about 4.5 percent this year, but the world still faces "very significant economic policy challenges. This is true, that oil prices have risen, driven by the political developments in the Middle East and North Africa, rapidly rising demand in emerging market and a muted supply response." This challenge in emerging economies is to deal with rising commodity and energy prices. This would mean in practice two things:

1. Those who will be directly affected are the poor amongst us. The poor will become poorer. For countries that are living in poverty, their suffering will be more. The poor, who now have so little to feed their children, will have to divide their share into smaller portions. What does the resurrection and the life mean to those people? What is our responsibility? On this Easter, we cannot ignore this fact. It calls us as individuals to repentance. It call us as churches to repentance, for we churches have also fallen short in the sharing of resources. It calls us to a repentance that does not think selfishly, but repentance that calls for equal resource sharing between North and South, East and West.

2. It teaches us that the resurrection of Christ that brought life—and life abundantly—connects us with the policies and circumstances of this life. It teaches us again that no one of us is independent, but all of us are interdependent. How can I enjoy life, if I know that my sisters and brothers in many parts of the world are deprived? How can I speak on life with dignity, when the dignity of others is deprived? The risen Christ calls us into this new interdependence to allow others to live in his dignity.

Doesn't this all go with the Easter message? At the tomb of Lazarus, Jesus spoke a powerful word: "I am the resurrection and the life." Jesus spoke, and Jesus acted with the greatest of signs. He called Lazarus forth from the tomb, bringing him from death into life.

Professor Karoline Lewis from Luther Seminary, recently wrote about this powerful word of Jesus in *Christian Century* magazine (April 5, 2011). She notes the omission of the word "life" from this pronouncement of Jesus in some ancient manuscripts. These variations in several old Bibles simply say, "I am the resurrection." Yet what is resurrection without life?

Sadly, this variant reading reflects the way some Christians lead their lives. For them, "I am the resurrection" means waiting patiently, with lots of prayer and singing, for the resurrection on the last day, yet with no life in the present. It means for some that Christianity is all about heaven above and beyond, and nothing about the here and now. This was the view of Martha who believed fervently that Jesus would resurrect her brother on the last day.

But there is more. Correcting Martha, Jesus said, "I am the resurrection *and* the life." And he acted to bring Lazarus from the tomb, to give Lazarus life, not just hope in a future resurrection.

And what does life mean for Lazarus? The resurrection is a gift from God, but Jesus says, "So is your life now." You are life in the midst of suffering and death. Your life is to be a message of hope in the resurrection. Your life is to provide comfort and relief for those who suffer, to be peacemakers in the midst of conflict and war, to be agents of reconciliation in the midst of division, to give sight to the blind, to help the lame to walk, to set the captive free. Hope in the resurrection means that Lazarus has life in the present, life abundant.

It means in the next chapter of John that Lazarus hosts a banquet in Jesus' honor. It means a close and intimate relationship with the one who gives life, and he sits close to him like the beloved disciple. It means a deepened spirituality. It means sharing his food with the hungry. It means a vibrant public witness to Jesus as Messiah.

And for us? It means, not just that we live in hope of the resurrection, but that we have the gift of life now—a life that embraces us with meaning and purpose in our present world, a life that calls us to speak a word of comfort in the midst of tragedy, a life that calls us to work for peace in the midst of war and strife, a life that seeks answers and solutions to global warming with its violent weather patterns, a life that commits to causes of justice and reconciliation, a life that hears the cries of the poor and answers them, a life that is not afraid of death.

People ask me about the Christians in the Middle East amidst all what is going on. The Middle East conflict is about life. It is unacceptable that some will have life at the expense of another. The situation requires a political will that will assure both Palestinians and Israelis that peace based on justice is possible—a peace that will allow all of us to have life and to have it abundantly. Arab Christianity is an integral part of the fabric of Arab society. What happens to others in the Middle East will now happen to us. But foremost is the fact that the resurrection of Jesus took place in Jerusalem. Arab Christians, as others, always are called to proclaim the good news of life with dignity, wherever we are called. This we do, in our witness in word and deed, in mission, education, and *diakonia*. Many have wondered how Arab Christianity survived through the 2,000 years, although our numbers are decreasing. We survived because of the hope in the resurrection that tells us that nothing can separate us from the love of Christ, "neither death, nor life, nor angels, nor rulers, nor things present, nor things to come, nor heights, nor depths, nor anything else in all creation" (Romans 8:38-39).

We survive because on the one hand we carry the hope of the resurrection and on the other hand the dignity of life. This is the reason that we ask you at this very time to continue to pray for us and support our ministries. We will continue to be a living witness through the power of his resurrection in a multi-religious and multicultural, globalized world. And our witness begins in Jerusalem and is shared outward to the rest of the world as we wish each other, joyfully and filled with life abundant,

Christ is risen.
He is risen indeed.
Christ is risen.
He is risen indeed.
Christ is risen.
He is risen indeed.

One in the Apostles' Teaching

Week of Prayer for Christian Unity

The Evangelical Lutheran Church of the Redeemer
Jerusalem • 25 January 2011

". . . and they continued in the apostles' teaching, in the breaking of bread, in fellowship, and in prayer" (Acts 2:42).

The grace of our Lord Jesus Christ, the love of God, and the communion of the Holy Spirit be with you all. Amen.

Dear sisters and brothers in Christ,

We are happy that we Palestinian Christians were asked by the World Council of Churches and the Vatican's Pontifical Council for Promoting Christian Unity to prepare this Week of Prayer for Christian Unity, that it came out from Jerusalem, from the local Christian churches. We as a committee thought it appropriate to focus on the life of the apostles in the early church: "And they continued in the apostles' teaching, in the breaking of bread, in fellowship, and in prayer" (Acts 2:42).

What started on that day of Pentecost in Jerusalem was a spirit of unity and ecumenism.

As I often say, to work for unity in Jerusalem is an art. We are in need of capable artists to produce something so beautiful. We all know the work required and the careful planning to design a Middle Eastern carpet. It is as if each of our churches is a different color of thread (or yarn), yet woven together the carpet becomes so much more beautiful than each strand of yarn by itself. The individual threads do not loose their identity or individual character. The beauty of their particular color remains intact. Yet coming together under the direction of an artist, the finished carpet is more beautiful than all of the individual strands. And it is none other than the Holy Spirit that guides this process of coming together to produce this beautiful, ecumenical carpet. Picture with me such a beautiful carpet hanging here on the wall—a beautiful carpet, perhaps with an image of the Lord's Supper with Jesus sitting in the middle. Imagine how beautiful this carpet would be.

If ecumenism succeeds in Jerusalem, it can succeed in the whole world. And so we are called to this purpose, for we are capable artists weaving together this beautiful carpet of the Holy Communion. It is not a burden or an effort. It is simply the duty to which we have been called, to answer Christ's priestly intercession so that we may be one as Christ and the Father are one (John 17).

When making a carpet, sometimes we make a mistake. Then we have to stop and make a correction before we can go on. And so it is in the church.

This past July in Stuttgart, Germany, The Lutheran World Federation came together in its Eleventh Assembly. After studying all the documents and all the historical facts about what happened among Lutherans and Mennonites, the Anabaptists of the Middle Ages, we made a historic decision. Although we may disagree on some theological issues, we as Lutherans felt it necessary to publicly repent for acts of persecution that we were responsible for in Europe that forced the Mennonites to emigrate to the United States and other lands. We assumed our responsibility to repent of the fact that we had failed to see in the other, our own brothers and sisters in Christ. No, we had not come to agree on every point of doctrine. Yet we had failed to recognize that we were children of the same heavenly father. It had been a mistake, yet more than a mistake—it had been a sin against God, who surely must have felt sorrow over God's divided children. And so we as the Lutheran communion publicly repented. Yes, with tears in the eyes of Lutherans and Mennonites, we sought reconciliation and pledged to live in the spirit of repentance and forgiveness with each other.

This can be an example of how Christian unity can take place here in Jerusalem. Ecumenism is not built on the shoulders of others, not on finding mistakes and disagreements with others. Nor is it in concentrating on particular events in our common histories. Unity starts when we are open to live in a spirit of repentance and forgiveness, and we ask our Lord to guide us. Unity is not uniformity. A carpet of all red threads is okay, or one that is all blue, or all green. But we all know that much more desirable in the market is that carpet which brings together various colors into one with a carefully designed pattern of the Holy Communion.

Each of the churches brings to our ecumenical carpet special gifts that benefit us all. Those of us from the Lutheran tradition stand in appreciation of the witness that each of you give:

- To the Orthodox we say thank you for your witness of steadfastness in faith.
- To the Armenian and Coptic, your example of faith in martyrdom.
- To the Syriac, the way that you have preserved a history going back to the Aramaic roots of our faith.
- To the Latin Catholic, your example of church order and the spirit of faithful obedience.
- To the Maronites, your ability to contextualize our faith.
- To the Greek Catholic, joining East and West together under one roof.
- To the Anglicans, your liturgical forms and hymnody.
- And I hope that you would say the same for our Lutheran zeal and fervor in preaching and especially our devotion to justification by faith and the priesthood of all believers.

We stand appreciative of each of you and your witness in the faith. And now that we have worked together for some time here in Jerusalem, we can only say that we cannot imagine for one moment trying to exist without each other.

Unity in a spirit of repentance and forgiveness calls us as reconciled diversity, seeing Christ in the other and finding a common witness here in Jerusalem. Why did God decide on that first Pentecost to make use of nineteen different languages, including Arabic? Why has God today placed us here in Jerusalem: Orthodox, Catholic, Oriental Catholic, and Orthodox, Lutheran Evangelical, Anglican? Why here in Jerusalem? Why us? Why these particular different churches? One thing is certain: God called us to be in Jerusalem to be a light to the world. It is a light that emanates from Golgotha and the empty tomb. It is a light reflecting this spirit of repentance and forgiveness. It is a light that calls us to show living witness and creative *diakonia* together.

The focus of this, the third day of this special week, is in the apostles' teaching. Think back to those early days of the church. I would have liked to sit at the apostles' feet. I would have liked to hear those very words coming from the mouth of Peter and Andrew, James and John, Matthew and Thomas, and all the rest—yes, and the words of young Mark and the words of Luke who followed them. What did they teach? How did they attract people to thirst and hunger for the Word of God? How did they read and interpret the Old Testament in a way that touched the peoples' hearts? Imagine! In just one single, didactic sermon of Simon Peter, 3,000 people came to believe.

The role of the church today is one that must continue the apostles' teaching if it is to continue to exist. And not just the traditions must continue, but the teaching of the apostles. The teaching of the apostles is the design of our carpet, the plan which brings all the individual threads together as a piece of art.

Teaching is a transformative power that can change the world. Read the history of my own church, for example—about our forefathers and foremothers at Schneller and Talitha Kumi Schools. They did not set out to establish a church but rather the transformative power of the education of society. It was none other than the same spirit of Paul when he said, "I am not ashamed of the Gospel, for it is the power of God to salvation." The experience of my church is the same as other churches' teaching. It is the apostolic vocation.

Today we are all challenged by the fact that Palestinian Christians are emigrating from the Holy Land. It is a cause of real concern. Today Christians are less than two percent of the total population. Surveys and research analysis say there are many reasons: the unsettled political situation, the absence of a horizon for peace, a lack of jobs, a lack of housing, the growth of political and religious extremism on both sides. Christians are emigrating. And what is our role as Christian churches in Jerusalem? What is our role as teachers of the church?

To put it simply, it is this: To rise up together to the challenges that we are facing here in Jerusalem. Maybe we are affected by what is happening in Iraq and in Egypt. Maybe we are concerned by questions raised in the Vatican synod on the Middle East. However, since that first Pentecost Christians have always resided in Jerusalem and have always presented a living and dynamic witness. We continue to encourage one another to be that witness as we are the fabric of society. Last month when I met with His Holiness Pope Benedict in Rome, we agreed that we must have a concerted effort, a common strategy, a greater voice, and a common witness. Our unity is our strength—unity, not to be used against one another, but unity for the benefit of the others, to be a light to the world.

We must have strategies and action plans. Most of all we are called to remain steadfast in the apostles' teaching. We all are responsible to deepen the understanding of our witness and presence in the Holy Land. We are called to educate our people:

- To know the Bible deeply.
- To understand its message.
- To emphasize the importance of Christian education.
- To know why we are here in Jerusalem and the Holy Land.
- To show the world that we in Jerusalem continue to be both the church of Golgotha and the church of the empty tomb, the church of suffering and the church of resurrection.

We are called to educate our people that what unites us is Jesus. We are called through this teaching to confess together that there is one body and one spirit, one hope in which we are called, one Lord, one faith, one Baptism, one eucharist, one God and Father of us all. We are called through this teaching to stand together, to present a common living witness.

Education is so important and so essential that it continues to transform the whole person and to make them capable of facing the emerging challenges ahead of us.

Today a whole host of writers—Muslim and Jewish authors, Arab and Israeli columnists—are saying that Christians are the balancing power in the Middle East. We Christians are called to be a source of moderation. We Christians are called to be instruments of peace, mediators of reconciliation, brokers of love. Only through our educational institutions can we transform society. We are here for a purpose—to turn injustice into justice; hatred into friendship, extremism into moderation, oppression into opportunities of equality and human rights, and to promote the role of women in society. This is Christ's will for all the churches.

We are called to bring transformation, reconciliation, and empowerment. And we can only do this when we live together in a spirit of repentance and forgiveness. We can only do this when we celebrate the gifts of each other. We can only do this when we are one, one in the apostles' teaching, the breaking of bread, in fellowship, and in prayer.

All eyes are on Jerusalem. People are looking to us for answers, for guidance, for leadership. I hope that none will look at us and see disagreements or divisions. Rather we pray that people will look at us and see our common witness; that people will look at us and say, "See how much they love each other!"

Brothers and sisters in Christ, are we ready? All eyes are upon us. The whole world is watching. What will they say about us? How will they tell the story of our common witness? I pray that they will say, "What a beautiful Middle Eastern carpet they make, what beautiful colors, what beautiful threads, what a beautiful design! Look how much they love each other."

Amen.

Living As the Children of Light

Lutheran World Federation General Assembly

Stuttgart, Germany • July 2010

"Live as children of light" (Ephesians 5:8).

Dear sisters and brothers in Christ:

It is a great privilege and honor for me to worship with you this morning. I carry two greetings to you:

1. The greetings of the LWF, where we are meeting as a Lutheran family, to strengthen our communion together in Stuttgart. This is the Eleventh Assembly of the LWF, and we are meeting under the theme, "Give us today our daily bread" (Matthew 8:8). This theme may seem simplistic, but in the last week we have learned that to ask for your daily bread means to share your resources with others. It also means bringing justice in order that others can pray for their daily bread. We are also encouraged to speak about the communion of Lutherans, which invites us to join forces in the world for creative mission and prophetic *diakonia*.

2. I bring to you the greetings of my church, the Evangelical Lutheran Church in Jordan and the Holy Land. We continue to be living witnesses in education, spiritual work, *diakonia*, ecumenism, and interfaith dialogue. We as Christians and especially as Lutherans have a role to play in the Middle East in reconciliation and interfaith dialogue. Although small in number, we continue to preach the Gospel and administer the sacraments, advancing God's kingdom for Christians and non-Christians alike.

Please pray that Palestinian Christians may not lose faith and leave the country. For who wants to imagine the Holy Land where Christ walked without Christians?

The text of this Sunday is bold and direct: "Live as children of light" (Ephesians 5:8). What was in the mind of St. Paul when he admonished the Ephesians to "live as children of light"? As you know, the early church expected the second coming of Jesus to come quickly. St. Paul observes that his coming did not take place as people expected. His letter is to a congregation trying to mold its identity, to disengage itself from the past in order to live as Christians. Paul as well as John describe clear contrasts between the darkness of pagan life and light-filled life of Christians.

St. Paul's words here are reminiscent of Jesus Christ's, when he said, "The light is with you for a little longer . . . believe in the light, so that you may become children of light" (John 12:35-36). This means a Christian is in communion with Christ, who is the light of the Christian. Through Baptism the children of light become "participants of the divine nature" (2 Peter 1:4).

This is why our Lord and Savior admonishes his followers, "You are the light of the world. . . . let your light shine before others, so that they may see your good works and give glory to your Father in heaven" (Matthew 5:14, 16), and St. Paul exhorts, "Live as children of light" (Ephesians 5:8).

It is the same challenge we face in our day. How can we live in this world and carry the light of Christ in us? This is the exact challenge that all churches and all Christians face daily. It is easy to intend to live in the light. But once we are confronted with a problem, are challenged by society, or are tempted to enact revenge, we see that this noble teaching remains a farfetched goal. Even so, with all our weaknesses, we are to live as children of light. Paul gives us a set of instructions: "The fruit of the light is found in all that is good and right and true. Try to find out what is pleasing to the Lord" (Ephesians 5:9-10).

Some may tell me that Christians have gone through many events that have led us to be different from the believers in Ephesus in the time of Paul. It is true that movements like the Reformation, the Enlightenment, modernity, and post-modernity have affected and shaped our Christian identity. But through all those movements and trends, the core question remains: How can we who are baptized in Christ live as children of light?

In these post-modern times, it is easy to label people as conservatives, liberals, ultraliberals, etc. Even Christians are categorized. I don't pay much attention to all these labels, because what I care about is if we Christian live as children of light.

In days gone by, bolts of cloth were stacked in dark rooms. The merchant would pull out a bolt and hold it up to the light so the buyer could inspect the weave and check for blemishes. In the same way, we Christians should stand in the light of Christ, so that we may see our flaws, our weaknesses—narrow-mindedness, judgmental attitudes, and hypocrisy—so that we might confess to the Lord that we have failed to live in his light. Such repentance will bring us back to our call to live as children of light.

One day as I was walking from my office in the Old City of Jerusalem to Jaffa Gate, a merchant stopped me and drew my attention to a passing woman and child. He knew she was a Christian and that the handicapped boy she carried came from a Muslim family. He was amazed that she would give such motherly care to a child not her own.

I answered him, "Yes, as Christians we are called to serve every human being, regardless of gender, race, ethnicity, religion, or political affiliation. We are called to be light. It is our witness and *diakonia*."

We are to live as children of light—and let our light shine—not to draw attention to ourselves or because our salvation depends on us. Rather, we live as children of light because Christ, our light, has given us special gifts to share with the world. We may not be able to convert the world to Christianity, but we can secure the world by sharing God's grace. We can secure the world by shining Christ's light into the darkness. We can serve the world by loving each other and all humanity.

This is why the church must be prophetic. It must not only condemn sin but dare to offer a vision of light to a dark world. It must take seriously the issues of the people it serves. It must embrace all of God's people, the children of light.

And as the church is made of Christ's followers, the church is also called to be light. That means that the church must not involve itself in a spirituality of escapism but in a spirituality that addresses human suffering and serves the world by being a light. Through witness and *diakonia*, the church is a servant, not a master, a carrier of the light and thus a living witness in every sphere of life. The church is to be light shining with the rays of faith, hope, love, and forgiveness.

As members of the church, we are called to refuse injustice and illuminate the world with God's light of justice. We are called to work to eradicate poverty, to secure the right to food, to promote the full inclusion of women in society, to condemn human trafficking, to call for just sharing of natural resources, to counter climate change and, above all, to work for justice. We are children of light when we promote justice, forgiveness, peace, and reconciliation. We are to be proactive in working to eliminate Islamophobia, xenophobia, and anti-Semitism. In this way the church, the communion of the children of the light, becomes a beacon of hope in hopeless situations.

I sometimes ponder the fact that there have been Christians in Palestine since the first Pentecost. Now we Palestinian Christians are less than 1.5 percent of the population. According to recent studies by Bethlehem University and the Diyar Consortium, Palestinians are leaving the country for three reasons: difficulties caused by the political conflict, a lack of jobs, and growing political and religious extremism.

Even so, Palestinian Christianity has survived 2,000 years. We have never ruled the country, nor were we ever in the majority. We do not have much property, power, money, or influence. Yet we have survived. And I believe we will survive another 2,000 years. We have survived for the simple reason that we have carried the death and resurrection of our Lord in our bodies, souls, and minds. Our strength has always been our witness, in spite of our weakness. The mystery of salvation keeps our hope and our living witness alive. By God's grace, we carry our light to the world, and we are ready to pay the price for this. This is why we do not focus on numbers but on the fact that our witness and *diakonia* are a light in our society. In spite of circumstances, we Palestinian Christians try to continue to be brokers of justice, instruments of peace, ministers of reconciliation, defenders of human rights including women's rights, and apostles of love. I only pray that Christ the light may continue to call us for this holy task of being light in the world, accompanying our sisters and brothers in the world and in Jerusalem.

We ask you to hold us in prayer that God may continue to use us to be light. Pray that the political situation will not prevent us from being living witnesses and extinguish our light. As sisters and brothers in Christ and fellow light bearers in the world, we should together let our lights shine so that the world might see Christ's light in us and glorify our Father in heaven. Amen.

Welcoming the Stranger

Christ the King Sunday

Denmark • 20 November 2011

"I was a stranger and you welcomed me. . . " (Matthew 25:31-46).

Dear sisters and brothers in Christ,

The Gospel for Christ the King Sunday presents the well-known scene of Judgment Day, where the king on his throne announces to one group of people, "I was a stranger and you welcomed me," while to another group he says, "I was a stranger and you did not welcome me."

This text can easily be misinterpreted by some preachers, turning themselves into judges of their congregations or of other groups of people. It is important to all of us to see how Jesus speaks to us directly.

Many of us have at one time or another found ourselves in the role of the stranger, alone in the world, away from home, in the midst of people we do not know. I remember shortly after 9-11 traveling in the United States when I was questioned at Chicago's O'Hare Airport. The young woman security officer looked at me in a strange way when she saw my name and my home listed on my passport. I was carrying my Bible with me as I always do, my Arabic Bible. She thumbed through it and asked, "Why are you carrying a *Qur'an*?"

I looked down to remind myself of my appearance. I had dressed that morning as I always do in my suit coat and my purple bishop's shirt. My pectoral cross was hanging from my neck. "This is my Bible," I explained.

"What language is this?" she asked.

"Arabic." I answered.

"So why are you carrying a *Qur'an*?" she asked a second time.

"I'm a Christian," I announced. "I always carry my Bible when I travel," I told her. And then I explained how I am an Arabic Christian from Jerusalem, where our families have been living for 2,000 years. She looked at me like she did not believe me, but eventually she allowed me to pass. That day, I really felt like a stranger, and there was no one there to welcome me.

I have come here today, a stranger, yet you have welcomed me. I have had plenty to eat, a warm bed, and most importantly the friendly handshakes, smiles, and warm words of greeting that make me, a stranger, feel welcome.

My childhood is one of being welcomed into the family of God. My parents were refugees from the 1948 war, and I grew up inside the Monastery of John the Baptist in Jerusalem's Old City. Many of my formative experiences took place in the Lutheran Boys Home in Beit Jala. I have told the story how my first experience with The Lutheran World Federation was through the chocolate milk they served. With our Jerusalem home just a stone's throw from the Church of the Holy Sepulchre and also the Lutheran Church of the Redeemer, what attracted me was the ministry of hospitality in a world where life was difficult. I was a stranger, and they welcomed me. Thanks for a church that embraced me so that I was not obliged to live my life in a refugee camp. Were it not for such a welcome, I wonder if I would have become a pastor and a bishop. If it were not for the hospitality I received as a child, I would not be here today.

I recently heard a story from Brazil about Izaete Romao Afujo. Most likely none of you will recognize her name. She was a little girl from the slums of Recife, Brazil, the fifth of eight children. Her mother was an alcoholic, and her father worked odd jobs. Izaete worked, too, as the maid for a rich family, and she washed clothes, scrubbed floors, and cooked meals. When she returned home, her mother would beat her. One day a neighbor invited Izaete's mother to attend a nearby Mennonite Church, where she was welcomed and loved. Within weeks, Jesus changed her life. Izaete too became involved in church and eventually went to college, became a pastor, and returned to minister to those in the slums where she grew up. She is a pastor, she says, because someone cared enough about her to welcome and accept her—a stranger, an outsider, a kid from the slums.

This story reminds me of the captured young Hebrew maidservant in 2 Kings 5, working for the wife of Naaman, the commander of the Assyrian army. This commander was very successful, but he suffered from leprosy and could find no cure. That young servant is only mentioned in a single verse of the Bible; her name is not given, and we really know nothing about her except that she offered a word of encouragement to the wife of Naaman the commander: "Tell him to go see the prophet Elisha where he can wash in the Jordan River" (2 Kings 5:5). As a result, this important leader was healed. This woman could have remained silent, she could have kept to herself, she could have minded her own business as so many people do today, she could have refused to get involved. But she didn't. She was a stranger who showed her master the way of God. And he was healed.

In the Hebrew Bible, the word *GER* is often translated as "stranger" or "alien," the foreigner who resides in the land of Israel. Several times—in Exodus 12:49, in Leviticus 24:22, and in Numbers 15:16—it is mentioned that same law should apply to the *GER*, the stranger, as to the natural-born citizen. In Leviticus 19: 18 and 34, an amazing transformation takes place: The stranger/foreigner becomes the neighbor. This takes place when you love the stranger (*GER*) as yourself because you once were strangers in Egypt (verse 34). You love the stranger as yourself (verse 34). You love the neighbor as yourself (verse 18). In the Bible, there are really no strangers, only neighbors.

In September 2007, 138 Muslim scholars from all Islamic countries and regions of the world published a statement describing what they believed was the fundamental Muslim teaching and also the common ground between Islam, Judaism, and Christianity. The document was called "A Common Word Between Us and You." They referenced passages in the *Qur'an* and in the Bible, and showed that the most fundamental core values between religions is the emphasis on loving God with our whole heart, soul, and mind, and loving the neighbor as oneself.

It is easy for an extremist to be fanatical or zealous for God, to claim to love God and to act in the name of God. Such fanatics claim to know and love God, as if only they understand God and God's will for humankind. But they have not seen and loved God through their neighbor. As it says in the first epistle of John: "Those who say, 'I love God,' and hate their brothers and sisters are liars; for those who do not love a brother or sister whom they have seen, cannot love God whom they have not seen" (1 John 4:20).

Today the greatest crisis in our world is a crisis of who is our neighbor. It is our human inclination to want our neighbor to look the same, to talk the same, to act the same—to have the same ethnicity, culture, language, and religion.

Yet the Gospel message begins with the incarnation, that Christ as a stranger becomes our neighbor, becomes one of us; that Christ was in the world, reconciling the world to himself; that while we were yet enemies,

Christ died for us as if we were friends, family, the familiar. Christ made the stranger into the neighbor by loving us without limit, without condition, without restrictions. We are no longer strangers, far off, but now we have drawn near to God, one in Christ. So Paul writes in Ephesians 2:19, "So then you are no longer strangers and aliens, but you are citizens with the saints and also members of the household of God."

"I was a stranger and you welcomed me," Jesus announced to one group of people, while to another group he said, "I was a stranger and you did not welcome me."

Estimates suggest that there are over fourteen million refugees and twenty-one million internally displaced persons worldwide; these are people displaced by fear of persecution. In addition, how many million are displaced for economic reasons? And today, as we speak, our thoughts are directed to the extreme famine in the horn of Africa. The Lutheran World Federation, on behalf of the United States, is currently operating a refugee camp at Dadaab on the border of Kenya, where it daily receives over 1,000 persons who have traveled an average of fifteen days without food or water and sometimes arrive half dead. The refugee camp, originally built for 40,000 Somali refugees is now home to 700,000.

Who is responsible? Is it the church that makes loud speeches, but never turns words into actions? Is it the church that sits quietly by, hoping that someone else will act in its place? Is it the church that thinks only for its own members or its loyal friends?

Why is it that the LWF is currently struggling to find even a relatively small amount as $700,000 to keep the Dadaab camp operational? Why in contrast do the governments of the world always manage to find funding for themselves, for banks and financial institutions, as the countries of Europe bail out Greece, while the suffering of Africa are all but forgotten. They are forgotten like a stranger. Who is responsible?

It was not by accident that Jesus had to challenge the common definition of "neighbor" with the parable of the Good Samaritan. The one who cares for the stranger, the one who treats the stranger with full humanity, the one who makes the stranger into a friend—that's who is neighbor.

Martin Luther King Jr. once said, "Any religion which professes to be concerned with the souls of people, but is not concerned with the slums that damn them, the economic conditions that cripple them—such a religion is a dry-as-dust religion."

"Dry-as-dust"—that's the life created by drought and famine in East Africa. Yet when we welcome the stranger, when we provide food for the hungry, when we offer shelter for the homeless, when we provide asylum or citizenship, we create a river of cool water that refreshes the earth and the spirits of people as the prophet Amos said, "Let justice flow down like water, and righteousness like an ever-flowing stream." The religion of the Bible is anything but a "dry-as-dust" religion.

Jesus made hospitality central to his ministry, welcoming the stranger and combating every form of xenophobia—whether it was Nicodemus or the Samaritan woman at the well, whether it was the nameless Canaanite woman or the seemingly insignificant child he placed in his midst, whether it was the thief on the cross or the soldier who crucified him. They were all strangers, and he welcomed them. And so he proclaimed, "As you did it to one of the least of these who are members of my family, you did it to me." One of the major issues facing Christians in the Middle East today is emigration. Although Christians have been living there for 2,000 years, Christians today are often treated as if they were strangers in their own countries. We cannot generalize between Iraq and Tunisia or between Egypt and Lebanon. And for the Christians in Jordan and the Holy Land, the situation is still different. Yet Christians are emigrating in large numbers, often because they feel like strangers when there is no justice, no security, no respect for human rights. In Palestine we see the problem of emigration because of the lack of a just peace, because of an increase in extremism, because of a lack of jobs and affordable housing. Still we encourage the Christian community to remain steadfast in their own countries; to continue, not as strangers, but as an integral part of the Arab fabric. Arab Christians are a very significant element in building a modern civil society, working for human rights, especially women's rights, for freedom of expression and freedom of religion in the midst of the Arab Awakening. Christ has called us to serve our people, to be brokers of justice, instruments of peace, defenders of human rights, and agents of reconciliation.

There is a story about a young boy who, in the Christmas season, was walking home in the street, carrying a special gift that had been given to him, when he encountered a strange man, dressed in ragged clothes and covered with sores on his body. When the boy drew near to the man, he turned to him and handed him the gift. "Why would you give this gift to me, a person that you do not even know?"

The boy answered, "Because I do not need the gift. I have all I need at home. Besides, I will be receiving other gifts."

"But you don't know me," said the stranger, "and I am all alone."

"Then you must come with me," said the boy, who proceeded to lead him to the church down the street where Christmas Eve services were taking place.

As they drew near to the door of the crowded church, the stranger protested, "I cannot enter. My clothes are torn and smelly."

But the boy persisted, "Never mind, I'll sit by you and I'll smell you."

And so it was that they sat together that Christmas Eve in church, and together they prayed the Our Father, and together they sang Christmas carols. And when it came to the time for communion and the breaking of bread, the boy saw that he was sitting with Christ himself.

Don't we read from the Bible that Christ is there with the poor, the vulnerable, the outcast, the sick, the hungry, the homeless, the displaced, the refugee, the emigrant, the stranger. When we welcome the stranger, Christ is in our midst.

May the peace which surpasses human understanding keep our hearts in Christ Jesus. Amen.

In Christ—Hope for the World

Lutheran World Federation
Meeting of Officers

Budapest, Hungary • 16 November 2011

Ephesians 1:15-23

Dear sisters and brothers in Christ.

It is a great joy to be with you today as we begin the meeting of officers of The Lutheran World Federation here in Hungary. And I am especially happy that this opening service has included so many of you from Budapest and other communities. A special word of gratitude to Bishop Tama Fabiny for his leadership and example as a servant of Christ, as well as Presiding Bishop Peter Ganc for the hospitality of the Evanglical Lutheran Church of Hungary.

I have heard about you.

Yes, I have heard of your faith in the Lord Jesus, as Paul says in his letter to the Ephesians. "I have heard about your faith, your love toward all the saints, and I pray. . . that you may know what is the hope to which he has called you." Faith, love, and hope—that same great triad of Christian virtues at the end of Paul's magnificent love chapter in 1 Corinthians. And I have heard about these same things among you—the faithful in the Lutheran Church in Hungary—just as I have heard the same about you, representatives of the Lutheran world communion who have come here for meetings today.

I have heard of your faith, a faith that has been tested under fire, a faith that has been steadfast and enduring in difficult and challenging circumstances. When we look to see the numbers of the faithful here in Hungary—seven and a half million Christians, 300,000 Lutherans—we can only give thanks to God.

Your history has been marked by times of struggle: the well-known decade of mourning in the seventeenth century; the two world wars in the first half of the twentieth century when over half of your church buildings were damaged and in need of repair.

After your government came under the cloud of totalitarianism, your 1956 uprising was met with repression. 20,000 were killed and a quarter-million citizens fled the country. These were difficult times, and yet your faith persisted. You never gave up. Together, your churches continued to witness the Gospel of Jesus Christ, to proclaim the Good News to believers and others, and to administer the sacraments.

I have heard of your faith.

In 1984, when the LWF held its Seventh Assembly here in Budapest, I was a youth delegate. I came and I saw and I heard. It was the first assembly behind the Iron Curtain. We heard of your faith, we gave thanks to God for you, and we prayed for you. I think of Paul's words in Ephesians 2: "Christ is our peace. . . and has broken down the dividing wall." You remained faithful. Your country has been transformed. You are now part of the European Union, still with struggles, especially the great economic recession of recent years, and you continue in the faith.

Before I left for the airport and was sitting in my Jerusalem office, I decided to open up on my computer the web page of the Lutheran Church in Hungary, and there was a short section with the heading: "What are Lutherans recognized by?" This question was followed by six characteristics:

They are open,
community people, not liking extremes,
cheerful,
resolute, but ready for compromises,
they love songs, music, and culture,
they hold together.

It is true. Aren't these characteristics that have joined us together in our Lutheran communion? Aren't these characteristics that make us a communion with all Christians? It is worth noting that it was precisely here in Budapest that The Lutheran World Federation became a communion of churches. In 1984 the assembly here voted that all the member churches should be in "altar and pulpit fellowship." From then on, no church could become a member of the LWF without entering into communion with all the other member churches. This decisive step happened right here!

In 1984, another important action was also taken. South Africa was still under apartheid rule, and Namibia—one of the strongest Lutheran countries in the world—was still just a province of South Africa. Meeting in Budapest, the LWF suspended the membership of two white South African churches due to their continued failure to end racial division in their churches. It was a sign of hope. The result was major political change, major attitudinal change in Africa.

Gathered in assembly in Budapest, the LWF held up a banner of hope: In Christ—Hope for the World.

In 1984, there was much to be done concerning the role of women in society and especially in the church. Yet there was hope. The LWF Assembly resolved that by the Ninth Assembly the ratio of male and female delegates would be equal. And in 1986 the Lutheran Church in Hungary showed us what it means to live in hope, and you accepted the ordination of women.

I also attended the youth gathering here in Budapest at the time of the LWF Assembly. And coming from Jerusalem, I felt encouraged. Allan Boesak addressed us on freedom and hope, which still seemed far off in the distance. Pastor Harald Brettschneider, the Saxon youth pastor of that time who was very much involved in peace activities, spoke of the end of injustice and communism. The Swedish rock band, Fjedur, led the singing. And they rocked us as we joined, swaying back and forth with the music. Was this a dream or reality? Had I been caught up in a vision of utopia? I still had feelings of ambivalence. When we looked outside, the people of Hungary were still living under communism. When we returned home, there were still problems. However, some five years later, strange enough—as if our prayers had been answered, as if God had said, "I have heard the cries of my people, the prayers of people believing in justice and filled with the hope of the Gospel"—the people of Hungary experienced freedom and new life.

As I look around the church today, I must say to all of you how I give thanks for your faith, for the joy of continuous growth for our churches in the South, especially our African churches; for the innovation and creativity of our Asian churches as you continue to seek ways to be a living witness in a region where Christianity is just a small minority; for churches in Latin America that continue to seek liberation in the Gospel; for churches in Europe and North America as you remain steadfast in difficult economic times and with many political challenges.

You are a living witness to the world today. In a world of individualism, you are community-minded; in a world of extremism, religious wars, and fanaticism, you seek moderation, you avoid extremes, you are resolute, but ready for compromise, yet never at the expense of the Gospel. You are cheerful, and you love your songs. I give thanks to God always for your faith and for your love to all the saints.

There was a second thing that struck me about the website of the Lutheran Church in Hungary. I was impressed to see in bold type, words of Dietrich Bonhoeffer: "The church is a church if she lives for the sake of others." And I am struck by your great focus on *diakonia*. Here in Hungary, you run thirty-seven educational institutions with about 7,000 students. In these difficult economic times, when the state can no longer operate many schools, there is an open door for expanding the role of churches in education,[137] programs for counseling and prison work, homes for the elderly and disabled, retreat centers for recreation, recognizing a wholistic ministry for the whole person.

We see the same vision here as in the Arab Awakening today—the vision that looks to education as a transformative, world-changing power. Many churches in the South have experienced that very thing, having been shaped not only through preaching, but also through education. We continue to educate because education transforms hatred into love, ignorance into knowledge, fear to trust, prejudice to love. Only education can bring the changes that will create a world of trust.

As we come together in this Lutheran world communion we must always ask ourselves this question: How can the church be a servant in our modern world? How can the church be a servant in a world faced with HIV/AIDs, malaria, and other pandemic diseases?

How can the church be a servant when the earth itself rises up in a seeming protest to the way we have mistreated God's creation, global warming, earthquakes, a world with contrasting disasters as drought and flood? In particular how can we continue to play an ever-growing role with the crisis of East Africa, the famine with people traveling fifteen days to the refugee camp at Dadaab on the border of Kenya, when a camp designed for 40,000 now numbers fifteen times that many?

How can the church be a servant when emigration changes the whole face of communities to become diverse in ethnicity, language, culture, and religion? How can the church be a servant during a time of economic recession, when entire countries are threatened with bankruptcy, when the division between rich and poor daily expands, when sufficient resources are no longer available for institutions to carry out programs?

I am concerned. I feel challenged. But I am not worried. As long as the church is the church that serves and does not live only for itself, the church will survive all turbulence, for the church does not preach itself, but Christ and him crucified. Again with Paul I say, "I have heard of your love for all the saints and for all humanity, and for that reason, I do not cease to give thanks or you as I remember you in my prayers." For the sake of our hope in Christ we must pray that the Spirit may continue to inspire and to empower the church to remain in faith, love, and hope. I pray that you may know the hope to which he has called you.

When the LWF met here in Budapest for its assembly, our theme was hope: "In Christ—Hope for the World." Coming as a youth delegate, I wondered, how can we as a Lutheran communion bring hope for the world, a world filled with seemingly insurmountable problems, a world where people had turned pessimistic, a world where hopelessness and despair were ruling the day.

I was a young pastor, filled with questions and concerns about my own country, my own people. I had just accepted a call to become the pastor of a congregation of refugees in Ramallah, The Evangelical Lutheran Church of Hope. I had to realize that it was not merely my abilities and my efforts which were necessary to succeed. It was a church of hope, the hope to which Christ had called me as pastor, the hope of the resurrection, witnessed from Jerusalem to the ends of the earth.

Our world today is living is a situation not so different from 1984. Many churches are suffering from persecution. Recession continues to stab like a sharp sword placed on the neck of the world economy, threatening to devastate the whole world. Extremists seem to be taking whole countries hostage. In the Middle East, there is little hope for peace and justice. Yet what can separate us from the love of Christ Jesus?

I believe that freedom is coming, as long as our trust remains in the living Christ. Coming from Jerusalem, it seems like there is no future, but we continue to hope for a resolution based on the 1967 borders with a shared Jerusalem, a peace based on justice, and reconciliation based on forgiveness. Pray for the peace of Jerusalem!

In our situation today, we look back to 1984, to Budapest and the LWF Assembly, and we are encouraged. "In Christ—Hope for the World." This is the Budapest legacy, a message of hope in the midst of challenges.

We come together twenty-seven years later in Budapest, and the challenges are no smaller. The issues of the church seem to overwhelm us. The problems of the world overshadow us. I am neither optimistic nor pessimistic about the future. But I am full of hope, hope in Christ.

This is why we have committed ourselves to our strategic plan for 2012-2017 with the theme, "With Passion for the Church and for the World."

Sisters and brothers, we come together in difficult times, but let us remember the hope to which Christ has called us. We live in hope. We are a communion of hope. I know who we are. "I have heard of your faith in the Lord Jesus and your love toward all the saints, and for this reason I do not cease to give thanks for you as I remember you in my prayers.

Please let us continue in our beloved communion to pray for each other, that this hope in Christ may remain alive.

May the peace of God, which surpasses all human understanding, keep your hearts and minds in Christ Jesus. Amen.

Planting a Tree for the Future
Tree Planting Ceremony in the Luther Garden

Wittenberg, Germany • 5 November 2010

" . . . and the dove came back to him in the evening, and there in its beak was a freshly plucked olive leaf; so Noah knew that the waters had subsided from the earth" (Genesis 8:11).

When Martin Luther was asked what he would do if he knew the world would end tomorrow, his response was that he would plant an apple tree. For Noah, the world had actually come to an end. The mythological world of the early chapters of Genesis was a thing of the past, drowned in the chaotic waters of the flood. Yet the presence of a living tree announced the promised future of a world transformed in God—not just any tree, but the freshly plucked leaf of an olive tree.

The catastrophe of the flood was no different from the threats that face our own existence: the effects of climate change, overpopulation, disappearing rain forests, the ever-present threat of nuclear war, world hunger, pandemic diseases like HIV/AIDS, earthquakes, hurricanes, monsoons, and tsunamis threaten us. Racism, sexism, classism, xenophobia, and homophobia run rampant in our world. In the face of them, the younger generations despair, rather than having hope for the future. And we human beings still have not learned to live at peace with one another, as evidenced by the individual acts of violence, by organized terrorism, and by societal acts of genocide.

Yet when Noah saw that branch of the olive tree in the mouth of the dove, he knew that God was smiling down upon the whole of creation and that there was hope for the future.

Today I am planting a tree here in Wittenberg. And today in our churches and institutions of the ELCJHL we are planting olive trees. We look to the olive tree as a sign of life and hope and peace. Its fruit is good to eat. Its oil is good for cooking, for medicinal purposes, and as fuel for lamps. Its branches and seeds are good for fuel. And out of the wood, our craftsmen create beautiful nativity sets or pieces of religious art. The olive is a staple of life. And with its twisted roots the olive tree takes hold in even the shallowest of soils, finding nourishment through the drought and finding stability against the winter winds. Ten million olive trees dot the West Bank. From one generation to the next, these trees are passed down through the centuries, some perhaps even lasting millennia. And although my generation will one day be dead and gone, we live in hope that the young olive trees planted today will see our great-grandchildren living in peace, *inshallah*.

It is easy to see why the olive branch long ago became a symbol of peace. It is also evident why our ancestors poured olive oil upon another's head to give them God's blessing.

Whenever I visit Gethsemane, people there tell me that several of the trees there are 2,000 years old, and sometimes I wonder whether agricultural science and techniques are really able to keep a tree alive for so long. But when I look closely, there is no doubt, these trees with their thick, gnarled trunks are indeed alive and still bearing fruit. I often wonder, "Perhaps this could be the tree under which Jesus knelt in prayer. For me this is a sign of two things:

First, it is a genuine sign of resilience that we take from the olive tree. No matter what the political situation, no matter what suffering and fear Palestinians and Israelis endure, no matter how slight the commitment there is for peace and justice, the olive tree is a steadfast sign. As long as it will take, the olive tree will continue to stand on Palestinian soil and assure us that justice, peace, reconciliation, forgiveness are possible in the Holy Land.

Second, for Lutherans especially, it is a sign that the word of God preached two thousand years ago in this place will never fade. The Good News we receive from Golgotha and the empty tomb continues to be as relevant and meaningful to us as in the early days of the church, since Martin Luther opened up and revitalized this Good News through the Reformation. The olive tree reminds us that the Gospel will always be green and fruitful, remaining fresh in our hearts.

Some say also that the tree on which Jesus was crucified was an olive tree, a dead stump of a tree, with no seeming signs of life. Yet the olive tree can be surprising. A single small shoot growing up from the bottom of an all but dead tree, can signify the beginning of a new era of abundant life, growing for centuries, and providing for generations of families not yet born.

When Noah saw the freshly plucked olive leaf in the beak of the dove and knew that the chaotic waters had subsided from the earth, he knew that God was present and there was hope for the future. So it is that the resurrected Christ is our life and hope and peace.

And so I plant this tree, along with other trees of member churches, as a visible symbol of the faith, love, and hope by which we pray that God may transform the world.

> But I am like a green olive tree in the house of God. I trust in the steadfast love of God forever and ever. I will thank you forever, because of what you have done. In the presence of the faithful I will proclaim your name, for it is good (Psalm 52:8).

Amen.

Publications by Munib Younan

Books

Witnessing for Peace: In Jerusalem and the World (Minneapolis: Augsburg Fortress; 2003).

The Augsburg Confession in Arabic (Jerusalem: Emerezian Est, 1993).

Chapters

"Beyond Luther: Prophetic Interfaith Dialogue for Life," in *The Global Luther: A Theologian for Modern Times,* ed. Christine Helmer (Minneapolis: Fortress Press, 2009).

"The Future of the Lutheran Reformation Tradition: From the Perspective of Palestinian Christians," in *The Future of Lutheranism in a Global Context,* ed. Arland Jacobson and James Aageson (Minneapolis: Augsburg Fortress, 2007).

"The Role of the Church in Peacemaking: Raising a Prophetic Voice," in *The Forgotten Faithful,* Ed. Naim Ateek, Cedar Duaybis, and Maurine Tobin (Jerusalem: Sabeel Ecumenical Liberation Theology Center, 2007).

"Theological Reflection and Theology," in *Theological Reflection on Accompaniment.* (Geneva: World Council of Churches, 2005).

Articles

"The Evangelical Lutheran Church in Jordan and the Holy Land: adapting to a changing environment while drawing strength from deep Christian roots," in *The Lutheran For*um, Winter 2011.

"Do justice, love kindness, walk humbly: Just Peace in the Middle East," in *The Ecumenical Review,* Summer 2011.

"Can religion solve conflicts in the Middle East? Bring religion back to the front lines of peace," in *The Washington Post*, September, 2010.

"The future of Palestinian Christianity and prospects for justice, peace, and reconciliation," in *Currents in Theology and Mission*, 34, October 2007, pages 338-351.

"Das Ökumenische Leben in Jerusalem" (The Ecumenical Life in Jerusalem), in *Jerusalem: Stadt der Freidens*, EMW Annual 2000 (Hamburg, Germany).

"Challenges of a Palestinian Church," in *Festschrift to Bishop Christian Krause* (Braunschweig, Germany, 1998).

"Prayer and Reconciliation in a Shared Land," in *Toward the Third Millennium–Trialogue in Jerusalem: Jews, Christians and Muslims (*Jerusalem: ICCI, 1998).

Endnotes

1. Kenneth Cragg, *The Arab Christian: A History in the Middle East*, (Louisville, Kentucky: Westminster John Knox Press, 1991), 282-285.
2. Munib Younan, *The Augsburg Confession (in Arabic)* (Jerusalem: 1993).
3. All the other congregations are in occupied territory: Redeemer congregation in Jerusalem which Israel declares as annexed to Israel, and Ramallah, Beit Jala, Beit Sahour, and Bethlehem congregations are under Palestinian Authority, but still under shared control with Israel.
4. Closures, difficulties in obtaining travel permits, and the twenty-five-foot separation wall are just some of the obstacles for our members under occupation.
5. Planning and funding are well underway for an eighty-six-unit housing project on the Mount of Olives.
6. http://www.acommonword.com/
7. Munib Younan, *Witnessing for Peace: In Jerusalem and the World* (Minneapolis: Fortress Press, 2003). Mitri Raheb, *I Am a Palestinian Christian* (Minneapolis: Fortress Press, 1995). Mitri Raheb, *Bethlehem Beseiged* (Minneapolis: Fortress Press, 2003).
8. Martin Luther, "The Leipzig Debate," in *Luther's Works: Career of the Reformer*: I, volume 31, eds. H.Grimm, H. Lehmann (Philadelphia: Fortress Press, 1957, 1999), 322. *Luther's Works: Career of the Reformer* II, volume 32, eds. J. J. Pelikan, H. C. Oswald & H. T. Lehmann (Philadelphia: Fortress Press, 1958, 1999).
9. The foreword to the Greek edition claims that it was translated by Paul Dolcius and that it was a rather literal translation from the German version. Wayne Jorgensen has demonstrated that the foreword was written to satisfy more conservative Lutheran readers. Clearly the translation was a revision with ecumenical accommodation in mind, and only Melanchthon was capable of such a work. *The Augustana Graeca and the Correspondence Between the Tübingen Lutherans and Patriarch Jeremias: Scripture and Tradition in Theological Methodology*, Wayne James Jorgensen, dissertation for the degree of doctor of philosophy (Boston University Graduate School, 1979), 31.
10. Berthold F. Korte, "Early Lutheran Relations with the Eastern Orthodox," *The Lutheran Quarterly*, volume IX, number I (February, 1957), 56.
11. Eve Tibbs, "Patriarch Jeremias II, the Tübingen Lutherans, and the Greek Version of the Augsburg Confession: A Sixteenth Century Encounter," Fuller Theological Seminary Lecture (March 9, 2000) at http://www.stpaulsirvine.org/html/lutheran.htm .
12. "Eastern Orthodoxy," in *The Oxford Encyclopedia of the Reformation*, ed. Hans J. Hillerbrand, four volumes (London: Oxford University Press, 1996).
13. George Mastrantonis, *Augsburg and Constantinople: The Correspondence between the Tübingen Theologians and Patriarch Jeremiah II of Constantinople on the Augsburg Confession* (Brookline, Massachusetts: Holy Cross Orthodox Press, 1982), 28. See also Eve Tibbs, "Patriarch Jeremias II, the Tübingen Lutherans, and the Greek Version of the Augsburg Confession: A Sixteenth

Century Encounter," Fuller Theological Seminary Lecture (March 9, 2000) at http://www.stpaulsirvine.org/html/lutheran.htm .

14 Mastrantonis, *Augsburg and Constantinople*, 306.

15 Mastrantonis, *Augsburg and Constantinople*, 313.

16 Linda Kay Davidson and David Martin Gitlitz, "Wittenberg" in *Pilgrimage: From the Ganges to Graceland: An Encyclopedia*, volume 1, (Santa Barbara, California: ABC-Clio, 2002), 686.

17 Armstrong, 352.

18 Anthony O'Mahoney, "The Religious, Political and Social Status of the Christian Communities in Palestine c. 1800 – 1930," in *The Christian Heritage in the Holy Land*, ed. Anthony O'Mahoney, Göran Gunner, and Kevork Hintlian (London: Scorpion Cavendish, 1995), 243.

19 http://www.lcje.net/bulletins/2003/72/72_02.html

20 Saul P. Colbi, *Christianity in the Holy Land: Past and Present* (Tel Aviv: Am Hassefer, 1969), 86.

21 http://conradschick.wordpress.com/basel-2/c-f-spittler/

22 One of Schick's first buildings in 1860 is what is now the German Lutheran Guest House on St. Mark's Road in the Old City.

23 Now the Swedish Theological Institute.

24 Another German Lutheran Missionary, Ferdinand Vester, built a house in 1868 on Mamillah Road (Argon Street) which would later become the home of the American Consulate. See http://conradschick.wordpress.com/architecture/.

25 August Strobel, *Conrad Schick. Ein Leben für Jerusalem* (Fürth: Flacius-Verlag, 1988).

26 The German Protestant Institute of Archaeology was founded on June 19, 1900, by the Deutsche Evangelische Kirchenkonferenz in Eisenach in order to "maintain, further and regulate the relations between the holy places of biblical history, on the one hand, and between the scientific inquiry and the interests of the Christian faith of the Protestant Church, on the other, in the fields of biblical and ecclesiastical archaeology." The first director was Gustaf Dalman, professor of Old Testament at the University of Leipzig, who also served as Lutheran pastor.

27 Mitri Raheb, *Das reformatorische Erbe unter den Palästinensern*, (Mohn: Gütersloh, 1990). Roland Löffler and Uwe Kaminsky, *Protestantism in Jerusalem: The Redeemer Church As a Focus of Common History* (unpublished paper), 5-6.

28 See http://conradschick.wordpress.com/jerusalem/syrisches-waisenhaus/.

29 Samir Akel, *Der Pädagoge und Missionar Johann Ludwig Schneller und seine Erziehungsanstalten (*Bielefeld: Surbir, 1978).

30 Later he was able to expand his deaconess program throughout Europe and to the United States with Florence Nightingale as his most famous graduate.

31 See http://www.talithakumi.org/Between1850-1950.html.

32 Kenneth Cragg, *The Arab Christian: A History in the Middle East* (Louisville, Kentucky: Westminster John Knox Press, 1991), 282-285.

33 Saul P. Colbi, *Christianity in the Holy Land: Past and Present* (Tel Aviv: Am Hassefer, 1969), 87.

34 Bernd Isphording, *Germans in Jerusalem*: 1830-1914 (Jerusalem: Passia, *2009),* 21. Mitri Raheb relates the story of his own Greek Orthodox grandfather who went to the Schneller School in 1868 when his parents died and was confirmed Lutheran a number of years later in *I Am a Palestinian Christian* (Minneapolis: Fortress Press, 1995), 7.

35 Saul P. Colbi, *Christianity in the Holy Land: Past and Present* (Tel Aviv: Am Hassefer, 1969), 88.

36 Pittman, 90-92. Saul P. Colbi, *Christianity in the Holy Land: Past and Present* (Tel Aviv: Am Hassefer, 1969), 88.

37 Pittman, 92.

38 See http://conradschick.wordpress.com/basel-2/friedrich-adolf-strauss/.
39 The school building in Madbaseh Square would remain in use until the year 2000 and adjacent to it was the site of the Evangelical Lutheran Christmas Church, built in 1891.
40 Centuries earlier this property had been given to the Emperor Charlemagne by Khalif Harun al-Rashid.
41 A 1967 attempt by twenty-five members to settle in Galilee ended in failure, with fifteen deaths in the first year.
42 At the turn of the century additional colonies were established near Bethlehem of Galilee— Wihelmina near Lod, Wahalla, and Waldheim. See http://en.wikipedia.org/wiki/Templers_(religious_believers).
43 The land was purchased by Matthaus Frank from Arab villagers of Beit Safafa.
44 Wilhelm Hoffmann died in 1873.
45 Colbi, 91.
46 Isphording, 20.
47 See http://www.enotes.com/topic/German_Colony,_Haifa.
48 Architect Paul Ferdinand Groth had responsibility for the actual project in the 1890s.
49 Pittman, 53-55.
50 Isphording, 26.
51 Isphording, 34.
52 Isphording, 36-37.
53 Roland Löffler and Uwe Kaminsky, *Protestantism in Jerusalem: The Redeemer Church as a Focus of Common History* (unpublished paper), 13-18.
54 Later he would serve as the first chief medical director of Augusta Victoria Hospital. Nashef, Khaled, "Tawfiq Canaan: His Life and Works," in *Jerusalem Quarterly* (November, 2002), 12-26.
55 Daoud Haddad, "Memoirs and History," 3-4.
56 Daoud Haddad, "Memoirs and History," 6-7.
57 The name would be changed to the Evangelical Lutheran Church in Jordan and the Holy Land in 2005.
58 The cost of production of this enterprise was subsidized by the Church of Sweden, the Finnish Evangelical Lutheran Mission, the Lutheran Church in America, and the LWF, a sign of the expanding global partnership of the ELCJ. Haddad, 9-10.
59 Similarly, the Anglican church in Jerusalem has had four Palestinian bishops, with the first installed in 1977.
60 Members of COCOP include the ELCJHL, the Berliner Missionswerk (BMW), the Church of Sweden (CoS), the United-Evangelical Lutheran Church of Germany (VELKD), the Finnish Evangelical Lutheran Mission (FELM), the Evangelical Lutheran Church in American (ELCA), the Evangelical Church in Germany (EKD), the Northelbian Evangelical Lutheran Church (NEK), the Church of Norway (CoN), the Evangelical Lutheran Church in Canada (ELCIC).
61 Munib Younan, *The Augsburg Confession (in Arabic)* (Jerusalem,1993).
62 *Mission in Context* (Geneva: Lutheran World Federation, 2004), 45.
63 Published as "Beyond Luther: Prophetic Interfaith Dialogue for Life," in *The Global Luther: A Theologian for Modern Times,* edited by Christine Helmer (Minneapolis: Fortress Press, 2009), pages 49-64.

64. Hans Küng; "No World Peace without Religious Peace," in *Christianity and the World Religions: Paths of Dialogue with Islam, Hinduism and Buddhism*, trans. Peter Heinegg (Garden City: Doubleday 1986), 443.

65. "Vulnerability and Security: Current challenges in security policy from an ethical and theological perspective," prepared by the Commission on International Affairs in the Church of Norway Council on Ecumenical and International Relations (Norway, 2002), 26; http://www.kirken.no/english/doc/kisp_vulnerab_00.pdf

66. Ibid.

67. Saint Augustine, *City of God*, Book. XVIII, Chapter 46. Cited in Augustine's *City of God*, abridged version, trans. Gerald G. Walsh et. al, ed. Vernon J. Bourke (New York: Doubleday, 1958), 417.

68. Mark U. Edwards Jr., *Luther's Last Battles: Politics and Polemics, 1531-1546* (Minneapolis: Fortress Press, 2005), 121; See also Rosemary Radford Ruether, *Faith and Fratricide: The Theological Roots of Anti-Semitism* (New York: Seabury Press, 1974); and Alan T. Davies, ed. *Antisemitism and the Foundations of Christianity* (New York: Paulist Press, 1979).

69. *Luther's Works*, American Edition, volume 45, eds. Jaroslav Pelikan and Helmut T. Lehmann (St. Louis: Concordia Publishing House and Philadelphia: Fortress Press, 1955-1986):195-230. Herafter LW.

70. LW 45:200.

71. LW 21:354 (to Luke 1:55).

72. LW 45:229. See also Ernst Ludwig Ehrlich, *Luther and the Jews* (Geneva: The Lutheran World Federation, 1984), 36.

73. Maurer published two major essays on Luther's understanding of Jews: Wilhelm Maurer, *Kirche und Synagoge, Motive und Formen der Ausseinandersetzung der Kirche mit dem Judentum in Laufe der Geschichte* (Stuttgart: Kohlhammer, 1953), and "Die Zeit der Reformation in Kirche und Synagoge," in *Kirche und Synagoge: Handbuch zur Geschichte von Christen und Juden. Darstellung mit Quellen*, volume 1, ed. Karl-Heinrich Rengstorf and Siegfried von Kortzfleisch (Munich: Klett-Cotta, 1968), 375-428.

74. LW 47:268-270, 273.

75. Roland Bainton, *Here I Stand: A Life of Martin Luther* (Nashville: Abingdon, 1978), 297.

76. Dietrich Bonhoeffer, *Letters and Papers from Prison*, trans. Reginald Fuller et al., ed. Eberhard Bethge (New York: MacMillan, 1971), 123.

77. Mark U. Edwards Jr. "Toward an Understanding of Luther's Attacks on the Jews," in *Luther, Lutheranism, and the Jews, A Record of the Second Consultation between Representatives of the International Jewish Committee for Interreligious Consultations and the Lutheran World Federation Held in Stockholm, Sweden, 11-13 July, 1983* (Geneva: The Lutheran World Federation, 1984), 27-28.

78. Richard Marius, *Martin Luther: The Christian between God and Death* (Cambridge: Harvard University Press, 1999), 482.

79. *Luther, Lutheranism, and the Jews* (Geneva: The Lutheran World Federation, 1984), 9-11.

80. "The Ways of God—Judaism and Christianity," a document for discussion within the Church of Sweden (endorsed by the Board of the Church of Sweden, September 19, 2001); http://www.sidic.org/fr/docOnLineView.asp?class=Doc00418

81. LWF Document No. 48, ed. Wolfgang Grieve and Peter N. Prove (Geneva: The Lutheran World Federation, 2003).

82. Online from 9 November 2000: http://www.ekd.de/ekd-texte/christen_juden_2000_vorwort.html (my translation).

83. https://www.lcms.org/pages/internal.asp?NavID=2166 (8 January 2008).

84 "It is important for the Lutheran Church, which knows itself indebted to the work and tradition of Martin Luther, to take seriously also his anti-Jewish utterances, to acknowledge their theological function and to reflect on their consequences," from "Christians and Jews: A Declaration of the Lutheran Church of Bavaria"/ "Erklärung der Evangelisch-lutherischen Kirche in Bayern zum Thema 'Christen und Juden,'" 24 November 1998, http://www.bayern.evangelisch.de/web/engagiert_dialog_interreligioeser_dialog_christlich_juedisch.phb (8 January 2008).

85 "Guidelines for the Lutheran-Jewish Relations of the ELCA," 16 November 1998, <http://www.elca.org/ecumenical/interreligious/jewish/guidelines.html> and "Declaration of the Evangelical Lutheran Church in America to the Jewish Community," 8 April 1994; http://www.elca.org/ecumenical/interreligious/jewish/declaration.html

86 Minutes of the LWF Council (4 September 2004), my summary, http://www.elcjhl.org/resources/newsletters/04/04sep.htm.

87 http://www.icjs.org/what/njsp/dabruemet.html.

88 The following are Luther's writings on Islam: "On War against the Turks" (1529), a pastoral piece written to teach people how to fight with a clear conscience, in LW 46:157-205; "*Heerpredigt wider den Turken*" *(*Sermon against the Turks, 1529), preached in the spring of 1529 in light of the Turkish threat to Vienna, in WA 30/2:160-197; "*Vorwort zu dem Libellus de ritu et moribus Turcorum*" *(*Preface to the Tract on the Religion and Customs of the Turks, 1530), in WA 30/2:205-208, trans. Sarah Heinrich and James Boyce, "Translation of Two Prefaces on Islam," *Word and World*, 16/2 (Spring 1996): 258-62; "Appeal for Prayer against the Turks" (1541), written to encourage resistance on the occasion of the resurgence of Turkish threats to Germany with Suleiman's conquest of Hungary, in LW 43:215-241; "*Verlegung des Alcoran Bruder Richardi, Prediger Ordens*" (Refutation of the Qur'an of Brother Richard, Preaching Order, 1542), a translation into German of a medieval tract against Islam, in WA 53:272-396; "*Vorrede zu Theodor Biblianders Koranangabe*" *(*Preface to Theodor Bibliander's Edition of the Qur'an, 1543), in WA 53:569-572, trans. Sarah Heinrich and James Boyce, "Translation of Two Prefaces on Islam," *Word and World*, 16/2 (Spring 1996): 262-66.

89 Gregory J. Miller, "Luther on the Turks and Islam," in *Harvesting Martin Luther's Reflections on Theology, Ethics and the Church*, ed. Timothy L. Wengert (Grand Rapids, Michigan: Wm. B. Eerdmanns Publishing Company, 2004), 185.

90 Heinrich and Boyce, "Martin Luther: Translations of Two Prefaces," 252.

91 LW 31:91-92.

92 LW 46:170-171.

93 Trans. Heinrich and Boyce, "Martin Luther: Translations of Two Prefaces," 259.

94 Trans. Heinrich and Boyce, "Martin Luther: Translations of Two Prefaces," 259.

95 Miller, "Luther on the Turks and Islam."

96 Trans. Heinrich and Boyce, "Martin Luther: Translations of Two Prefaces," 256.

97 See his *Preface to Theodor Bibliander's Edition of the Qur'an,* "Martin Luther: Translations of Two Prefaces," trans Heinrich and Boyce, 262-66.

98 LW 22:500 (Sermons on the Gospel of St. John; to John 3:35: 1537-1540).

99 LW 24:349 (Sermons on the Gospel of St. John; to John 16:11).

100 LW 24:242 (to John 15:8).

101 LW 24:371 (to John 16:14).

102 LW 22:350 (to John 3:16).

103 LW 22:18 (to John 1:3).

104 LW 22:137 (to John 1:16).

105. LW 22:394 (to John 3:16).
106. LW 22:468 (to John 3:32).
107. Miller, "Luther on the Turks and Islam," 197.
108. LW 46:181 ("On War against the Turks").
109. Robert O. Smith, "Luther, the Turks, and Islam," in *Currents in Theology and Mission* 34/5 (October 2007): 335.
110. Resolution on Israel-Palestine, LWF Council (2004).
111. There are signs of hope. A code of conduct aimed at finding common positive values between religions was signed in January 2008 at a conference in Amman, Jordan, as a response to the 2005 Muhammad cartoon controversy that began in Denmark. Roman Catholic, Orthodox, Eastern Orthodox, and Evangelical Christians in Palestine, Jordan, Syria, Lebanon, Egypt, and Iran pledged respect for all religions, their prophets, holy writings, and doctrines; the security of access to all holy places; the freedom of expression that does not harm the other's beliefs or sentiments; and the initiation of dialogue in order to achieve justice, peace, development, and human dignity for all: http://www.coexistencejordan.org/APP/Public/News/ArticleDetails.asp The "Amman Message," developed by King Abdullah of Jordan in 2004, seeks to strengthen the moderate voices of Islam by holding up common values of justice, compassion, and non-violence and standing against extremism and violence in the name of religion:

    http://www.coexistencejordan.org/Amman_msg.shtm A similar initiative was issued by 138 Muslims to Christians in the fall of 2007. The text, *A Common Word Between You and Us*, quotes both the Bible and the Qur'an, claiming that religion's essence is the love for God and the love of neighbor as one's self: http://acommonword.com

112. Lissi Rasmussen, *Diapraksis og Dialog mellem Kristne og Muslimer –i lyset af den afrikanske erfaring* (Aarhus: Aarhus Universitetsfolge 1997), "From Diapraxis to Dialogue: Christian-Muslim Relations," in *Dialogue in Action: Essays in Honor of Johannes Aagard*, ed. Lars Thunberg et. al. (New Dehli, 1988).
113. *Lutheran World Information Magazine* 4 (2005): 4; Ingo Wulfhorst, LWF study secretary for the church and people of other faiths, explains further that: "Diapraxis involves dialogue, thus theological discourse on what is commonly shared as well as the differences in the respective faith traditions can never be excluded, despite the inherent complexities, deep-rooted prejudices and conflicts. By sharing their common pain, people of different faiths are enriched by the 'otherness' of the other," *Lutheran World Information Magazine* 4 (2005): 5.
114. Munib Younan, *Witnessing for Peace: In Jerusalem and the World*, ed. Fred Strickert (Minneapolis: Fortress Press, 2003), 123-124.
115. LW 13, "Commentary on Psalm 82," 53.
116. LW 43, "Whether One May Flee a Deadly Plague," 113-138.
117. LW 43:121.
118. LW 13:53-54.
119. LW 13:53.
120. LW 13:54.
121. LW 13:54.
122. Martin Luther, "Explanation to the Apostles Creed."
123. The term is, as we know, especially common among Lutherans, having emerged from the Institute for Ecumenical Research in Strasbourg, and affirmed by the LWF Assembly in Dar-es-Salaam in 1977.
124. " The Blessed Sacrament of the Holy and True Body of Christ, and the Brotherhoods." LW 35, 50-51.
125. The Blessed Sacrament, 57–58.

126 Closures, difficulties in obtaining travel permits, and the twenty-five-foot separation wall are just some of the obstacles for our members under occupation.

127 *Oriental Orthodox Churches:*
The Coptic Orthodox Church
The Armenian Apostolic Church - Catholicosate of Cilicia
The Syrian Orthodox Church of Antioch and all the East

Eastern Orthodox (Chalcedonian) Churches:
Greek Orthodox Patriarchate of Alexandria and All Africa
Greek Orthodox Church of Antioch and All the East
Greek Orthodox Church of Jerusalem
Greek Orthodox Church of Cyprus

Catholic Churches:
Maronite Church of Antioch
Greek Catholic Melchite Church of Antioch, Alexandria and Jerusalem
Armenian Catholic Church of Cilicia
Syrian Catholic Church of Antioch
Coptic Catholic Church of Alexandria
Latin Patriarchate of Jerusalem
Chaldean Catholic Church of Babylon

Evangelical Churches:
The Evangelical Synod of the Nile
Union of the Armenian Evangelical Churches in the Near East
National Evangelical Synod of Syria and Lebanon
National Evangelical Union of Lebanon
Episcopal Church in Jerusalem and the Middle East
Evangelical Lutheran Church in Jordan and the Holy Land
National Evangelical Church in Kuwait
The Synod of the Evangelical Church in Iran
Evangelical Church in Sudan
Episcopal Church in the Sudan
Presbyterian Church in the Sudan
Protestant Church in Algeria
Eglise Reformée de France en Tunisie

128 On the issue of forgiveness of sins in Judaism, I refer you to Rabbi David R. Blumenthal's illuminating piece "Repentance and Forgiveness" (http://www.crosscurrents.org/blumenthal.htm).

129 Cf. the piece adapted from *Tide of the Supernatural* by Kundan Massey (http://www.leaderu.com/isr/articles_resources/forgivenessofsin.html).

130 Joachim Jeremias, *The Central Message of the New Testament* (Philadelphia: Fortess Press, 1981)

131 Karl Barth, *Church Dogmatics*, volume 2 (Edinburgh: T & T Clark, 1957), 386. See also James Limburg, *The Prophets and the Powerless* (Atlanta: John Knox Press, 1977).

132 Charles Kimball, *When Religion Becomes Evil: Five Warning Signs* (San Francisco: Harper and Row, 2008).

133 Delbert R. Hillers, *Hermeneia Commentary: Micah* (Minneapolis: Fortress Press, 1984).

134 Charles Kimball, *When Religion Becomes Evil: Five Warning Signs* (San Francisco: Harper One, 2008).

135 Martin Luther King Jr., *Strength to Love* (New York: Harper and Row, 1963), 37.

136 Auxiliary Bishop William Shomali of the Latin Patriarchate of Jerusalem, *The Middle Eastern Synod in its Geopolitical and Pastoral Context* (Zenit.org, May 22, 2010).

137 http://www.evangelikus.hu/articles/in-recession-hit-hungary-churches-take-over-state-schools

www.ingramcontent.com/pod-product-compliance
Lightning Source LLC
Chambersburg PA
CBHW050315120526
44592CB00014B/1918